Empowered Without Power
Women and Leadership in the Basel Mission and Presbyterian Church in Cameroon

Michael Kpughe Lang

Langaa Research & Publishing CIG
Mankon, Bamenda

Publisher:
Langaa RPCIG
Langaa Research & Publishing Common Initiative Group
P.O. Box 902 Mankon
Bamenda
North West Region
Cameroon
Langaagrp@gmail.com
www.langaa-rpcig.net

Distributed in and outside N. America by African Books Collective
orders@africanbookscollective.com
www.africanbookscollective.com

ISBN-10: 9956-551-42-2

ISBN-13: 978-9956-551-42-2

© Michael Kpughe Lang 2020

All rights reserved.
No part of this book may be reproduced or transmitted in any form or by any means, mechanical or electronic, including photocopying and recording, or be stored in any information storage or retrieval system, without written permission from the publisher

Table of Contents

Acknowledgements v
List of Photographs, Maps and Tables vii
Abbreviations ix
Introduction xi

Part I: Women in Traditional Religion and Basel Mission Church in Cameroon

1. Goddesses and High Priestesses:
Women's Status in Cameroonian Traditional Religions 3

2. Basel Mission, Patriarchy and
Missionary Deployment to Cameroon 23

3. Controversial Emancipation: Christian
Housewifisation of Local Women 45

4. Discrimination Against Women in Leadership
Structures of the Basel Mission Church 69

Part II: Women in Presbyterian Church in Cameroon Power Structure

5. Women's Work in the PCC: Empowerment
for Leadership? 97

6. Women in PCC's Ordained
Ministry Leadership 121

7. Female Eldership in the Presbyterian
Church in Cameroon 151

8. Called to Serve: Nuns in the Presbyterian
Church in Cameroon.. 175

9. Conclusion: Women's Role Reconsidered....................... 193

Bibliography... 203

Acknowledgements

I wish to thank the many people who were involved in the preparation of this book. I am immensely indebted to Verkijika G. Fanso, Simon Ngenge Tata, Canute A. Ngwa, Nixon Kahjum Takor, Henry Kam Kah, Confidence Ngam Chia, Mark Bolak Funteh, Wilibroad Dze Ngwa, Edouard Bokagne Betobo, and Kingsly Awang Ollong for sharpening and challenging my thinking. Several people have offered valuable suggestions and correctives in the process of revising sections of several chapters. I am grateful to Noah Tabi Ameli, Protus Mbeum Tem, and Paul Animbom for reading portions of early drafts and for their criticisms and suggestions. Jacob Fongang proofread the entire manuscript and made numerous very useful suggestions. I am glad to extend my thanks to workers of the Presbyterian Church in Cameroon Central Archive and Library for facilitating the exploitation of archival materials. Ignatius Tabi was usually quick in satisfying my requests for relevant documents and read portions of the manuscript. I offer my gratitude to those pastors, elders, sisters, and CWF members I interviewed and who are named in the list of informants at the end of this book. Elders Gladys Shang Viban, Lilian Njalla Quan, Catherine Tamanji, Gladys Diale Ngoe, and Reverends Agnes Ngwa, Cynthia Asenek, Margaret Nchoupouh Azange, Immaculate Neba, and Theresia Uso deserve special thanks for replying to the questionnaire. I am grateful to my students, who have challenged me to present these ideas in a clear manner. I thank especially those in my graduate course on women in African history and development at The University of Bamenda, Cameroon. Considering that writing a book is a family project, I am especially grateful to my wife, Bisherine, for adjusting to my demands. Finally, the highest praise remains for Anthony Ndi for taking me under his wings during my doctoral program. With consistency, he has affirmed my scholarly inquiry since 2010 when we met. I dedicate this book to this mentor, father and friend. In spite all this assistance, I take responsibility for any mistakes of fact or judgment in this book.

List of Photographs, Maps and Tables

Photographs
1. Anna Wuhrmann with female pupils in Foumban, 1911 60
2. Gohring-Kalmbach Margarethe with female pupils in Douala, 1906 61
3. Wildi-Suter Rosli delivering a sewing lesson to females in Buea, 1928 62
4. Students at Basel Mission Girls' School Victoria in 1938 63
5. Zurcher-Roggli Emmy in a practical knitting lesson, 1939 64
6. All-male General Synod Meeting of the Basel Mission Church in Cameroon 79
7. Rev. Grace Dashako and Church Elders at her Induction as Presbytery Treasurer, 2018 143
8. Rev. Agnes Ngwa, Pioneer President of PCC Female Pastors' Conference 147
9. Female Pastors pose with Moderator, Synod Clerk and Secretary of PCC, 2016 149
10. Elder Gladys Shang Viban, Chairperson, East Mungo North Presbytery 162
11. Elder Elizabeth Mbiwan, Teacher at Basel Mission Girls' School, Victoria 170
12. Sisters at Emmanuel Sisterhood in Bafut 189

Map(s)
1. Basel Mission Stations in Southern Cameroons 40

Table(s)
1. Male and Female Enrolment in the PCC Seminary, 1987-2014 131

Abbreviations

AACC	All African Conference of Churches
AICs	African Independent Churches
AMFCO	Association of Meme Female Counsellors
ATR	African Traditional Religion
BODA	Bali Old Boys Association
CBS	Christian Broadcasting Service
CDC	Cameroon Development Corporation
CMF	Christian Men Fellowship
CPC	Cameroon Protestant College
CRTV	Cameroon Radio and Television
CWF	Christian Women Fellowship
EEC	Eglise Evangélique du Cameroun
ETTC	Elementary Teacher Training College
LBMS	London Baptist Missionary Society
NAB	National Archive Buea
NAVDEV	Nkong Hill Top Association for Development
PCC	Presbyterian Church in Cameroon
PCCCALB	Presbyterian Church in Cameroon Central Archive and Library, Buea
PCSA	Presbyterian Church in South Africa
PEM	Paris Evangelical Mission
PTS	Presbyterian Theological Seminary
WCC	World Council of Churches
WEEP	Women's Education and Empowerment Programme
WTTC	Women's Teacher Training College
WWD	Women's Work Department
WWH	Women's Work Helper
YWCA	Young Women Christian Association

Introduction

For over two thousand years, Christianity has had a global impact on the status of women. In the early Christian era, women exercised significant roles, given that the period is replete with examples of women who committed themselves to the Great Commission task in ways that made their participation in the continuous growth of the church indispensable. In religion historian Elizabeth Clark's words, women served as "owners of the houses in which early Christians gathered and as patrons of monasteries, churches, and the poor throughout the patristic and medieval periods."[1] Clearly, Christ's liberating teachings exemplified a more egalitarian form of Christianity before the trajectory of women's demotion set in following the institutionalization of the church. From this moment through to the emergence of various brands of Protestant faiths, as scholarship reveals, there was a struggle within the church on roles for women.[2] As centuries passed, the church remained in the path of patriarchalization in which women were further pushed to the margins of power and leadership.[3]

In Africa in general and Cameroon particularly where there had been a culture of female involvement in traditional religious matters as priestesses and ritual experts, the white missionary era was a moment when women began losing religious status and power. The Basel Mission and other mission agencies that laboured to plant Christianity in Cameroon patriarchalized the mission church, with a second-class citizenship status offered to female faithful. This explains why scholars of women in the history of Christianity in Africa associate the white mission agency era with female demotion. In the slow process of granting autonomy to its mission church in

---

[1] Elisabeth A. Clark, "Women, Gender, and the Study of Christian History", *Church History*, 70 (3), 2001, p. 398.
[2] Margaret Bendroth, "Gender and Twentieth-Century Christianity", in *A People's History of Christianity, Vol. 7, Twentieth-Century Global Christianity*, edited by Mary Farrell Bednarowski, Minneapolis, Fortress Press, 2008, p. 307.
[3] Ronald L. Johnstone, *Religion in Society: A Sociology of Religion*, Fourth Edition, New Jersey, Prentice Hall, 1992, p. 197.

Cameroon, the Basel Mission, just like other mission bodies, left behind a female-hostile legacy, which was inherited and perpetuated by the Presbyterian Church in Cameroon (PCC). So, both the Basel Mission and the PCC resisted including women in leadership positions. Following the rise of Christian feminism, the demand for inclusiveness in ecclesial ministry and authority, as was the case in the early Christian church, gained propensity. The PCC was obliged by this international crusade for women's empowerment in Christian organizations to rethink its gender policy. This amounted to the opening of the ordained ministry to women and the implementation of other gender policies that were intended to roll back the exclusion of women from its power structure. Tacitly, therefore, the PCC recognized the damage it had done to women, and opted to dismantle the structures that have kept women at the margins of the Eucharistic ministry and authority. This revision of church policies towards gender and its degree of effectiveness in the ecclesial empowerment of women cannot be examined without engaging it with existing scholarship, especially the Christian feminist debate.

The twentieth century was marked by a rich scholarly debate about the intentions and effectiveness of Christian feminism as a movement for women empowerment in the church. While observers of this movement admit that feminist ideas created awareness among Christian women and roiled Christian organizations, there are two opposing paradigms on the intentions and effectiveness of the association of the female folks with the church power structure. The first school is the egalitarian, which advocates a level playing field for men and women in Christian organizations.[4] Subscribers to this school argue that similar opportunities ought to be opened to both sexes in all matters of church life, especially in the leadership structure.[5] In intellectual

---

[4] Johanna Wood, "Patriarchy, Feminism and Mary Daly: A Systematic-Theological Enquiry into Daly's Engagement with Gender Issues in Christian Theology", Doctor of Theology Thesis, University of South Africa, p. 3.
[5] L. Japinga, *Feminism and Christianity: An Essential Guide*, Nashville, Abingdon Press, 1999, p. 43.

terms, therefore, the level playing field empowerment approach was forcefully peddled and justified.

In the 1970s, the Christian feminist debate took a new twist, specifically from those who doubted the capacity of women to function properly in the positions of church leadership that were resulting from the female empowerment crusade. Referred in Christian feminist literature as complementarianism, exponents of this school, while accepting the feminist ideal of knocking down ecclesial gender biases, pressed that men have an advantage to monopolize power in non-child related positions. Steven Goldberg supports this view by arguing in *The Inevitability of Patriarchy* that men's gushing testosterone gives them an aggression advantage which enables them to monopolise power in all high-prestige non-child-related positions in the social order. This pushed Goldberg to suggest that women should be prevented from seeking such positions through the imposition of sex roles.[6] He notes that the elimination of sex roles through egalitarian feminism will expose women to frustration since they are doomed to failure. What can be gleaned from this line of thinking is the inevitable conclusion that women cannot live up to the task of church leadership, especially the priesthood. Simply put, their admission into the leadership structures of the church, argues Goldberg and other complementarianism theorists, would be disruptive to the church. This radical pessimistic attitude towards the inclusion of women in the power structure of the church was what caused some scholars to herald a utilitarian backing against female demotion in Christian organizations. The utilitarian perspective simply accords more credibility to the egalitarian paradigm by insisting that the church's utility is diminished by the absence of full female involvement in church administration.[7] Utilitarians make it clear that the restriction of women from ordination negatively affects the church's utility

---

[6] Stevens Goldberg, *The Inevitability of Patriarchy*, New York, William Morrow & Company, 1973.
[7] Read Isabel Apawo Phiri, "Doing Theology in Community: The Case of African Women Theologians in the 1990s", *Journal of Theology for Southern Africa*, Vol. 99, 1997, p. 73.

since it undeniably loses the contribution of women whose gifts are suited to church leadership from which they are excluded.

Although I subscribe to the egalitarian school, this book generally builds on the paradigmatic Christian feminist debate, a field of marked scholarly disagreements: egalitarianism, complementarianism and utilitarianism to analyse the gender question in the Basel Mission Church and Presbyterian Church in Cameroon. This unfolding debate has the potential to richly inform the contentions and analysis of this study. This explains why the book seeks to sustain and enrich this gender debate from the Christian faith perspective by examining the evolutionary dynamics of women's status in the PCC from the era of the Basel Mission. I use the Basel Mission and PCC as Christian organizations for the testing and enrichment of the Christian feminist debate. Surely, the persisting voices for and against the empowerment of women for leadership in the PCC is a clear manifestation of the current Christian feminist theoretical disagreement among scholars of women in Christianity. In 2015, my research on female pastors in the PCC featured in the second edition of *Ibadan Journal of Gender Studies*. The findings of the study revealed that clergywomen were confined at the margins of the church's leadership, despite their call for leadership inclusiveness.[8] Later in 2016, another study on women in the PCC found that opportunities for female leadership in the PCC are more limited than for males, and these limitations have produced a composite picture of women that at least suggests leadership marginality.[9] This book, which pays particular attention to the changing status of women in both the Basel Mission and

---

[8] Michael Kpughe Lang, "The Long Trip to the Front Alter: Women in the Ordained Ministry of the Presbyterian Church in Cameroon, 1957-2010", *Ibadan Journal of Gender Studies*, Vol. 2, 2015. The first draft of this paper was presented at the International Colloquium on Women and Development in Africa in Yaounde, Cameroon from 24-26 June 2015. I am grateful to the organisers for the invitation and the participants at this academic gathering for their useful comments, which helped me to improve on this work.

[9] Michael Kpughe Lang, "Women and Christianity in Cameroon: The Case of the Presbyterian Church in Cameroon since the Basel Mission Era, 1886-2010", *Afro Asian Journal of Social Sciences*, Vol. 7, No. 4, 2016, pp. 1-24.

PCC, took its inspiration in some substantial part from these previous researches.

In addition to the Christian feminism discourse, this book builds on the analytical insights of a large scholarship on women and leadership in Protestant churches, especially the works that have demonstrated the connection between patriarchy and female subordination. Within this broad field, scholars have traced female repression in these churches to gender hierarchies that were promoted by mission agencies, attributing the improvement of women's status in recent decades to female activism.[10] Hannah Mellemsether points to the efforts that were made to give authority to women in the Norwegian Mission in South Africa after many years of exclusion and subordination.[11] This is, to some extent, the case with the Basel Mission in Cameroon and the PCC, whose female members were kept at the margins of power. But while female advocacy in some mission churches permitted women to access power, female activism in the Basel Mission and PCC failed to dismantle the all-male authority. Thus far, most of this scholarship has said very little about female activism's inability to challenge patriarchy. Rather, more attention has been given to successful cases, marked by women's rise to higher echelons of power in churches with a history of male ascendancy and female subservience.

Besides, there is little scholarship on women's place in the Basel Mission and PCC. Some of the scholarship has concentrated on the emancipation of local women by Western missionaries, which significantly transformed their morality, sexuality, economic power, and political participation in the wider society. Fiona Bowie, for

---

[10] See L. Nyhagen Predelli, "Contested Patriarchy and Missionary Feminism: The Norwegian Missionary Society in Nineteenth Century Norway and Madagascar", Faculty of the Graduate School, University of Southern California, 1998; Ulrike Sill, *Encounters in Quest of Christian Womanhood: The Basel Mission in Pre- and Early Colonial Ghana*, London, Brill, 2010; Inger Marie Okkenhaug, ed., *Gender, Race and Religion: Nordic Mission, 1860-1940*, Studia Uppsala, Missionalia Svecana XCI, 2003.

[11] Hannah Mellemsether, "African Women in the Norwegian Mission in South Africa", in Inger Marie Okkenhaug, ed., *Gender, Race and Religion: Nordic Mission, 1860-1940*, Studia Uppsala, Missionalia Svecana XCI, 2003.

example, examines the setting up of what was known as 'Sister Mammy' Settlement by Mill Hill missionaries in an attempt to define women's roles in British Southern Cameroons.[12] Bowie's work, which completely ignores the Basel Mission situation, is silent about how such emancipation impacted women's status in the church. Adams examines the links between colonial and missionary policies and women's participation in public life in British Southern Cameroons.[13] She submits that the propagation of Western notions of domesticity by missionaries provided women with constraints and opportunities for participation in public life. While the home became the operational space for many women, others used the skills to participate in political and economic life. Simply put, missionary policies were both empowering and domesticating. In a recent study, Jacqueline-Bethel Mougoue examines women's participation in the Anglophone Cameroonian nationalist movement from 1961 to 1972. Formally educated women, argues Mougoue, were active participants in the struggle to protect the cultural values and the self-determination of the Southern Cameroons state.[14] Existing research has therefore concentrated on women's agency in public life in Cameroon, with no focus on how they were represented in church leadership structures. In fact, Basel Mission history in Cameroon has been written from a male-perspective, obviously because patriarchy had yielded male preponderance.[15]

---

[12] Fiona Bowie, "The Elusive Christian Family: Missionary Attempts to Define Women's Roles: Case Studies from Cameroon", In Fiona Bowie, Deborah Kirkwood and Shirley Ardener, eds., *Women and Missions: Past and Present: Anthropological and Historical Perceptions*, London, Bloomsbury Publishing, 1993.

[13] Melinda Adams, "Colonial Policies and Women's Participation in Public Life: The Case of British Southern Cameroons," *African Studies Quarterly*, Vol. 8, No. 2, 2006.

[14] Jacqueline-Bethel Mougoue, Gender, Separatist Politics, and Embodied Nationalism in Cameroon, Michigan, University of Michigan Press, 2019.

[15] See for example Mathew Basung Gwanfogbe, *Basel Mission Education in Cameroon, 1886-1968*, Bamenda, Quality Printers, 2018; J. N. Dah, "Missionary Motivations and Methods: A Critical Examination of the Basel Mission in Cameroon 1886-1914", PhD Thesis in Theology, University of Basel, 1983; J. N. Dah, "The Vision and Challenges of an Autonomous Church", In Jonas N. Dah ed. *Presbyterian Church in Cameroon: 50 Years of Selfhood* (Limbe: Presprint, 2007), 15-55; E. Hallden, *The Culture Policy of the Basel Mission in the*

This book tells a different story of women and the church in Cameroon, which complements and extends the existing scholarship in this field. Using two case studies, it outlines a new analytical framework that examines the ineffectiveness of female activism to challenge discriminations against women in church executive structures. It focuses on the repression and exclusion of women from positions of leadership in both the Basel Mission in Cameroon and the Presbyterian Church in Cameroon. The book's core arguments and observations complicate some established contentions about the status of women in Christianity in Africa. First, I argue that women were reserved an admired status in African Traditional Religion (ATR), as opposed to the view that they were marginalized. Rather, the status of women in religion began to diminish in Cameroon, just like elsewhere in Africa, with the advent of Western Christianity – a religion with an entrenched system of patriarchy that kept women in a narrowly defined place. Second, this book sees Western missionary women empowerment initiatives as a flawed approach that kept women at the margins of church leadership. I posit that historians researching on Cameroon have overlooked the role of Western Christian mission agencies in diminishing the status of women. I point out that Basel Mission's pursuance of the policy of training women in fields like motherhood, domestic science and marriage made the home to become the narrowed space for women. This yielded a pattern of predominantly male leadership in the structures of the Basel Mission.

Third, although scholars like Adams and Mougoue[16] argue that some of the colonial and missionary policies yielded unintended opportunities to women for education, salaried employment, and political activism, they overlook how this influenced women's participation in church leadership. Hu Weiqing has used the

---

Cameroons 1886-1905, Lund, Berlingska Boktryckeriet, 1968; and Keller Werner, *The History of the Presbyterian Church in Cameroon*, Victoria, Presbook, 1969.

[16] Melinda Adams, "Colonial Policies and Women's Participation in Public Life: The Case of British Southern Cameroons", *African Studies Quarterly*, Vol. 8, No. 2, 2006, pp. 1-22.

Chaozhou community in South-East China as a case study to argue that women were placed at the margins of power in the Presbyterian congregation, attributing the gender inequality to the sacred division of labour in terms of gender in the congregation.[17] Here I argue that a careful analysis of the domesticity empowerment approach of mission agencies like the Basel Mission reveals that, while women used the skills attained in domestic science centres to increase their participation in public life, their participation in church leadership structures remained low. In Cameroon, the Basel Mission did not associate women with church leadership. Clearly, the secular society was friendlier towards women than the missionary church. Fourth, I argue that the Presbyterian Church in Cameroon (PCC) and many other African churches that emerged from Western mission agencies found it difficult to dismantle the patriarchal culture they inherited from their founding missions. After close to six decades of empowerment, women have largely remained at the margins of PCC's leadership structure from top to bottom, with men bossing them.

Despite consistent recourse to controversial women's empowerment models within the PCC, the resultant marginalization of its female faithful is little known to Presbyterians or to the society at large. This partly results from the flawed impression that women participate in church leadership by belonging to the various social groups that have been created to accommodate them. It is also believed that women's access to the ordained ministry has empowered them for leadership in the church. But the truism is that women have been groomed to accept their marginal status in the structures of the church. So, a comprehensive analysis of the changing status of women in the PCC since the era of the Basel Mission is long overdue. Knowledge about how controversial gender policies have occasioned the discrimination of women is important to Presbyterians and non-Presbyterians alike. This should concur with Bendroth's contention that the Christian church "has

---

[17] Weiqing Hu, "The Mode of Misery: Women Evangelists and their Witnesses to Christian Doctrines in Modern Lingdong Region," *Journal of Hanshan Teachers College*, Vol. 4, 2001.

followed dominant cultural models, assigning women the obligation of self-sacrifice and men the power to lead, regardless of the strain this might impose on both."[18]

As part of my research, I spent the whole of 2018 consulting archival materials and interviewing more than a hundred Christians and officials of the PCC, including many female pastors and elders as well as some former and current church leaders. Letters, reports, speeches and meeting minutes gotten from the PCC Central Archive in Buea as well as interviews with women, men and church officials have provided data on women's experiences in the structures of the Basel Mission and the PCC. Female Christians and clergywomen were particularly interested to talk about their experiences as members of a church with an entrenched patriarchal culture. Most of my quotations are from these interviews, as I have tried to allow these women to speak for themselves. We gathered from the interviewees information about the way the structures of the PCC have kept women at the margins of leadership in a context of controversial empowerment models inherited from the Basel Mission. In fact, this book builds on an astonishing range of archival, oral and secondary data to argue that women were marginalized in the structures of the Basel Mission and PCC due to the implementation of problematic empowerment initiatives. The premise of the book is that over the last several decades, starting from 1886 when the Basel Mission began evangelical work in Cameroon, the PCC and its founding mission agency have pursued gender policies that kept women at the margins of church leadership. The book, therefore, is about women's struggle for empowerment and resultant minimal participation in the leadership structures of both churches.

The Meaning of Sex and Gender

The understanding of gender and sex in both Western and African contexts can inform analysis on women's changing status in the power structures of the Basel Mission and later the PCC. Generally construed as the biological and anatomical separation of

---

[18] Bendroth, 2008, p. 307.

human beings into males and females, sex is determined at birth. In fact, biological differences which are evidenced by varying body organs, have divided humanity into men and women. Because of beliefs about sex differences, societies ascribed dissimilar roles and responsibilities to men and women based on their values and beliefs about gender. So, analysing women's roles and responsibilities in the Basel Mission and PCC requires an understanding of the term "gender".

Often confused with the term "sex", gender is a social construction of what it means to be male or female in a given society. In all societies, male and female roles are determined by how gender is construed. This implies that the values of a given society and its conception of gender roles have a bearing on the status of men and women. Little wonder gender is not uniformly construed across cultures, and gender roles, which are anchored on group expectations, differ from one society to another. Ann Oakley attributes human roots to gender, insisting that it is a social construction even though its meaning is shaped by male and female anatomical variations. This acclaimed feminist sociologist acknowledged the gender-culture nexus and described gender as the "social classification of men and women into masculinity and feminine."[19] In other words, gender refers to the social and cultural understanding of biological sex differences, and this determines the rights and functions of men and women in human societies.

This social and cultural conception of gender roles changes from culture to culture and over time and circumstances. Gender was construed in different ways across Western societies, and it shaped women's public roles. In most societies, the social definition of women's functions was restrictive and oppressive. In the Western world, there was a heterogeneous gender system which was generally favourable to men. It has been established that women in Western societies were traditionally ascribed a nurturing role. Based on a biased definition of femininity and masculinity, Western societies became intensely male-dominated, and the female sex was

---

[19] Read Ann Oakley, *Sex, Gender and Society* (Revised Edition), Farnham, Surrey, Ashgate, 2015.

construed as less capable in public life. Throughout the nineteenth century, gender was a social and cultural construct that defined the conscriptions of women in taking part in public life. According to Towns, women's exclusion from public life had become a standard of civilization in Europe in the eighteenth century.[20] It was socially constructed in a way that placed women at the margins of church governance structures. Intended to challenge this patriarchy, Western feminism attributed women's subordination to capitalism and erroneously claimed that this was a defining feature of all human societies.

Such universalization of women's subservience to men is challenged by evidence from some non-Western societies. In African traditional life, roles and functions determined the way gender was construed, and this differed from one society to another and over time and circumstances. The social and cultural construction of gender in African societies caused women to be conspicuous in public life, contrary to their Western counterparts who hardly functioned beyond the home. Culture shaped gender in ways that led female and male purviews to be construed as separate and complementary.[21] Ifi Amadiume challenges the universal subordination of women assumed by Western feminists and builds on evidence from the Nnobi community in South Eastern Nigeria to argue that the social construction of gender guaranteed women power.[22] In Cameroon, every community had socially constructed norms and beliefs about the appropriate role of women in society. Developed through socialization, gender roles reflected expectations that were associated with roles ascribed to men and women. As Phyllis Kaberry explains, gender roles in the Cameroon

---

[20] Ann Towns, "The Status of Women as a Standard of 'Civilization'", *European Journal of International Relations*, Vol. 15, No. 4, 2009, p. 686.

[21] See Niara Sudarkasa, "The Status of Women in Indigenous African Societies", *Feminist Studies*, Vol. 12, No. 1, 1986; Afisi Oseni Taiwo, "Power and Womanhood in Africa: An Introductory Evaluation", *The Journal of Pan African Studies*, Vol. 3, No. 6, 2010, pp. 229-238.

[22] Read Ifi Amadiume, *Male Daughters, Female Husbands: Gender and Sex in an African Society*, London, Zed Press, 1987.

Grassfields were socially constructed and negotiated.[23] Based on the conception of gender as complementary, women actively participated in public life, even though their public roles varied across ethnic communities. The cross-cultural variation in gender role norms and attitudes notwithstanding, the agency of women in political, economic and religious life was a hallmark of all indigenous societies. So, gender roles for women permitted them to play active roles in society. Among the Laimbwe in northwest Cameroon as noted by Kah, gender socialization of girls anchored on matriliny and began during childhood and adolescence, and it was intended to mould them into self-sufficient, assertive, and active members of the community.[24] No wonder Laimbwe women assumed a variety of public roles just like elsewhere in Cameroon and Africa. Matriliny and patriliny were the two principal gender constructions in Cameroon; under both systems, women played public roles.[25]

Building on the foregoing discussion, I use the term "gender" to denote the social prescriptions associated with biological sex in regard to rights and functions. Acknowledging the centrality of gender to the Christian missionary movement, this study describes unequal power relationships in church governance structures and discusses how this found expression in the Basel Mission and Presbyterian Church in Cameroon. Put differently, the ways in which gender was conceived of and deployed determined women's degree of participation in both Christian organizations. Based on evidence from the Basel Mission and PCC, this study uses gender to describe a power system in which women were subordinated to men and restricted from playing power roles. Gender affects women's participation and entitlements in decision-making within the church. It eases the comprehension of the unequal structure of

---

[23] Phyllis M. Keberry, *Women of the Grassfields: A Study of the Economic Position of Women in Bamenda, British Cameroons*, New Edition, London, Routledge, 2004.

[24] Read Henry Kam Kah, *The Sacred Forest: Gender and Matriliny in the Laimbwe History (Cameroon), C. 1750-2001*, Munster, LIT Verlag, 2015, pp. 40-41.

[25] For a detailed discussion of matriliny and patriliny as gender constructions, read Emmanuel Yenshu Vubo, "Matriliny and Patriliny Between Cohabitation-Equilibrium and Modernity in the Cameroon Grassfields", *African Study Monographs*, Vol. 26, No. 3, 2005, pp. 145-182.

power that underlies the relationship between men and women, and helps explain the marginalization of female Christians in the PCC. An insightful analysis of women's changing status in both the Basel Mission and PCC supports the claim that gender is dynamic.

The cultural contexts that produced Western and Cameroonian conceptions of gender roles along sex lines influenced rights and functions that were ascribed to women. Shaped by these Western gender norms, the Basel Mission fashioned a power structure that was intensely male-dominated. This Western patriarchal culture became a central element of missionary enterprise in Cameroon, and little or no attention was given to the indigenous conception of gender as complementarity. Missionaries deployed to Cameroon by the Basel Mission were products of this Western gender system, which led them to restrict women from participation in the executive structures of the mission church. As argued in this book, these foreign missionaries overlooked and downplayed the local culture and historical circumstances which had yielded a gender system friendly to women. They introduced the culture of barring women from religious (church) governance and later handed it down to male Cameroonian clerics.[26] No doubt PCC's leadership structures were initially defined as exclusively for men, with women facing exclusion as in the era of the Basel Mission. In these churches, particular traits and statuses were ascribed to the female sex, and this amounted to their marginalization in governance. This book builds on this social conception of gender to analyse women's participation in the power structures of these churches. It takes the social construction of gender into the heart of our understanding of women's leadership roles in the Basel Mission and later the Presbyterian Church in Cameroon.

The book is divided into two major parts. Part one consists of four chronologically and thematically structured chapters which examine the status of women in the Basel Mission Church in

---

[26] This concurs with Ifi Amadiume's observation that colonialism and Western Christianity imposed patriarchal systems on African societies which eroded women's power. For a detailed of how Western religion narrowed women's space in Africa, read Ifi Amadiume, *Re-Inventing Africa: Matriarchy, Religion, and Culture*, London, Zed Press, 1997.

Cameroon. Chapter one examines the status of women in a Cameroonian indigenous religious context. It looks at the world of Cameroonian women before its encounter with Western Christianity. By engaging the religious status of women in pre-Christian Cameroonian societies from the perspective of their role as priestesses, ritualists, and mediums, I advance the argument that African Traditional Religion did not discriminate against women. The chapter demonstrates that indigenous religious traditions in societies across Cameroon offered women opportunities to act as ritualists, leaders and priestesses. It serves as a foundation for understanding the great changes that occurred in women's status as members of the Basel Mission Church and later PCC since the late nineteenth century.

Chapter two provides a historical context of the Basel Mission as a leeway to appreciate women's status in Christianity in Cameroon since the last quarter of the nineteenth century. The historical roots of the Basel Mission are examined in view of appreciating how patriarchy got entrenched in its system to the point of placing women at the margins of mission work and power structures. This will reveal the context in which the Basel Mission exported to Cameroon, like elsewhere, controversial women's emancipation and empowerment mechanisms that were detrimental to their active participation in its leadership structures.

Chapter three investigates the exportation and implementation of controversial Western women's empowerment ideologies by European missionaries sent to Cameroon by the Basel Mission. It demonstrates the encounter between "the Christian Home" model and local Christian women, showing how it was expressed through the diffusion of Western knowledge on marriage, childcare, and domestic science. It is this chapter's thesis that such empowerment, informed by Western domestic ideals and the entrenched patriarchy in the structures of the Basel Mission was controversial in ways that were detrimental to the participation of women in the leadership structures of the Basel Mission. It was an empowerment policy that narrowed the woman's space to the home, while leadership in the Basel Mission Church in Cameroon, like in other mission territories, was the preserve of men.

Chapter four takes the reader into the patterns of discrimination against women in the leadership structures of the Basel Mission from 1886 to 1968. It explores what the domestic empowerment doctrine analysed in chapter three meant with respect to gender relations in the leadership structures of the Basel Mission, arguing that it yielded a seemingly all-pervasive male dominance over women. In fact, female church adherents were predominant in the Basel Mission church, but males dominated church leadership.

In part two, women's status in the Presbyterian Church in Cameroon is examined. Chapter Five is devoted to the treatment of women's work in the PCC in view of appreciating its bearing on women's participation in the church's leadership structures. The first section examines women's empowerment through the activities of the Christian Women Fellowship CWF under the coordination of the Women's Work Department. The section pays particular attention to the operation mechanism and activities of the CWF, arguing that the church group has not been able to roll away patriarchy in the power structures of the church. In section two, I examine PCC's empowerment of women in the context of the Ecumenical Decade of the Churches in Solidarity with women launched in 1988 by the World Council of Churches. In the final section, the role of the Women's Education and Empowerment Programme (WEEP) in the empowerment of women for leadership is analysed. Overall, the chapter seeks to demonstrate that, in spite women's empowerment initiatives through the CWF, the Ecumenical Decade of the Churches in Solidarity with Women (1988-1998), and the WEEP, interactions between men and women in the PCC have this far, coursed within an imbalance of power, with women largely remaining subservient to male leadership hegemony. Indeed, the progress made in associating women with leadership through women's work is meagre, and represents only a slight shift from the all-male Basel Mission power structure.

Chapter Six critically explores the bases and changing trends of women's participation in the ordained ministry of the PCC in view of appreciating the extent to which it has enhanced the empowerment of female pastors for full participation in the leadership of the church. It pays particular attention to the extent to which elective and appointive leadership positions are accessed by female pastors. It argues that the PCC opened its ordained ministry to women but put restrictions on their access to leadership positions. In fact, opportunities for female pastors to access the church's executive structures are more limited than for male pastors, and this discrimination has produced a consistent marginalization of clergywomen in the church's power structures.

In Chapter Seven, church eldership is presented as one of the rare spheres in which women have been prominent in the power structure of the PCC. The chapter sustains the argument that although patriarchy remained entrenched within the PCC, women's participation in the eldership revealed the remarkable gifts and skills they possessed. This is a clear case of how male-female complementarity can be beneficial to church governance and growth. To better articulate this argument, the chapter examines the requirements for the eldership. It further examines the responsibilities of female elders and their participation in decision-making structures of the church. It ends with an analysis of the limitations of eldership as a tool for women's association with the church's power structure.

In chapter Eight, the role of nuns of the Emmanuel Sisterhood in the power structure of the PCC is examined. I argue in this chapter that although the nuns have responded to the human and societal needs of Presbyterians and non-Presbyterians, they were/are consistently placed at the margins of leadership in the church. The vowed sisters were/are not assigned to positions of responsibility and their leadership roles were/are mostly limited to the administration of the convent. Just like the female pastors, Emmanuel Sisters did not question the institutional structures that perpetuate their marginalization in the church. Simply put, the nuns are meek servants who have consistently displayed submission to the church patriarchy.

Chapter Nine concludes the study.

Part I:

Women in Traditional Religion and Basel Mission Church in Cameroon

Chapter 1

Goddesses and High Priestesses: Women's Status in Cameroonian Traditional Religions

The crafting of the numerous ethnic communities in Cameroon was the joint effort of men and women who played complementary roles as migrants in search of a permanent home. The peopling of various parts of the country by these migrants gave birth to an aura of ethnic communities in which men and women were expected to function in collegiality for their collective wellbeing. There was evidence of gender relations deeply rooted in traditions and customs fashioned over time and circumstances.[1] These customs and traditions which emanated from the collective initiatives of the people hinged on beliefs, values, attitudes, religions, roles and possessions. It was in this context of a shared culture that ethnicities across Cameroon, just like elsewhere, were structured along political, economic, social, and religious lines. The functional mechanisms within each of these cultures had a bearing on women's status in society. They defined the manner in which women were associated with governance, succession, economy, healthcare, marriage, education, and indigenous religious observances. Overall, women, just like their male counterparts, were prominent in traditional societies. They held roles of political, economic, social, and religious authority. This is an indication that women held political and social roles of authority beyond the domestic sphere to which Western Christianity eventually confined them. In this chapter, an effort is made to explore the status women had in indigenous religions in pre-Christian Cameroonian societies. The main contention, intended to further complicate outmoded and problematic Western notions on African gender systems, is that indigenous religions of Cameroonian ethnicities had long offered

---

[1] Read Emmanuel Yenshu Vubo, ed., *Gender Relations in Cameroon: Multidisciplinary Perspectives*, Bamenda, Langaa RPCIG, 2012.

women leadership opportunities in their structures before the coming of Western Christianity.

Before the encounter with Christianity, African Traditional Religion (ATR) was the dominant faith tradition in Cameroon just like in many other societies across Africa. As an expression of the people's customs and beliefs that were inbuilt in their culture, ATR resulted from the intellectual acumen and creative endeavours of the indigenous people in Cameroon. The religious beliefs and practices of the numerous ethnic groups were important for enabling the people to cope with the complex world in which they lived. According to Mbaku, religion permits people to address emotional problems and provides answers to questions about the meaning of life.[2] In pre-Christian Cameroon, there was a diversity of indigenous religions which was a reflection of the multi-ethnic reality of society. The ethnographic landscape of Cameroon at the time was comprised of a complex network of ethnic groups: the Tikar, the Widekum, the Chamba, the Fang-Beti, the Sawa, the Fulbe, among others.[3] Today, Cameroon is a blend of more than 250 of such ethnic entities, with each having a Traditional Religion traced to the origin and settlement of the people. The religious beliefs and practices of each ethnic entity were characterized by prayer, ritual, sacrifice and an aura of beliefs that were/are embedded in the culture of the people. Each group was further broken up into sub-groups that have made Cameroon to be described as a hugely multi-ethnic country. Although each society had its own religion, they nonetheless shared many common religious beliefs and practices. This explains why ATR is considered in this study as a single religious tradition that enjoyed a communal and an absolute status throughout much of the pre-Christian period in Cameroon.

There were many cross-cutting features of ATR such as the belief in a Supreme Being whose appellation was as varied as the ethnic groups. For example, among the Gbaya, God is *Gbaso* (Great

---

[2] John Mukum Mbaku, *Culture and Customs of Cameroon*. London: Greenwood Press, 2005.

[3] V. G. Fanso, *Cameroon History for Secondary Schools and Colleges, Vol. 1, From Prehistoric Times to the Nineteenth Century*. London: Macmillan, 1989.

Spirit and Creator). Among the Nso, God is *Nyuy* while the Fang-Beti call Him *Zambe*. So, God was actually worshipped in ATR in pre-colonial Cameroon. Other common features included the belief in spirits/divinities, belief in life after death, the existence of religious personnel and sacred places and numerous magic practices. Generally, Traditional Religion affected all aspects of life, from farming to hunting, from travel to courtship, and from birth to death. No wonder John Mbiti underlines the religious notoriety of Africans.[4] Prior to the introduction of other faith traditions, ATR had permeated all aspects of societal life: political, economic and social. As Moyo writes, traditional religion was "a way of life in which the whole community is involved, and as such it is identical with life."[5] Undeniably, therefore, ATR influenced the lives of many people in Cameroon through its absolute and communal ritual practices. The religious authorities exercised jurisdiction over many aspects of spiritual life.

In considering women's status in pre-Christian Cameroonian ethnicities, one is confronted by the diversity in societal complexity ranging from the northern Sahel to the coastal forest polities. And considering that Basel Mission work never covered the whole of Cameroon, I chose to focus the discussion on the status of women in traditional religious systems to the ethnicities that constituted the former British Southern Cameroons. This choice is further inspired by the fact that though the Basel Mission began work in Cameroon in 1886 during the era of German colonialism, her sphere of operation covered only the southern part of Cameroon. Due to the First World War, fought in Cameroon from 1914 to 1916, the German missionary enterprise in the territory was significantly altered. All missionaries with German roots were forcibly deported in the course of the war. This orphaned the Basel Mission, while Britain and France sought to officially terminate the work of these missions and to invite loyal agencies to take over. Recourse to this policy was accelerated following the Anglo-French partition of

---

[4] John S. Mbiti, *Introduction to African Religions*, London, Heinemann, 1975.
[5] Ambrose Moyo, "Religion in Africa". In April A. Gordon & Donald L. Gordon, (ed.). *Understanding Contemporary Africa*, Second Edition, London, Lynne Rienner Publishers, 1996, p. 12.

Cameroon in 1916. In the French section, the Paris Evangelical Mission (PEM) succeeded the Basel Mission. Efforts to put a final end to Basel Mission work in the part of Cameroon under British administration met with fierce resistance. This caused the British government to lift the ban on the Basel Mission in 1924. In 1925, the Basel Mission resumed work in British Southern Cameroons, while France maintained the prohibition on the German mission agency to missionize in French Cameroon.[6] From 1925 to 1957, therefore, Basel Mission work covered only Southern Cameroons which constituted less than one fifth of the Cameroonian territory. Consequently, the discussion on women's status in indigenous religions will give attention to societies in the part of Cameroon that eventually became known as British Southern Cameroons.

The female divinity system inbuilt in some indigenous religions is a lens through which women's status in traditional societies can be appreciated. Cameroonian societies display a plurality of divinities that are united under one Supreme Being. The female divinity system in Cameroonian ethnicities is rooted in the African mother image. This conception of God as female in some communities could have resulted from the flawed perception of childbirth as the sole responsibility of a woman. Small wonder women were portrayed in many local proverbs as indispensable to the wellbeing and sustenance of society due to their procreative and nurturing abilities. There was/is a belief among Weh people that Women were partners with God in the creation of human life. Among the Bali Nyonga people in the northwest of Cameroon, a woman's pregnancy was described as "God (*Nyikob*) has licked her." The expression meant that pregnancy was understood as a blessing from God.[7] The resultant conception of God as female served as a basis for gender cohesion in Cameroonian ethnicities. In fact, Goddesses

---

[6] For more information on the mistreatment of German missions in Cameroon in the First World War context, read Michael Kpughe Lang, "The Plight of German Missions in Mandate Cameroon: An Historical Analysis," *Brazilian Journal of African Studies*, Vol. 2, No. 3, 2017.

[7] George Fochang Babila, "An Exploration of the Conception of God among the Bali Nyonga and its Impact upon Their Contemporary Christian Practice with Particular Reference to Hymnody and Prayer," Masters Dissertation in Theology, University of KwaZulu Natal, 2004, p. 53.

are indispensable in indigenous religiosity as they are directly connected with the divine creation abilities of women. Bankole writes that "African goddesses are most associated with the process of human creation in terms of womanhood, fertility, childbirth, and pregnancy."[8] This is more of a divine recognition of the indispensable role of women in pre-Christian African societies. Segueda who makes a case for women's respect in traditional African societies says that "many natural processes related to women, such as childbirth, were considered mysterious, and thus women enjoyed great prestige."[9] In some Cameroonian societies where goddesses were powerful, special shrines, temples and ritual observances were reserved for them. They were omnipotent, omnipresent beings who performed the same functions as God. Their control and influence affected the lives of male and female mortal beings without distinction. This centrality of women in the indigenous conception of the Supreme Being provided the context for women's participation in traditional religious leadership structures.

The fact that there existed both male and female divinities was an indication that women had a special religious status in some communities in Cameroon. This should not surprise anybody given the collective portrayal of the woman at the time as the mother of children, mother of the community, and mother of humanity. Among the Weh in Cameroon's northwest, divinities were held to be responsible for all the good and evil that occurred. This accounted for the regularity of sacrifices to divinities by male and female ritualists in an effort to attract prosperity, good health, protection, wives, husbands, children and other forms of good fortunes. The intention was to appease the divinities to avoid any misfortune that could come from an embittered divinity. It was

---

[8] Katherine Olukemi Bankole, "Goddesses" in *Encyclopedia of African Religion*, edited by Asante, Molefi Kete and Mazama, Ama, London, SAGE Publications Ltd., 2009, p. 293.

[9] Wendpanga Eric Segueda, "Imported Religions, Colonialism and the Situation of Women in Africa," *Schriftenreihe Junges Afrikazentrum*, Vol. 3, 2015, p. 4. This belief resulted from society's initial ignorance about the sex-birth connection. The creation of new life was thus misunderstood to be the sole preserve of women, with men having nothing to do with it.

believed that failure to offer sacrifice or show gratitude could result in the punishment of the individual or entire community by a particular divinity. Female ritualists, just like their male counterparts, officiated sacrificial observances that attracted good fortunes from divinities.

The co-existence of patriarchy and matriarchy in the traditional society amounted to complementary roles for men and women in indigenous religious professions. The prophetic roles of women in their societies were huge. Their power and status in traditional religious structures found expression in the roles they played as priestesses, queen mothers and ritual specialists. This implies that Cameroonian indigenous religious traditions have long offered women leadership opportunities in their structures. Women in traditional communities were known to be powerful queen mothers and priestesses, with religious responsibilities spanning the entire society and affecting both males and females. While most queen mothers were born into their roles like those in Bafut, Aghem, Mmen, Nso, Bamileke country and in many other traditional societies, some gained such leadership status by appointment. Among the Nso, for instance, the High Priestess (*Yewon*) and the queen mother (*Ya*) assisted in governance and in the observance of ritual ceremonies. Hierarchically, they come next to the King (*Fon*). The *Ya* was the mother, sister, or daughter of the *Fon* who were conferred the title upon the succession of a *Fon*. The title was conferred upon the sister or daughter only if the *Fon's* mother was dead. In commemoration of mothers of departed *fons*, the title of *Ya* was conferred upon other women of the royal lineage.[10] This is almost similar to what was done in the Chamba fondom of Bali-Gham. Here, the natural mother of the ruler (*manfon*) or her princess representative was conferred the title of queen mother upon the enthronement of a new ruler. Among the Chamba polities, queen mothers were dressed in male royal attire and were offered a special royal stool. In the absence of the king for war or diplomatic visits, the queen mother's stool was taken to the palace

---

[10] P. M. Kaberry, *Women of the Grassfields*, London, Routledge, 2004, p. 9.

since she acted as regent.[11] Among the Aghem, the dwelling house of the queen mother (*natum*) was the *nduni*. It was a ritual lodge were kings were buried and a place where important governance and spiritual issues were discussed. The *natum* attended the *nduni* when it was in session except when war was discussed.[12] The *kefab*, a female regulatory society that was headed by the *natum* had powers to check the excesses of the king, with the possibility of deposing him.

For context, the position of queen mother in the traditional governance system is possibly traced to what Molefi Kete Asante describes as the first ancestor, founding family, founding mother, or divine clan lineage. These female royals who were vested with leadership responsibilities were infused with special supernatural power of divinity. This made them indispensable in the traditional governance system, given that it was through their ritual functions that the society kept its bond with the Supreme Being. As such, queen mothers carried influential spiritual power as leaders of ceremonies and rituals. This explains why they were in charge of shrines and cultic centres. As religious officials, queen mothers and other women served as high priestesses and performed rites of passage such as birth, puberty, marriage, death, and mourning. They were also involved in supplication rites for rain, good health, children, and good harvest. They also had responsibility over purification and thanksgiving rites for various achievements in the community. Overall, women were associated with ceremonies which were special occasions that marked particular social, economic, political, or historical moments in a society's experience. This lends credence to the claim that traditional religion shaped women's lives and status in the pre-Christian society.

Among the Weh, the queen mother and other noble women performed cleansing rituals for children. It hinged on the belief that spirits and gods are a solution to barrenness. The Weh put in place special symbols, gods, rituals and ceremonies intended to check childlessness among men and women. To address the problem of infertility, the Weh observed the *Kengbeum* ritual that was officiated

---

[11] E. M. Chilver and P. M. Kaberry, *Traditional Bamenda: The Pre-colonial History and Ethnography of the Bamenda Grassfields*. London, 1967, p. 74.
[12] Ibid., p. 76.

by high priestesses. The latter served as intermediaries between those who were infertile and the ancestors and Supreme Being. Those who officiated at the ritual were principally ritual priestesses who belonged to the prestigious women's society called *Kefab*. This domination by female priestesses who went by the name *na'tum* can be explained in two ways. First, this frontline role of women probably resulted from the fact that the dilemma of barrenness in Weh as elsewhere in the grassfields weighed more on women than men. In an interview with Taiheart Akwo, he said that the Weh believed that a man's ability to produce children depends on the fertility of the woman.[13] This information goes to support Mbiti's view that the sorrows of being childless go very deep in the wife.[14] Given that a woman could be divorced, stigmatized, psychologically depressed, and forced to look for other wives for her husband because of flawed understanding of infertility, women probably took upon themselves to fight the problem. Second, procreation played an important role in defining the status of women in the Weh society. In fact, childless women were not allowed to gain membership into prestigious societies especially *Kefab*. As observed by Geary, barren women could not become *Kefab* members and were exempted from all the social and economic advantages that accrued from it.[15]

Irrespective of the explanation we give to female dominance, the *Kengbeum* ritual was conducted by the *na'tum* after consulting the Fon and elders who were members of the Weh traditional council called *Ndau-tse*. It was quite often necessitated by the inability of many couples to bear children. When the *Ndau-tse* had given its accord for the ritual to take place, the *na'tum* spread the news of the *Kengbeum* through various channels: quarter heads and country-wide town crier. On the day of the ritual, the *Ndau-tse* lodge was destroyed and reconstructed. This is because the mud with which the house was constructed was an indispensable item required for

---

[13] Interview with Taiheart Akwo, Member of Ndau-tse, Weh, 27 April 2013.
[14] John Mbiti, "The Role of Women in African Traditional Religion", *Cahiers des Religions Africaines*, no 22, 1988, pp. 69-82.
[15] Christraud Geary, "Traditional Societies and Associations in We (North West Province, Cameroon)", *Paideuma*, no 25, 1979, p. 69.

the ritual. It was only at this stage that male ritual officiants were involved in the *Kengbeum*. The senior members of *Ndau-tse* including the Fon offered sacrifices to the departed elders at the lodge in view of soliciting their intervention for the success of the *Kengbeum*. Still on this day, the Fon visited the collective royal grave at the palace where he poured palm wine from the sacrificial cup of the village (*sou inah*) and said prayers intended to attract children from the Great Being and ancestors. As earlier pointed out, Geary limited the role of Weh indigenous religion as a fertility determinant to the sacrifices performed by the Fon on the royal grave.

The sacrifices and prayers were followed by the reconstruction or renovation of the *Ndau-tse* building by senior Weh notables who were mostly members of cult associations such as *Ndau-ifa, Ndau-mbaa, ndau-kenyi, ndau-ibamme, and ndau-keze*. They were supervised by the members of *Ndau-tse* who assisted the Fon in his ritual tasks. As the construction of the lodge was ongoing, all the members of the *Kefab* society (*na'tum*) led by the overall *na'tum* who was the most senior woman in the Weh society (the Fon's senior wife) went round the village to gather all men and women suffering from infertility. While singing songs of praise to the ancestors, the *nat'tum* conveyed the women to the Fon's palace where the construction of the *Ndau-tse* lodge was taking place. At the palace, the barren men and women were undressed and displayed at the esplanade. The leftover of the mud with which the lodge was constructed was used in rubbing the participants and was accompanied by prayers offered by the priestesses (*na'tum*). In this prayer, the priestesses brought before the Supreme Being and ancestors the problem of barrenness. According to Christiana Nnam, one of the *na'tums* I interviewed, the belief was that the ancestral spirits of the departed members of the *Ndau-tse* and *Kefab* exercised healing power especially by conveying the fertility request to the Supreme Being. In fact, the prayer offered on behalf of the barren by priestesses showed how they solicited relief for infertility from the spirit-world.

From the palace, the officiants and barren people journeyed to a ritual stream called *Dzu Wai*. Those officiating hung special herbs round their necks and led the crowd to the stream. At the stream, prayers that were similar to those said in the palace were recited by the *na'tum*. The visit to the stream was necessitated by the belief that the ancestors and Supreme Being had responded positively to their prayer. So, they went to the stream to further pray and wash away all what was responsible for the infertility. The ritual at the stream ended with the offering of invocations and the placing of a special herb on the necks of all participants. This can be compared to the traditional religious prayers offered by women in Burundi to relief infertility described by Mbiti.[16] The Weh believed that the herbs could prevent the misfortune from re-engulfing those who took part in the *Kengbeum*. From the stream, the participants led by priestesses sang songs of joy on their way back to the palace. It was upon their return to the palace that the final phase of the ritual commenced. It was marked by the rubbing of the participants with camwood mixed with palm oil. This was followed by eating and drinking in the course of which all participants received blessings from the Fon. After this, the people retired to their homes with the strong belief that the misfortune had been washed away and that they were to be blessed with children by *Keze* and ancestors.[17]

Women in other communities also played important roles in fertility rituals. Among the Meku, Befang, Fungom, Fang, and Aghem of the northwestern grassfields, there existed lodges whose role was to perform religious rituals to relief infertility in women.[18] In Meku for instance, the *Ndea-tsha* lodge was responsible for the preparation of pregnancy medicine. This was intended to lure unborn children to come and "feed on the chief's oil" and be conceived by barren women. Nkwi and Warnier go on to observe

---

[16] Mbiti, 1988.

[17] It is worth noting that the pre-colonial manifestation of the *Kengbeum* has been reconstructed principally from interviews we conducted with ritual priests and priestesses alongside other elderly and dignified people in Weh. They include Miselele Akwa, Kum Moses Mughe (Chief Priest of purification rituals), Christiana Nnam (*na'tum*), Taiheart Akwo (a notable), Big Ejuh, among others. Most of the interviews were conducted in March and April 2013. The reliance on information accruing from interviews resulted from the absence of scholarly works on the *Kengbeum* ritual prior to the imposition of colonial rule. The works of Christraud Geary that largely pay attention to pre-colonial Weh do not make any allusion to the *Kengbeum*.

[18] Paul Nchoji Nkwi and Jean-Pierre Warnier, *Elements for a History of the Western Grassfields*, Yaounde, SOPECAM, 1982, 196.

that the ritual that was performed for infertility was quite often accompanied by the sacrifice of a black dog at a stream. Among the Nso' as Banadzem records, ancestors were invoked by the High Priestess (*Yewon*) to bestow many children on the lineage during the burial of notables.[19] In most cases, fertility rituals as earlier noted were performed by ritual priestesses who acted as intermediaries between the Supreme Being and the people. They possessed powers circumscribed on them by the will of the gods and ancestral spirits. So, the fertility of the people depended largely on the ritual actions of these high priestesses. Through ritual, high priestesses were able to maintain or re-establish harmonious connection with spiritual beings whose influence on fertility was not in doubt. The religious quest for children in traditional societies was attainable through ritual observances led by women in collegiality with men.

Female ritual specialists also played central roles in agricultural rites. In all Cameroonian ethnicities, the concept of agriculture was viewed through the prism of religion. Acknowledging the inextricable connection between religion and agriculture, Falvey says that agriculture had a bearing on the codification of traditional belief systems.[20] Probably without any exception, ethnic communities developed longstanding reputation for farming and faith. Since the peopling of the territory, agriculture and religion have interacted together. The Tikar, Aghem, Chamba Widekum, Bakossi, Bakweri, Bangwa, Ejagham, Fang-Beti and other people successfully brought their own ideas to notions of agricultural development and progress. These ideas were articulated in a religious idiom, perhaps, because the notions of agriculture and African Traditional Religion have so much in common. The agricultural cycle was shaped by seasons and religious observances since farming was considered a religious act. The entire farming cycle was marked by ritual practices which included sacrifice to, and appeasement of, the spirits or God; prayer and requests for

---

[19] Banadzem, Joseph Lukong, "Catholicism and Nso' Traditional Beliefs", In Fowler, Ian and Zeitlyn, David, (eds.), *African Crossroads: Intersections between History and Anthropology in Cameroon*. Oxford: Berghahn Books, 1996, p. 130.

[20] Lindsay J. Falvey, *Religion and Agriculture: Sustainability in Christianity and Buddhism*, Adelaide, The Institute for International Development, 2005, p. 1.

communal intercession. In every community, there existed male and female traditional religious specialists whose roles were connected with agriculture. They carried out religious observances throughout the year in an annual cycle of rituals intended to promote agriculture.

In the Tikar fondom of Nso, planting and harvest were preceded by special rituals since agriculture is considered as a real religious experience. According to Banadzem, the Fon of Nso in collaboration with the high priestess (*yewon*) performed farming rituals at the Kovifem sacred site and other alters spread across the fondom.[21] At Kovifem, the Fon and his ritual associates performed the major sacrifice to the ancestors and to *Nyuy* (God) to ensure the fertility of all Nso land. Among the Nso, the link between *Nyuy*, the earth, and the people who live on and cultivate the earth, is a close one and is expressed in moral and ritual terms.[22] Evidently the rituals carried out at Kovifem and other alters in Nso by lineage heads who had control over farmlands were an expression of dependence on the supernatural and of appreciation for good harvest. In the Nso palace, there is a lodge called *fai shishwaa* in which apotropaic medicines are prepared at irregular intervals during the growth period. The medicines are often distributed at cross-roads and on some farms.[23] At the beginning of the farming season, women take their hoes to the *fai shishwaa* for blessing. Among the Aghem, the queen mother (*natum*) who was a member of the *nduni* cult presided over some annual agricultural rituals intended to ensure the fertility of the farmlands; among the Wimbum, ritual priests and priestesses carried out farming rituals in the *ndamgang* (house of the country) in March and December every year.

Though the principal intercessors with spiritual beings for the fertility of the farmlands were male priests, female priests (*yewon* and *ya*) were also given primary farming ritual responsibilities. While some women played frontline roles as priestesses, others served as suppliants, ritual assistants, and mediums. This is illustrative that the

---

[21] Banadzem, 1996, p. 132.
[22] Kaberry, 2004, p. 33.
[23] Chilver & Kaberry, 1967, p. 103.

priesthood in traditional religion was not the preserve of men. Complementary male and female ritual roles in agricultural rites (with women acting as principal officiants and participants in some cases) attracted blessings from the spiritual beings. Resultant good harvest was interpreted as blessings from an appeased God.

Women's religious status was also expressed through the ancestral cult that is entrenched in African traditional religion and culture of people across Africa. In cultures across Cameroon, there were ancestral cults through which male and female ancestors were venerated. The veneration of female ancestors reflected the status of women in the society, especially their spiritual strength. Generally, African societies conceived of their female ancestors as intervening in their everyday life. Such intervention that could either enhance wellbeing or bring misfortune depended on how these female ancestors were treated. This is evidence that male-female complementarity continued in the spirit world. Just like their male counterparts, female ancestral spirits were/are interested in what goes on in the world of the living. This explains why male and female members of a given society venerate these female ancestors through special ritual ceremonies. Among the Nso, the ancestors (*anyuy*) were referred to as "father" or "mother" and were mostly noble men and women who lived exemplarily.[24] To qualify as a female ancestor, such women must have led a transparently good moral life as dictated by the customs and traditions of the society. Little wonder the people had great reverence for their ancestors, an indication that the status of women in traditional religion was high.

Finge people in the North West Region of Cameroon venerated their female ancestors through a ritual practice called *wainabe*. Aimed at venerating and remembering the mother of the family head, the *wainabe* practice had to do with the first-born female of the man heading the family. From birth, even when the paternal grandmother was still alive, the first-born female was declared *wainabe* and remained single all her life. This first-born female was named after the paternal grandmother. Through the *wainabe*, the

---

[24] Tatah Mbuy, *The Faith of Our Ancestors: New Perspectives in the Study and Understanding of African Traditional Religion*, Bamenda, Archdiocesan Print Media, 2012, p. 91.

entire family, it is believed, maintained a bond with the ancestral spirit of the departed grandmother. Hence, the *wainabe* received the respect and honour reserved for paternal grandmothers. She took the place of her father's mother in the family and was not permitted to get married. This ensured that these ancestors were continually pacified in order to keep them in good humour.

Wainabe was the mother-grandmother of the family who was attributed ancestor status upon her demise.[25] The death of such females was followed by ritual ceremonies aimed at venerating and respecting these ancestors. Their death was not understood as complete separation from the family. It was collectively held by the Finge that departed mothers of family heads, as ancestors, continued to participate in social relationships. It was the duty of the head of the family to properly bury his deceased mother for her to become an ancestor. This made procreation, death and proper burial preconditions to becoming an ancestor. Rituals and rites organized around female ancestors involved the offering of sacrifices to them for the protection given to their families. In the course of the sacrifices the elderly man in the family, who served as the officiating priest, named one of his female children after the departed mother. Such a female child became a *wainabe* and through her, the departed mother was felt to be still present, watching over the household, and directly concerned with the wellbeing of the family. "It is the *wainabe*", says Linus Toh, "who ensures the interaction between the living and the death."[26] Female ancestors play an intercessory role between their living children and the Supreme Being. The foundation of the *wainabe* ancestor cult is the belief that departed females have a spiritual status that empowers them to promote fruitful interaction between the physical and metaphysical worlds. When interviewed on the relevance of rites associated with the ancestral cult, John Tofibam, a Family Head (*Njindau*), said that "I know that the spirit of my dead mother can do harm and good to the living, and I always sacrifice fowls to her

---

[25] Interview with Nkoh Joseph, Finge Notable and Practitioner of Traditional Religion, 86 Years, Interviewed in Finge, August 20, 2017.

[26] Interview with Toh Linus, Teacher and Catholic Christian, 47 Years, Interviewed in Finge, August 20, 2017.

spirit, so that I may not fall sick, and ask her for good fortune."[27] This was done by each family among the Finge as it was supposed to be under the direct protection of its ancestors.[28]

The ancestral cult, in light of the foregoing, was a gender-friendly spiritual feature of African religiosity. It offered women a dignified spiritual status, as they were able to intercede for their people after journeying to the spirit world. This amounted to a sacred female ancestorship which offered women to become dignified servants of the Supreme Being upon their demise. This sensitivity to gender also found expression in the healing rituals of the people. The healing practices were built into the people's worldview, anchoring particularly on their beliefs. It was believed in indigenous Cameroonian societies that there existed a natural connection between religion and disease/illness. This causation, justified or not, served as a basis for the fashioning of traditional healthcare practices couched in spiritual terms. It was an encompassing healing system that went beyond the illness by paying attention to the person. Illnesses were believed to be punishment emanating from embittered divinities, ancestral spirits, witches, wizards, and sorcerers. Small wonder solutions to these illnesses involved healing ritual practices officiated by diviners and healers acting as interlocutors between the physical and the spirit worlds. Interestingly, some of these diviners and healers were women who performed healing rituals to surmount illnesses in their communities.

Among the Bali-Nyonga, a Chamba polity in Cameroon's northwest, medicine and religion were derived from the same philosophical foundation. In this community, ritual priests and priestesses performed a plethora of healing functions. They were endowed with spiritual powers to treat physical and psychological problems. Ngwainmbi confirms that Bali Nyonga priestesses were experts at the use of herbs as well as in the nature of

---

[27] Interview with Tofibam John.
[28] For details on the wainabe ancestral practice, read Michael Kpughe Lang, "Finge Ancestral Practices and the Christian Faith: A Historical Study of the *Wainabe* Cult", *Journal of Studies in Social Sciences*, Vol. 17, No. 1, 2018, pp. 46-69.

communication.[29] The healers or medicine women used divination to diagnose illnesses and to determine the appropriate treatment. Hence, diagnosis, treatment, and ritual were intertwined, causing diviners/healers to be seen as indispensable religious officials. They were tied to specific deities in charge of divination and healing. Female healers had knowledge of hundreds of roots and leaves and mastered their application in curing various illnesses. Among the Oku, illness and death were attributed to transcendental powers rather than natural causes. This resulted in a healthcare system rooted in Oku world view in which men and women played complementary roles as diviners.[30] In this community, the High God (*Feyin*) and ancestors revealed themselves with the living through the medicines they gave to them for health and protection against witchcraft. While women were excluded from most masquerading lodges that produced medicine for protection against enemies, they played a central role in *Kefuh myin*, a healing ritual primarily concerned with the health and well-being of children. Before the encounter with Western Christianity and colonialism, women were the owners of *Kefuh myin*, which was found throughout the chiefdom. Inherited matrilineally from a mother to her daughters, the *Kefuh myin* healing ritual had a female officiant who carried out a sequence of ritual actions. She prepared the various leaves and roots, greeted the ancestors, and engaged in a long prayer which explained the reasons for performing the ritual and asked the ancestors for their help. After this stage of the ritual, the patient was given some medicine and final prayers were said to mark the end of the healing ceremony which usually took from two to three hours. But in recent years, ownership of *Kefuh myin* has gradually shifted from women to men in a context of heightened patriarchy. Today,

---

[29] Emmanuel Komben Ngwainmbi, "Bali", in *Encyclopedia of African Religion*, edited by Asante, Molefi Kete and Mazama, Ama, London, SAGE Publications Ltd., 2009, p. 96.

[30] Emmanuel Neba Ndenecho, "Traditional Health Care System and Challenges in Developing Ethnopharmacology in Africa: Example of Oku, Cameroon," *Ethno Med.*, Vol. 5, No. 2, 2011, p. 135.

the ritual is exclusively carried out by men, with women playing subordinate roles.[31]

In general terms, the central role women played in pre-Christian healthcare systems needs not be doubted. As diviners/healers, they were endowed with the power to connect with the spiritual realm. Through divination, they looked for disturbing events in the past, which could amount to misfortunes if left untreated. These women knew the virtues of the plants and had a mastery of the rituals through which the High God and ancestral spirits were caused to intervene in the healing process. In a book focused on women and their medicinal knowledge in Mauritius, Rodrigues, and La Reunion, Laurence Pourchez, says women combined their knowledge of plants and rituals to address illnesses in these small islands of the Indian Ocean.[32] This knowledge was passed down from woman to woman, with men kept at the fringes.

The active role of women in traditional religion notwithstanding, critics charge that traditional religious leadership structures were dominated by men. In an almost outdated paper published in 1976, Kilson alluded that women rarely play primary ritual roles in communal cults. "Almost without exception," notes Kilson, "the principal intercessor with spiritual beings on behalf of human beings is a male priest."[33] This scholar limits women's important religious role to personal rituals of status transformation associated with birth, puberty, and death. In her book published in 2002, Mercy Oduyoye, an acclaimed theologian, notes that women are placed in secondary roles in traditional religious structures despite the fact that some of them play key roles in shrines and cults.[34] This female theologian further advances the claim that most of the rituals for women are probably underpinned by a veiled intention to

---

[31] For a detailed account of the Oku Kefuh myin ritual, see Hans-Joachim Koloss, "Kefuh Myin: A Therapeutic Medicine in Oku," *JASO*, Vol. 26, No. 1, 1995, pp. 69-79.

[32] Laurence Pourchez, *Women's Knowledge: Traditional Medicine and Nature - Mauritius, Reunion and Rodrigues*, Paris, UNESCO, 2017.

[33] Marion Kilson, "Women in African Traditional Religions," *Journal of Religion in Africa*, Vol. 8, No. 2, 1976, p. 138.

[34] Mercy Amba Oduyoye, *Beads and Strands: Reflections of an African Woman on Christianity in Africa*, Yaounde, Editions Cle, 2002, p. 79.

stall the active participation of women in societal affairs. Linda Ankiambom Lawyer's essay on female missionaries' involvement in the redefinition of gender roles points to the fact that customs and traditions in societies across the Bamenda Grassfields of Cameroon were patriarchal and male dominated.[35] Kasomo has even argued controversially that the improvement of African women's status in religion started only in the era of Western Christianity in the continent.

While these claims may seem tenable, the stark reality is that women were adequately represented in the leadership structures of indigenous religions in pre-Christian Cameroonian ethnicities. Male and female ritual roles were not inspired by an intention to obtain gender equality or male dominance, but by a role differentiation system operating in a context of gender complementarity. As such, religion which was built into local cultures was a male-female collaborative spiritual venture intended for the collective good of the society. Clearly, describing African Traditional Religion in the pre-Christian era as a man's world is a claim laden with flaws. The charge misses or overlooks the male-female role differentiation principle that found expression in a context of complementarity in traditional societies where communality of life was the norm. The co-existence of patriarchy and matriarchy in these traditional societies and which served as a basis for gender complementarity in indigenous religious professions is downplayed by these critics. For them, especially Oduyoye, women's religious roles as high priestesses, queen mothers, diviners, and healers hardly equalled those performed by men. This is unfortunate because there was equal ease of access to religious leadership positions regardless of gender. In communities across Cameroon, like elsewhere in Africa, there was a consistent balancing of power among genders to ensure full participation of members in governance structures. Obtaining equality between male and female members was not always the intended agenda. So, gender equality was not a fundamental

---

[35] Linda Ankiambom Lawyer, "The Christian Women Fellowship of the Presbyterian Church in Cameroon and Women Empowerment in the Bamenda Grassfields, 1961-2001," *Pan-Tikar Journal of History*, Vol. 1, No. 2, 2013, p. 86.

organizing principle. It gained prominence as a defining factor for social roles only from the twentieth century thanks to advocacy by Western feminists who used it as a lens for interpreting gender in African culture and belief systems.

Oduyoye's seemingly tenable argument that traditional religion places women in secondary roles as mediums and suppliants is not enough to challenge the reality of women's leadership in shrines, cult centres and divine healing. In fact, women, just like men, had access to the High God and supernatural spirits. Sackey's work on women's status in African Independent Churches (AICs) supports the thesis of women's high status in traditional religion. She maintains that Ghanaian indigenous religious traditions have long offered women leadership opportunities in their structures.[36] Empirical studies among the Igbos and Yorubas of Nigeria, and the Dinkas of South Sudan have also exposed that roles in spirit possession cults such as diviners and mediums were public ritual roles available to women. This yields the thinking that women gained status in highly patriarchal societies through their religious roles. Peach declares that "although African religions in general are highly gender segregated, this segregation does not necessarily mean that men dominate and control all aspects of religious life."[37] Women's access to religious training and education resulted in opportunities for leadership roles. This reality of effective women's role in the power structures of indigenous religions stands at odds with the already mentioned complementarianist thinking that the admission of women into religious leadership structures would be disruptive to religion. Rather, women's leadership roles in traditional religious power structures strengthened these religious traditions in ways that were beneficial to these societies. There is no evidence that the association of women with ritual observances disrupted the longstanding intertwined relationship between the people and their spirit world. On the contrary, women's participation made possible the observance of supplication rituals for rain, good health, children, as well as passage rites linked to

---

[36] Brigid, Sackey, *New Directions in Gender and Religion: The Changing Status of Women in African Independent Churches*, Lanham, MD, Rowan and Littlefield, 2006.
[37] Lucinda Joy Peach, *Women and World Religions*, Paris, Pearson, 2001, p. 306.

birth, puberty, marriage, and death. This should accord credence to the feminist utilitarian paradigm whose apologists argue that religion's utility is diminished by the absence of full female involvement in leadership.[38] The exclusion of women would have caused indigenous religions to lose their contribution, given that they are endowed with gifts suited to leadership in general.

So, contrary to Lawyer's observation that women in indigenous Cameroonian societies were dominated in patriarchal religious structures, it is clear that women's status was high. Western Christianity was therefore brought into an African religious landscape with an entrenched culture of respect and high status for women. Men and women played complementary roles in ritual and healing structures. The demotion of women's status in religious circles began with the coming of Western Christianity in the hands of European missionaries groomed in a context that was not gender friendly. Arrogantly and ignorantly, they labelled local populations as "uncivilized" and resolved to recourse to a civilizing agenda couched in Western terms. The net outcome of this approach was the promotion of Western gender systems that were hostile to women. This was reflected in the exclusion of controversially empowered women in the leadership structures of Western mission agencies. In this light, the remainder of the book uses the Basel Mission and PCC as case studies of Christian organizations that pursued problematic women's empowerment approaches which kept women at the margins of their executive structures.

---

[38] Read Isabel Apawo Phiri, p. 73.

Chapter 2

Basel Mission, Patriarchy, and Missionary Deployment to Cameroon

This chapter examines the general background to the mission work of the Basel Mission in Cameroon. The chapter proceeds from the origins of the Basel Mission through the patriarchalization of its leadership structures and the timid inclusion of women to the establishment of the excessively male dominated mission agency in Cameroon. With this historical background, the reader is introduced to the workings of the Basel Mission: its attitude toward women, its concept of the Christian home, its connection with the "civilizing mission" of colonialism, and its arrival and expansion in Cameroon. The exposition of the broad scope in which Basel missionaries did their work in Cameroon is the rationale of this general survey. It is argued that patriarchy in the European society (particularly in Germany and Switzerland) into which the Basel Mission was borne as well as the patriarchal beliefs and practices that shaped its policies and structure all combined to place the status of local Christian women in its structures in Cameroon on a bad course.

Origins and Gender Policy of the Basel Mission

Though the sixteenth century reformation is the broad context from which the Basel Mission emerged, its actual beginnings are traced to the revival of Pietism in Protestant Germany and Protestant Switzerland in the first quarter of the nineteenth century. This pietistic revival came as a response to the negative bearing of rationalistic enlightenment on Christianity. Defined as a direct relationship between the individual and God, Pietism had gained prominence in Germany and Switzerland, especially in Wurttemberg and Basel respectively. As such, the establishment of the Basel Mission in 1815 was the initiative of prominent Pietists who had significant influence on the power structures of religious and secular organizations in their communities. A majority of these resourceful Pietists were men holding power positions in a Western society that was hostile towards women.[39] They had wielded considerable economic and political power influence over close to two hundred years. The combined bearing of their wealth, political influence, and pietistic commitment enabled them to play a frontline role in the establishment of the Basel Mission. Hastened by the Napoleonic wars of the first quarter of the nineteenth century, the Basel Evangelical Missionary Society was formed on 25 September 1815, with Rev. Nicholas van Brunn as its pioneer President.

Given that the primary objective of this missionary society was to train and send missionaries to mission fields across the world especially to Africa, China, and the Indian West coast, a theological college was created in 1816. However, women were excluded from the missionary profession, which was a reflection of their low status in the Western society. This was the initiative of the Committee that was created as the governing body of the Basel Mission. Generally, it was this all-male Committee that fashioned the operational rules of this mission agency. This exclusion of women from serving as missionaries and from participating in the governing structures of the Basel Mission initially went unchallenged because of the huge dependence on funds allotted by influential pietists who sat on the Committee. It was even believed that the will of the Committee was the will of God that could not be challenged. Hence, the male-dominated hierarchy of the mission agency and the anti-female laws it enacted were believed to be endorsed by God. Simply put, the Committee was perceived as an infallible earthly instrument of the will of God.[40] Missionaries that were engaged by the Basel Mission were subordinated to this Committee, which held unchallengeable ruling power. Expectedly, the missionaries simply implemented decisions emanating from the Committee. This made the evangelical work in the mission fields a shared responsibility of the Committee and the missionaries it recruited.

---

[39] Waltraud Haas, "The 19th Century Basel Mission and its Women Missionaries," *Mission History from the Woman's View*, No. 13, Basel, Basel Mission, 1989.
[40] Ibid.

The low status of women in the leadership structures of the Basel Mission came on the heels of their subordination to male leaders of Pietism and the gender insensitive Western culture. In the Western society, there was an entrenched patriarchal culture in which men and women were not viewed equally. Even in the democratic Greek society, considered by many as the base of Western civilization, women were marginalized from all aspects of public life.[41] While women played public roles in the Roman society, the rise and institutionalization of Christianity offered limited space for female adherents. Halsall observes that "the Church came to entrench certain patterns of male power."[42] Overall, Greco-Roman cultures that contributed to the rise of Western civilization valorised masculinity and marginalized women despite isolated cases of female public roles.[43] So, patriarchy was a hallmark of Pietism despite the fact that women served as patronesses and writers of devotional manuals and hymns. The Basel Mission was formed in an era of open advocacy for women to remain subjected to men as a leeway to ensure the sustenance of patriarchal norms. It was a missionary society established by pietist leaders who were strong advocates of patriarchy. Dominated by pietists, the Committee of the Basel Mission used the divine powers it arrogated to itself to declare the missionary profession as a man's world. Little wonder it was an all-male mission agency in the first decades of its existence. And being single was a condition which new male recruits had to fulfil. This hinged on the shared view that male-female contact in the mission field could be disruptive to mission work. Considered as a distraction for male missionaries, women were discriminated

---

[41] Read Paul Halsall, "Early Western Civilization under the Sign of Gender: Europe and the Mediterranean", In Teresa A. Meade and Merry E. Wiesner-Hanks (eds.), *A Companion to Gender History*, Melbourne, Blackwell Publishing Ltd, 2005, p. 290.

[42] Ibid., p. 297.

[43] Neculaesei observes that gender and sex are distinctively construed in Western societies, stressing that both concepts "delineate anatomical and cultural differences between men and women. While sex is a biological concept, gender is culturally determined. For more on the Western construction of gender and sex, read Angelica-Nicoleta Neculaesei, "Culture and Gender Role Differences", *Cross-Cultural Management Journal*, Vol. 1, No. 7, 2015, pp. 31-35.

upon as they were prohibited from having missionaries as husbands and from joining the missionary profession.

Later on, knowledge of single male missionaries' inability to administer to women who were members of the intended Christian communities led to a review of the marriage policy. Male missionaries were now allowed to have wives carefully selected for them by the Committee. Women with a displayed mastery of pietistic values were privileged. The opening of the marriage institution to male missionaries gave birth to the controversial concept of missionary wives. What made this concept controversial was the simple fact that women who were married to missionaries were sent to the mission field as missionary wives, not as missionaries in their own right. They were commissioned to educate local Christian women in the "womanly skills" of good housekeeping and to turn them into submissive Christian housewives. In fact, it could be interpreted as recourse to a policy through which marginalized missionary wives were used to produce submissive and low status Christian housewives in the mission territories. Simply put, these missionary wives carried out controversial women's emancipation systems borrowed from their pietistic Western context.

The discrimination to which missionary wives were subjected within the system of the Basel Mission was further evidenced by the fact that they were not formally employed, and were not on the pay roll of the Basel Mission. However, mission duties were shouldered by these women, who were bossed by their well-paid husbands. The heavy load placed on missionary wives coupled with their household and childcare burdens, caused their husbands to consistently request for the deployment of single female missionaries. By sending such requests to the Basel Mission Committee in Basel, male missionaries who coordinated work in mission fields wanted to shift the responsibility of emancipating local Christian women from their wives to single missionaries.[44] Though opposing voices led to hesitation, the Committee

---

[44] Ulrike Sill, *Encounters in Quest of Christian Womanhood: The Basel Mission in Pre-and Early Colonial Ghana*, London, Brill, 2010.

eventually endorsed the recruitment and deployment of single female missionaries to the mission fields. It is worth stressing that the work of this new category of female mission workers was not dependent on marriage to a male missionary. Though their mission work among local women was judged independently of that of their male counterparts, women's marginalization in the structures of the Basel Mission persisted.

Evidently, the decision to knock down laws barring women from participation in the overseas activities of the Basel Mission was not an outcome of field challenges. The reform was not motivated by an effort to ameliorate the status of women who had suffered under an entrenched patriarchy. Rather, it came on the heels of feminist agitation for women's empowerment in the second half of the nineteenth century, coupled with complaints from male missionaries that their wives were overworked. In 1841, the Basel Women's Association was created as an institution for the promotion of women's mission. Pressure from this association challenged the barring of women from participating in the missionary profession. Its representative in the Basel Mission Committee caused the mission agency to start sending single female missionaries to the field.[45] As an auxiliary society to the Basel Mission, the association promoted the ideals of domesticity. Female missionaries were expected to act as exemplars of proper Christian femininity and as teachers in informal and formal empowerment institutions in the mission fields.

Overall, the deployment of single female missionaries led to a rethinking of women's place within the Basel Mission. In Africa, India, and China, single female missionaries performed mission work among local women. Their work in the mission field was interpreted by the all-male Committee in Basel as victory for women. This yielded the false impression that patriarchy was no longer a defining feature of the internal workings of the Basel Mission. In fact, it has been established that even single female missionaries were placed at the margins of the leadership structures of the Basel Mission in the mission fields and at the level of the

---

[45] Ibid., pp. 54-73.

Committee. They were not statutory attendees of missionary conferences and station meetings. These gatherings were strictly reserved for their male counterparts. According to Waltraud Haas, a male leadership attitude was entrenched in the Basel Mission system throughout the nineteenth century.[46] Indeed, the Basel Mission incorporated into its system and work, the patriarchal standards of the Western world in ways that caused its leadership to be defined as male. In mission territories, missionary wives and independent female missionaries had a very low status. Their secondary role was hugely dependent on a male-led leadership. Specifically, male missionaries hailed the exclusion of women from leadership structures and their marginalization in the missionary profession as civilized measures. The patriarchy was harmful to the status of single female missionaries and the local women among whom they worked.

Though presented as an emancipation initiative, the domesticity empowerment work carried out by single female missionaries was harmful to the status of local Christian women. I insist that this emancipation approach drawn entirely from a female hostile Western context was controversial, yielding little or no occupational options and opportunities for local women to participate in the power structures of the Basel Mission. In the Cameroonian mission field, with its entrenched culture of women's leadership role in traditional religious institutions, domesticity as an emancipation ideal was detrimental to their status. Furthermore, though the Basel Mission Committee had endorsed the association of women with the missionary profession, the female and male missionaries who worked in Cameroon ordained only men as pastors to assist them. The patriarchy that had eaten deep into the European society and into the Basel Mission system also found expression in its work in Cameroon. By accepting to work under male leadership, female missionaries actually helped in promoting the patriarchal structure of the mission and the patriarchal beliefs and practices that sustained it. This placed local Christian women at the mercy of such Western patriarchal practices, beliefs, and structures. This is the

---

[46] Haas, "The 19th Century Basel Mission", p. 47.

context in which the discrimination of women in the structures of the Basel Mission in Cameroon as well as in the PCC can best be understood.

Women's Exclusion as a Standard of Western Christianity

Of course, it should be emphasized that the marginalization of women in the leadership structures of the Christian church is of Western origin. It was a gradual process marked by a shift from women's full participation in the early Christian church to their almost total exclusion in the nineteenth century. Some scholars have used The New Testament to argue that women had a high status in the days of Jesus. The history of Christianity is also replete with examples of women who provided incalculable contributions in spreading the gospel in various parts of the world. Grudem notes that men and women were active in the ministry of the church during the time of Jesus, though women's roles were not very pronounced.[47] Clearly, Christ's liberating teachings exemplified a more egalitarian form of Christianity before the trajectory of women's demotion set in following the institutionalization of the church.

The biased interpretation of biblical texts and the cultural and institutional set-up of the Christian church offered society with a patriarchal image of God which served as a basis for the marginalization of women in Christian churches and organizations. In the Western society, the mutual influence between Christianity and the patriarchal culture resulted in a similar status of women in the church and society.[48] It was a decreased status of women within Christianity caused by the strong influence of patriarchal values which were characteristic of Western societies. Women's position in the modern Western society has been studied by scholars. Ivy

---

[47] Wayne Grudem, *Evangelical Feminism and Biblical Truth*, Multnomah, Inter Varsity Press, 2004.
[48] Kamila Klingorova and Tomas Havlicek, "Religion and Gender Inequality: The Status of Women in the Societies of World Religions," *Moravian Geographical Reports*, Vol. 23, 2015, p. 2.

Pinchbeck viewed the specialization of male and female roles into breadwinner and housewife as evidence of a low female status. This made women powerful in the domestic sphere, which came with opportunities for them to engage in childbearing tasks. Towns observes that women's exclusion from political, economic, social, and religious public spheres was an endorsed behaviour in the Western world.[49] In church circles, clerical leaders took measures to emancipate women along these controversial lines, based on the belief that women's talents were primarily domestic. This attitude yielded what Bendroth describes as an age-old pattern of predominantly male leadership in Christian churches.[50] It validates the contemporary depiction of missionary societies as patriarchal and sexist. As a matter of fact, women across the dauntingly diverse world of modern Christianity continued to sit in pews and work in kitchens in the way as their mothers and grandmothers many centuries before. This long history of second-class citizenship for women within Christianity was in part fed by St. Paul's perception of women.[51] In fact, this Paul's view of women as inferior to men was entrenched and reinforced throughout much of the history of Christianity.

Expectedly, women were exposed to all sorts of discrimination in Christian organizations as they were not allowed to exercise their spiritual gifts as well as to respond to God's call. This was the context in which the custom barring women from the missionary profession flourished in Western Christianity. Consequently, mission service across the world was mostly a male province since the exclusion of women from positions of leadership and theological influence was a welcomed practice in Christian institutions.[52] In fact, the standards of Western civilization that informed mission agencies' behaviour were not female-friendly. In

---

[49] Ann E. Towns, "The Status of Women as a Standard of 'Civilization'," *European Journal of International Relations*, Vol. 15, No. 4, 2009, p. 684.

[50] Margaret Bendroth, "Gender and Twentieth-Century Christianity", in *A People's History of Christianity, Vol. 7, Twentieth-Century Global Christianity*, edited by Mary Farrell Bednarowski, Minneapolis, Fortress Press, 2008, p. 308.

[51] Johnstone, *Religion in Society*, p. 204.

[52] Read H. E. Baber, "Feminism and Christian Ethics", Paper Presented at the April 1993 Meeting of SEAD at Virginia Theological Seminary.

the words of Dana Robert, "church planting and the subsequent relationship between church and mission was rarely part of women's public missiological agenda."[53] This was an outcome of the patriarchal dispositions of the Western society in which Christianity developed.

In Catholic and Protestant circles, opposition to the holding of leadership positions by women was entrenched. The society in general and churches in particular emphasized the distinctive contribution of women as mothers in the domestic sphere. This made the empowerment of women to be informed by the domestic roles they were expected to play. Broadly, as Towns notes, "The advancement of civilization was best assured with women in the domestic sphere and men occupying public positions."[54] Women's voice was almost absent in the structures of the Basel Mission because its birth was rooted in such patriarchy. The most severe restrictions on women in mission circles were visible in the structures of the Basel Mission.

Interestingly, this marginalization of women in Christian churches was put to question when the women empowerment project which was fed by feminism engulfed the church. The significant changes for women in society brought by the feminist movement represented a challenge to the Christian community. The latter, under the influence of Christian feminists, was forced to consider afresh the role of women in their relationship to men in the church.[55] Christian feminists launched the argument that in Christian churches, marginalized women are kept down and disempowered.[56] In spite the Christian feminist movement, progress towards the inclusion of women in the missionary profession and

---

[53] Dana L. Robert, "The 'Christian Home' as a Cornerstone of Anglo-American Missionary Thought and Practice," Dana L. Robert, ed., *Converting Colonialism: Visions and Realities in Mission History, 1706-1914*, Grand Rapids, Michigan/Cambridge, UK, William B. Eerdmans Publishing Company, 2008, p. 409.

[54] Towns, "The Status of Women", p. 699.

[55] Paul W. Felix, "The Hermeneutics of Evangelical Feminism", *The Master's Seminary Journal*, Vol. 5, No. 2, Fall 1994, p. 159.

[56] Zohreh Abdekhodaie, "Letty M. Russell: Insights and Challenges of Christian Feminism", Master of Theology Studies Thesis, Waterloo, Ontario, Canada, 2008, p. 1.

other roles in the Christian church was slow. Mission agencies in the example of the Basel Mission were hesitant to initiate reforms aimed at removing restrictions on women. Hence, Christianity was exported from its historical Western base to mission fields in Africa and other parts of the world when it was still a conservative force. This came on the heels of Western evangelical awakening in the late and early eighteenth and nineteenth centuries respectively, and coincided with European imperialism.

The "Christian Home" Ideal as Cornerstone of Basel Mission Evangelism

The missionary enterprise and colonialism were locked in a circle of mutual influence, with Christian missionaries partnering with colonial officials to implement the "civilizing" agenda of imperialism. For context, the "civilizing mission" hinged on cultural pride and triumphalism among Western citizens, and was dictated by the chained events of enlightenment, scientific discoveries and the industrial revolution. The missionaries deployed to Cameroon and elsewhere by the Basel Mission and other mission agencies were proud of the cultural and material achievements of the Western world. According to Njoku, "European missionaries generally participated in the buoyancy and cultural pride and went to the missions walking as on heels."[57] This feeling, justified or not, turned missionaries into promoters of the glories and riches of Western culture in mission territories. The Basel Mission accepted to enforce colonialism's "civilizing mission" in Cameroon by colluding with German and British colonial agents. The cultural arrogance unfolded in a dual context of near total ignorance about the glories and riches of African culture and unjustified claims about the superiority of Western culture over other cultures. Basel missionaries to Cameroon lacked the capacity to grasp the intersection of culture, traditional religion, and gender in societies across the territory. This served as context for the propagation of Western gender patterns in Cameroon.

---

[57] Chukwudi A. Njoku, "The Missionary Factor in African Christianity: 1884-1914," In *African Christianity: An African Story*, edited by Ogbu U. Kalu, Pretoria, University of Pretoria Press, 2005, p. 228.

The bringing of the Western Christian faith to Cameroon, just like elsewhere, by the Basel Mission was therefore construed as a civilizing mission. The adoption of Christianity by local women also meant acculturation into the gender patterns of Western civilization. The missionaries deployed by the Basel Mission worked hard for this goal to be attained. This was preceded by the fashioning of a theology of marriage and family which inspired the manner in which local women had to be transformed. It was a theology inspired by Martin Luther's understanding of marriage as an important institution that was much in crisis as the church. He therefore advocated the reformation of the marriage institution by stressing the dignity of women, seeing them as the foundation of marriage and family. As noted by Asare-Danso, "Luther believed that women were capable of transforming society by moulding women and the youth through the institution of marriage."[58] The adoption of this theology coincided with the heydays of the family claim paradigm, which described efforts by women to mark their presence in the public domain as detrimental to the family. There was a conflict between women's personal fulfilment and the demands of the family. The family claim paradigm required that the family should have priority over women's personal fulfilment. The home was their narrowed space, where they engaged in domestic responsibilities hinged on marriage and motherhood.

This Western family claim had a bearing on Basel Mission work among women in mission territories. Little wonder its marriage and family theology was exemplified in the concept of "the Christian home". The later was the cornerstone of Basel Mission missionary thought and practice. The Basel Mission believed that the home was the woman's space which it considered to be at the centre of the universe. The theology of marriage and family brought about the need to emancipate local Christian women. The emancipation was intended to introduce women to a respectable domestic sphere of proper female activity. According to Dana Robert, "issues addressed by the concept of the "Christian Home" included

---

[58] Seth Asare-Danso, "Historical Study of Girl Child Education in Ghana (1828-2014): A Review of Basel Mission Educational Policy," *International Journal of Scientific Research and Management*, Vol. 5, No. 4, 2017, p. 7439.

relationships between husbands and wives, principles of child-rearing, and a whole range of tangible components such as cleanliness, clothing, and domestic tasks."[59] This domesticity ideology was meant for local Christian women whom European missionaries assumed to be lacking in modern aspects of home care, childcare, cookery and the like.

This "Christian Home" mission agenda, couched in Western terms, played a crucial role in inspiring missionaries and in shaping their attitude to the peoples and the mission fields in which they worked. This caused local Christian women to experience controversial transformation in their families and societies. The emancipation women received secured them a new status often defined in terms of dressing, cooking, and child-rearing, not full participation in church leadership. In fact, the limitations of the domesticity empowerment ideology and the resultant effects on the status of women in mission fields were huge. Women's sphere of activity was narrowed to the home and family. This outcome of the diffusion of Western women's emancipation norms by European missionaries could be described as the "housewifisation of African women." This was at the origin of women's leadership woes in the church in mission fields. It contributed in further deepening patriarchy in the leadership structures of the Basel Mission in its areas of operation. As a mission agency at the mercy of Western gender beliefs and practices, the Basel Mission played a central role in shaping gender expectations in its mission fields in Africa, especially Cameroon. Through its work, the mission enforced boundaries between male and female roles in ways that were detrimental to the status of women. This was to be in stark contrast with the privileged positions women occupied in traditional religious structures in most African societies. This complicates the claim that the empowerment of women began in the Western world. Rather, it is the exclusion of women from the leadership structures of the church that is attributable to Western society.[60]

---

[59] Robert, "The Christian Home", p. 136.
[60] The initiation of reforms to roll away restrictions to women's full participation in the public sphere was the outcome of sustained protest by social movements.

Generally, the emergence of the Basel Mission, its patriarchal beliefs and practices, its controversial "Christian Home" ideal, and its endorsement of the "civilizing mission" of colonialism were all tied to the Western context. The latter serves as a broad background to women's marginalization in Western mission agencies, particularly the Basel Mission. The Basel Mission incorporated into its system and work, the patriarchal standards of the Western world, causing its leadership and mission work to be defined as male. The establishment of the mission agency and gender policies cannot be dissociated from the gender conditions of the Western society. The Basel Mission represented a Western Christian enterprise through which the transformation of local Christian women was to occur in mission territories. With this patriarchal structure and policy, the Basel Mission began sending missionaries to mission fields in Africa, China, India, and Japan. Missionaries embraced these patriarchal beliefs and practices and sought to promote them in mission fields such as Cameroon.

Advent and Establishment of the Basel Mission in Cameroon

The Cameroon mission of the Basel Mission was started in 1886 when it resolved to undertake the duties begun by the London Baptist Missionary Society after the territory became a German protectorate in 1884. This happened in the context of the launching of German colonial enterprise in Cameroon and Basel Mission's desire to heighten its presence in mission territories. The close relationship between the Basel Mission and the German Government hinged on what has been described as the nationalization of religion and religionization of Germany.[61] In the last quarter of the nineteenth century, German missionary societies were willing to collaborate with the government in territories that were brought under German colonialism. As such, German annexation of lands abroad came with opportunities for the Basel Mission and other German missions to send missionaries to

---

[61] Michael Kpughe Lang, "World War One in Africa: Implications on Christian Missions," *Contemporary Journal of African Studies*, Vol. 4, No. 2, 2017, p. 38.

mission territories. In 1885, the All-German Missionary Conference saw the launching of German colonial enterprise as a "great opportunity for missionary work among the millions of the heathens living in the lands now brought under German protectorateship."[62]

The annexation of Cameroon in 1884 was interpreted in German mission circles as the opening of a new door for mission work, and Cameroon quickly gained the status of a German mission territory. But this was complicated by the fact that Western missionary work in the territory preceded its annexation. As early as 1841, the London Baptist Missionary Society (LBMS) began sending missionaries to Cameroon at a time when British commercial influence in the territory was on the rise. By the time Germany annexed the territory, the LBMS operated many mission stations, educational facilities, and health centres. The intention of Germany was to terminate the mission work of this British missionary enterprise at a time when it was practically budding. Anglo-German colonial rivalry caused German colonial officials to take measures aimed at stalling the work of the LBMS. While this hostility dragged, the Basel Mission was lured by the All-German Missionary Conference to continue the work of the LMBS in Cameroon. Meeting in Bremen from 27-29 October 1885, the Conference resolved that mission agencies with German roots should consider sending missionaries to Cameroon. The appeal was motivated by the fact that public opinion in Germany held that access to German territories be limited to German missions.

This hostility towards non-German missions in German possessions was enough evidence that the LBMS could not pursue its work in Cameroon. The All-German Missionary Conference was pushed by public opinion and its close ties with the German government to invite the Basel Mission to take over the work of the LBMS. The Basel Mission was the lone German mission with a good track record in mission work in foreign lands. It had successfully established mission stations, schools, and health

---

[62] J. N. Dah, "Missionary Motivations and Methods: A Critical Examination of the Basel Mission in Cameroon 1886-1914", PhD Thesis in Theology, University of Basel, 1983, p. 61.

facilities in China, India, and in the Gold Coast. By becoming a German colonial mission, the Basel Mission worked hard to surmount the financial and health challenges that had yielded an initial hesitation. The LBMS had already been forced by the constraints placed on its work by the German government to express the desire to handover to the Basel Mission. At the same time, the German government publicly announced her readiness to grant the Basel Mission free scope to missionary work.

It was in this context of colonization that the Basel Mission sent the first team of missionaries to Cameroon. Comprised of Rev. and Mrs. Gottlieb Munz, Rev. Christian Dilger, Rev. Johannes Bizer, and Rev. Friederich Becher, the team arrived in Cameroon on 23 December 1886. Rev. Becher's death barely four days after his arrival confirmed Basel Mission's initial hesitation on grounds of health, though it rather served as motivation for his three colleagues to plant Christianity in the territory. These Basel missionaries took over budding Baptist churches, schools, health centres, pupils, and Christians from the LBMS.[63]

After settling down, the all-male missionary team and the lone missionary wife embarked on the opening of mission stations. They intensified their activities on the Cameroon coast by opening mission stations in Magamba, Bonaberi among others. In April 1891, they extended their activities to the Sanaga Maritime region under the leadership of Bohner and Schuller. In 1895, Rev. Lauffer opened a new mission station in Buea[64]. New stations emerged as the number of Christians increased. They made their presence felt on the coast of Cameroon in domains like evangelization, education, health and economic transformation. Thereafter, the authorities of the Basel Mission decided to penetrate the grassland region. This was dictated not only by the need to evangelize the people but also by the coming of the Roman Catholic German-

---

[63] Anthony Ndi, *Mill Hill Missionaries in Southern West Cameroon*, Nairobi, Paulines Publications Africa, 2005, p. 21.
[64] J. A. Arrey, "Missionary Activities in the Upper Cross River Region: The Basel Mission in the Banyangland 1912-1957", Maitrise Dissertation in History, University of Yaounde, 1991, p. 34.

based Pallotine Fathers to Cameroon in 1890 led by Father Henrich Vieter.[65]

The presence of the missionaries in the grassland led to the opening of the Bali Mission Station in 1903 by Reverends Schuller, Spellengberg and Keller.[66] The station became the main centre from where other interior areas were reached. In 1908, Rev. Ernst baptized thirty-two converts in the Bali Station. These Christians then assisted white missionaries in expanding Christianity into other interior parts of Cameroon. This expansion was evidenced by the opening of new interior Basel Mission stations in Bafut in 1904, Bamoun in 1906 and Babungo in 1914.[67] Unfortunately, the expansion of the Basel Mission was temporarily halted by the outbreak of World War I in 1914. In Cameroon, the war continued until 1916 when the Germans were finally defeated and forced to take refuge in Fernando Po and Rio Muni. During the war, all missionaries of German origin together with colonial authorities were interned and ousted. As such, Basel missionary activities in the coastal and grassland regions were continued by indigenes who were already converted before the war under the supervision of ordained Cameroonians. In 1916, Cameroon was provisionally partitioned between Britain and France, causing both powers to invite their mission agencies to replace German ones.

In the French section of Cameroon, recourse to the policy of de-Germanization led to a permanent ban on mission work by German mission agencies, whose work was taken over by French societies. The work of the Basel Mission was taken over by the Paris Evangelical Mission (PEM).[68] In the British sphere, similar measures were taken to permanently terminate the German missionary enterprise. Britain was successful in replacing German Catholic missions (Sacred Heart Fathers and Pallotine Fathers) with

---

[65] H. O. Ojong, "Missionary Activities in Kumba Division 1916-1961: A Study of their Presence", Maitrise Dissertation in History, University of Yaounde, 1987, p. 36. For more information on this subject, read B. Omgba, *Histoire de l'Eglise Catholique au Cameroun*, Yaoundé, SOPECAM, 1985, pp. 12-15; Mveng, *Histoire des Eglises*, p. 36.
[66] Werner, *The History of the Presbyterian*, pp. 62-64.
[67] Ibid., pp. 62-64.
[68] Ibid., p. 48.

the London-based Mill Hill Mission. Recourse to British missions to replace German Protestant missions met with fierce ecumenical resistance. Basel Mission authorities condemned the policy, arguing that it was underpinned by selfish British colonial desires. In 1924, during the Conference of Missionary Societies in Europe and America held in Birmingham, obstacles to evangelization in Africa were discussed. The agenda to replace German missions with British ones, especially in Cameroon was denounced. In response, the British government in 1924 lifted the embargo on mission work by German missionaries in its possessions. The Colonial Office then abolished all restrictions which had been placed on the Basel Mission since the war. In December 1925 Reverend Adolf Vielhauer arrived Cameroon from Basel to coordinate Basel Mission work in British Cameroon. This caused the mission territory of the Basel Mission to be limited only to the British sphere.[69]

Working in partnership with indigenous evangelists, Basel missionaries reopened abandoned stations and intensified activities in Buea, Victoria and Bali. These stations became the main centres from where virgin fields were reached. The result was the emergence of new mission stations like Weh Station which was opened in 1932, Bafut Station in 1937, Bamenda Station in 1957 among others[70]. As a matter of fact, the massive involvement of the indigenous evangelists in Basel Mission activities was already a sign of maturity for independence. But the 1939-1945 World War II came with serious challenges. During the war, missionaries of German origin were expelled, and their work was halted for the second time. However, the post war era was marked by multiplied determination to spread the gospel on the part of both the white missionaries and indigenous evangelists. More indigenous pastors

---

[69] In the initial years, Basel Mission's Cameroon mission territory covered the entire German protectorate of Cameroon. However, its mission work during the German era from 1886 to 1916 was limited to the southern zone, given that its missionaries were prohibited from extending into the Muslim-dominated north. But following Anglo-French partition of the territory during the First World War, its mission territory was reduced to the British sphere (See map 1).

[70] Werner, *The History of the Presbyterian*, pp. 58-64.

were ordained, and the Basel Mission Church in Cameroon was on its way to autonomy[71]. The indigenous clerics were armed and determined to take up full responsibility of spreading the gospel as negotiations for the granting of independence commenced[72].

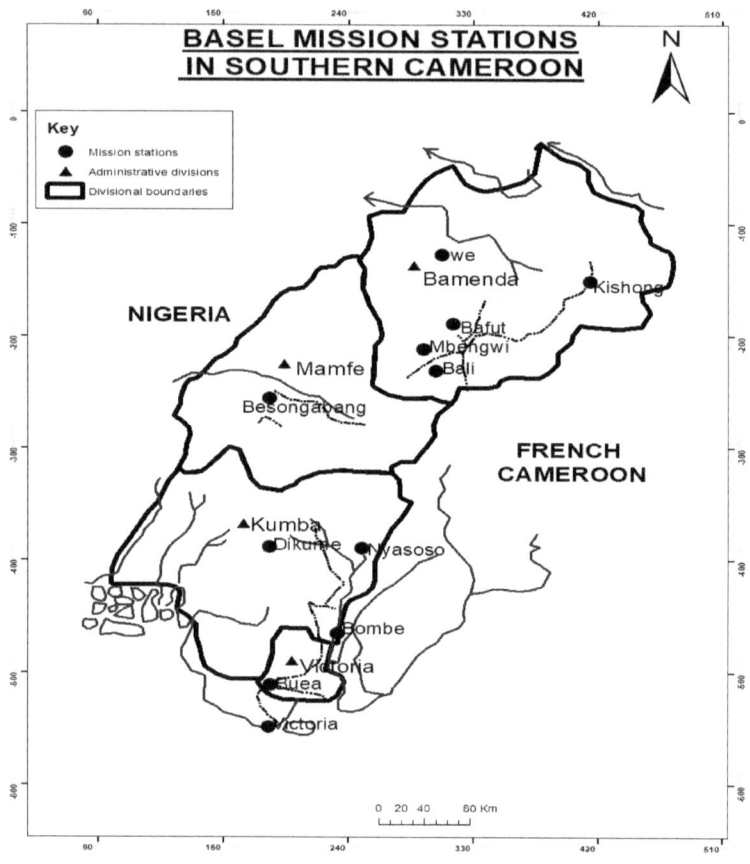

The Basel Mission was conscious of the fact that independence would one day be granted to the indigenous Christians. Consequently, measures were designed to prepare Cameroonians towards autonomy. The Basel missionaries started training and arming more indigenous workers (pastors, teachers, health personnel, administrators and finance experts) with required skills to enable them replace the white missionaries. Consequently, the

---

[71] Ibid., pp. 79-82.
[72] Ibid., p. 82.

journey towards autonomy was commenced in 1935 when the first official constitution of the Basel Mission Church in Cameroon was drafted and adopted. The constitution did not only lay down guiding principles of the church, but also integrated and linked the numerous Basel Mission stations and churches with one another. The structure of the Church in ascending order was comprised of Local Congregations, Stations, Districts and the General Synod[73]. As a matter of fact, leadership was to be gradually passed down to Africans at the different levels of church organization as well as at the helm of educational and medical institutions. The highest governing body of the church was the General Synod which before 1949 had a membership of 25 (9 white missionaries and 16 indigenous pastors and elders)[74]. Thus, Cameroonians could now make their voices and opinions heard whenever Church issues were discussed during General Synod meetings. But the entrenched patriarchy in the system of the Basel Mission made its leadership structures an all-male affair.

Basel missionaries, however, accorded much priority to the training of African pastors who were expected to act as frontrunners in the evangelistic endeavours and administration of the would-be independent church. Before 1937, the founding mission had only two ordained Cameroonian pastors. They were Revs. Joseph Litumbe Ekesse and Peter Essoka Diso ordained in 1917 and 1929 respectively[75]. In order to foster the drive towards autonomy, Rev. H. Stahl ordained twelve other male indigenes between 1937 and 1945[76]. It was thanks to the efforts of these African ministers that the churches were kept alive after the ousting of missionaries of German origin during World War II. Indeed, the church had embraced the path towards self-determination especially as the number of ordained pastors further increased thanks to the Theological Training Centre at Nyasoso opened in 1952[77]. Admission into this theological college was limited to men given

---

[73] Dah, "The Vision and Challenges", p. 34.
[74] Ibid.
[75] Werner, *The History of the Presbyterian*, p. 78.
[76] Ibid., pp. 79-79; Dah, "The Planting of Christianity", pp. 82-83.
[77] Ibid.

that Basel missionaries barred women from the ordained ministry. This sex-segregation in the ordained ministry limited women's access to leadership within the church. As preparations for independence intensified, leadership was gradually transferred from white missionaries to indigenous male clerics.

As earlier highlighted, the second global confrontation of 1939-1945 created administrative loopholes in the Basel Mission Church in Southern Cameroons, caused principally by the internment of missionaries of German nationality. This was a long-awaited opportunity for African pastors to prove their worth since plans were made for them to take over leading posts within the church's set up. The idea of appointing indigenous Christians to important positions was first suggested to the General Synod in 1946 by the Field Secretary, Rev. E. Peyer. He insisted that it was time for a Cameroonian to be appointed as Chairman of the General Synod so as to promote the handing over of more and even delicate responsibilities from the mission to the church[78]. This was followed by serious discussions between 1946 and 1950 when the proposal finally materialized. It was a non-negligible break through as Revs. Essoka Diso and Aaron Shu became Chairman and Vice Chairman of the General Synod respectively[79]. Similar transfer of authority was witnessed at the level of the presbyteries, mission stations and schools. Crucial posts such as treasurers and financial secretaries became placed under the command of Africans.

Later in 1953, the General Synod established an all-male committee charged with the revision of the constitution. The work of the committee led to the convening of an all-male General Synod in Bali from 10 to 15 November 1957.[80] Deliberations focused on the issue of independence, ending with the unanimous adoption of the constitution which granted a quasi-autonomous status to the Basel Mission Church in Cameroon under the name Presbyterian Church in Cameroon. The autonomous church, as we shall discuss later, inherited patriarchy from the Basel Mission.

---

[78] Werner, *The History of the Presbyterian*, p. 80.
[79] Ibid., p. 81.
[80] Werner, *The History of the Presbyterian*, p. 82; Dah, "The Vision and Challenges", p. 35.

The development of the Basel Mission in Cameroon, from 1886 when its pioneer missionaries arrived in the territory to 1957 when partial autonomy was granted to the local church, was influenced by patriarchy. The roots of this patriarchy are traced to the emergence of the Basel Mission, its patriarchal beliefs and practices, its controversial "Christian Home" ideal, and its endorsement of the "civilizing mission" of colonialism discussed earlier in this chapter. In Cameroon, the Basel Mission incorporated into its system and work, the patriarchal standards of the Western world, causing its leadership and mission work to be defined as male. In the power structure of the Basel Mission which comprised hierarchical organs from the Station through to the General Conference, the voices of women were virtually absent. These governing structures alongside those in charge of education and health served as instruments through which women were marginalized in the system of the Basel Mission in Cameroon. This patriarchal structure of the mission and the patriarchal beliefs and practices of the missionaries it sent to Cameroon, led to a controversial emancipation of local Christian women and their marginalization in the leadership structures of the church. The presence of a few missionary wives and single female missionaries in the Cameroon mission field rather increased the marginalization of women. It is shown in the next chapter that the controversial women's empowerment measures carried out by these female missionaries contributed in narrowing women's sphere of influence and increasingly confined them to the home and family.

Chapter 3

Controversial Emancipation: Christian Housewifisation of Local Women

The Basel Mission commenced work in Cameroon in 1886 at a time when the "Christian home" ideal was being implemented in its mission fields. Through this policy, the Basel Mission aimed at transforming gender patterns in areas where it operated. As such, the Christianisation of women went concomitantly with their emancipation along Western gender lines. This was situated in the context of pietism, patriarchy, and colonialism's civilizing mission to which Western Christianity subscribed. Missionary wives and single female missionaries who were commissioned to spread the concept of the "Christian home" ideal had a pietistic background, which had shaped their status in the internal workings of the Basel Mission.

This chapter discusses the female missionaries to Cameroon as a point of departure for analysing their controversial emancipation work among local Christian women. There were two categories of agents of women's emancipation in Cameroon. It was begun by missionary wives who were later joined by single and married female missionaries. A brief sketch of the biographies of these women and the circumstances under which they came to Cameroon are handled in the first section of this chapter. The second section analyses domesticity as a controversial approach to the emancipation of women. The emancipation project anchored on the flawed assumption that indigenous women were oppressed and marginalized in a patriarchal and conservative society, and had as hallmark female education. The chapter ends with an examination of vocational empowerment initiatives of the women missionaries, arguing that they failed to grant women access into the power structure of the Basel Mission. The main contention of the chapter is that in emancipating local Christian women, missionary wives and female missionaries gave considerable attention to the ideals of female domesticity, with little focus on empowerment for leadership in the mission church.

Women Missionaries to Cameroon

The Home Board of the Basel Mission sent two categories of women missionaries to the mission fields. The first category comprised of missionary wives at a time when the Basel Mission understood the missionary profession as the preserve of men. The second category was made up of single and married female missionaries who had received the training required for qualification to join the missionary profession. This intervened at a time when pressure accruing from the Christian feminist movement had pushed the Home Board to revise the gender policy of the Basel Mission. In this section, the deployment of these two categories of women missionaries to Cameroon is discussed. They are presented as agents of controversial emancipation among local Christian women.

The deployment of missionary wives to Cameroon began in 1886 when the Basel Mission sent a pioneer all-male team of missionaries to take over from the London Baptist Missionary Society.[81] The female missionaries had a pietist background and were brought up in a German society where a distinction existed between formal male and informal female spheres. This low status of Western women coincided with the era when there was entrenched patriarchy in the leadership structures of the Basel Mission. These women accepted the low status of missionary wives because of the possibility of uplifting their welfare. Most of them were from middle-class families in which patriarchy was the norm. Apart from wanting to secure a new status, these women were probably attracted to male missionaries by the financial support made available to missionary wives by the Basel Mission.[82] In her "Reclaiming Women's Presence", Bowie describes a Basel

---

[81] This pioneer team was deployed from Gold Coast where the Basel Mission had worked among the local population since 1828. Rev. Friederich Becher died of malaria four days after his arrival in Cameroon. As leader of the team, Rev. Munz became the pioneer Field Secretary in the Cameroon mission field.

[82] Sill, *Encounters in Quest of Christian Womanhood*, p. 81.

Missionary as a male noun, presenting it as a male action and male sphere of service.[83]

From 1886 to 1936, missionary wives were the only women missionaries working in Cameroon. The evangelical work of the Basel Mission was started in Cameroon by a team of four male missionaries and one missionary wife. This team comprised of Rev. and Mrs. Gottlieb Munz, Revs. Christian Dilger, Johanness Bizer, and Friederich Becher. They arrived in Cameroon on 23 December 1886. This made Mrs. Munz the first missionary wife to work in the Cameroon mission field. Before coming to Cameroon, Mrs. Munz spent her childhood years in a German Christian home where she received her calling and was trained as a mission bride. As a co-worker of her husband, Mrs. Munz had a plethora of tasks given that she served as wife, mother, teacher, nurse, etc. Her primary role was to serve as an exemplar of the ideal of Christian femininity. As an unpaid worker alongside her ordained husband, the task of this missionary wife was to serve as teacher for local Christian women and girls. This was partly predicated on the idea of evangelical womanhood which developed in Europe and America in the second half of the 19th century. The concept emphasized the Protestant "virtuous woman" ideal, which portrayed women as nurturing and sensitive to injustices in society. So, by associating missionary wives with mission work in the fields, the intention was to export this ideal of evangelical womanhood to other parts of the world. The goal was not to challenge the male-dominated hierarchy of the church. Little wonder missionary wives underwent special training which made them not to find fault with women's marginalization in the structures of the Basel Mission. Women's mission, especially their teacher/trainer roles were conceived and professionalized through training. Missionary brides had to complete compulsory courses before deployment to the field with their husbands. One of such courses was a five-month midwifery course which started in 1896.[84]

---

[83] F. Bowie, "Reclaiming Women's Presence", in Bowie, F; Kirkwood, D& Ardener, S. (eds.), *Women and Missions: Past and Present: Anthropological Historical Perceptions*, USA, Berg Publishers, 1993, p. 2.

[84] Haas, "The 19th Century Basel Mission", p. 3.

For half a decade (1886-1891), Mrs. Munz was practically the lone woman missionary working in the Cameroon mission field. The major reason for this was that most of the male missionaries were not yet married, given that being a missionary bride was the main opportunity women had to be deployed to the mission field. Despite the fact that the Basel Mission had endorsed the recruitment and deployment of single female missionaries, it took male missionaries many years to overcome the initial reaction that marrying was a weakness and disruptive to mission work. Most of them continued to see marriage in negative terms. Besides, it was not obligatory for male missionaries to marry. So, mostly single male missionaries were sent to Cameroon in the last quarter of the 19th century. Of the four pioneer male missionaries, only Rev. Gottlieb Munz was married. In 1896, Cameroon received a second missionary wife in the person of Greta Kalmbach.

At the turn of the century, the Basel Mission sent more missionary couples to Cameroon, which increased the number of missionary wives in the territory. In 1903, for instance, Hedwig Arndt from Zurich married Gottlieb Spellenberg and was sent to Cameroon. Other missionary wives who arrived in Cameroon in 1903 were Mrs. Walker-Anner Otilie and Mrs. Sophie Basedow-Hiller. In 1904, two other missionary brides, Mrs. Hulda Hoffmann-Muller (wife of Rev. Hoffmann Georg Max Alfred) and Mrs. Hies-Muller (wife of Rev. Wilhelm Hies), began work as women missionaries in Bonaku. At the Bonaberi mission station in Douala work among local women was started in 1905 by Margarethe Gohring-Kalmbach. She served in Douala and its environs until 1911 when she was redeployed to Foumban. Later in 1909, Katherine Link, who was born in Wurttemberg in 1875, was sent to Cameroon after undergoing training as a nurse.[85]

Worth stressing is the fact that before 1903, missionary wives and their husbands were stationed only in the coastal mission stations, given that the Basel Mission had not yet extended its activities into the interior part of the territory. This changed in 1903

---

[85] Paul Jenkins, "Everyday Life Encapsulated? Two Photographs Concerning Women and the Basel Mission in West Africa, c. 1900," *Journal of African Cultural Studies*, Vol. 15, No. 1, 2002, p. 50.

when the Basel Mission was established for the first time in the grassfields after an earlier working session in 1902 between the Fon of Bali Nyonga and missionaries Schuler, Keller, and Spellenburg.[86] The presence of these missionaries led to the creation of the Bali Mission Station, thus necessitating the deployment of missionary couples to the area. In fact, the significance of the mission station as the main centre from where other interior parts of the western grassfields were reached led to the stationing of six missionary wives between 1903 and 1910. These missionary brides comprised of Anna Geprags-Merkle, Anna Leimbacher-Brunner, Margaretha Schwarz-Vogel, Friederike Widmaier-Gutekunst, Clara Schultze-Reinhardt, and Katharina Keller-Schnetzer. These women missionaries intensified female domesticity and vocational training activities in Bali-Nyonga and its environs. They engaged in the transformation of indigenous culture and society, especially for local women. Most of these missionary wives made Bali-Nyonga their home up to 1915 when they were forcibly deported with their husbands as a result of the outbreak of the First World War.[87]

From the main hinterland station in Bali Nyonga, efforts were made by Basel missionaries to plant the church in other polities in the western grassfields. Resulting from these initiatives was the establishment of two mission stations: Bafut in 1904 and Foumban in 1906. Considering that the setting up of mission stations in the grassfields was partly intended to stall the advance of Islam from the north, the Basel Mission took swift measures to deploy missionaries to Bamoun where the Muslim faith had just been officialised by King Njoya. This led to the redeployment of Margarethe Gohring-Kalmbach and her husband to Foumban in 1911. The year 1911 also witnessed a major shift in the category of

---

[86] Paul Nchoji Nkwi, *The German Presence in the Western Grassfields 1891-1913: A German Colonial Account*, Leiden, African Studies Centre, 1989, p. 56.

[87] These missionaries were arrested, interned, and forcibly deported British forces under the command of General Charles Dobell. For more on this subject, read Michael Kpughe Lang, "The First World War in Cameroon: An Historical Analysis of its Implications on the Territory's Christian Religious Landscape", In *Cameroon and the Great War (1914-1916)*, Proceedings of the 1st National Colloquium of Military History, Douala, 05-08/08/2014, Paris, L'Harmattan, 2017, pp. 241-258.

women missionaries the Basel Mission was deploying to Cameroon. For the first time, an unmarried woman missionary was engaged and sent to Cameroon. I am talking about Anna Wuhrmann who worked as a missionary teacher for the Basel Mission in the Bamoun Chiefdom from 1911 to 1915. Born in 1881 in Marseille, France, of Swiss parents, she received her education in Switzerland and was trained as a teacher. The Basel Mission engaged her in 1910 and she was deployed to Cameroon in 1911. For four years, Missionary Anna Wuhrmann served as Principal of the Basel Mission Girls' School in Foumban. In 1915, she returned to Switzerland under the weight of anti-Basel Mission policies during the First World War. Later in 1923, she continued teaching in Germany and got married to her German colleague. She died in 1971.[88] By 1914 when the First World War broke out, there were 31 missionary wives and nine single female missionaries working in Cameroon under the Basel Mission.[89] Female missionaries were required to remain single for at least four years after posting before they could marry. This rule anchored on the fear that marriage at the beginning of such a career could be disruptive to mission work.

The extension of the First World War to Cameroon in 1914, as earlier noted, led to the internment and forceful deportation of all Basel missionaries from the territory. From 1916 to 1925 when Britain permitted Basel missionaries to resume work in Cameroon, mission work in the territory was orphaned, thus temporarily bringing to an end the emancipation of local Christian women. Indeed, the experience of the war destroyed the foundational work of mission work carried out by women missionaries.[90] On the eve

---

[88] For more information on Anna Wuhrmann, read Gerald H. Anderson, ed., *Biographical Dictionary of Christian Missions*, Cambridge, William B. Eerdmans Publishing Company, 1999, p. 564.
[89] Dah, "Missionary Motivations and Methods", p. 117.
[90] The period 1914-1916 which was marked by the unfolding of military operations in Cameroon was one of severe trial for Christianity. Efoua observes that almost all missionaries were deported to the Queens Ferry concentration camp from where they were repatriated to their countries of origin.[90] It was indeed a serious setback to the growth of the church in Cameroon considering that missionaries were abruptly cut off and their work orphaned. In addition to these deportations, church buildings, farms, schools and residences of the missions were destroyed during the war. For details on

of the war in 1914, women missionaries were active in mission stations such as Douala (Bonaberi, Bonaku, Mangamba, and Lobetal), Sakbayeme, Bombe, Nyasoso, Victoria, Buea, Besongabang, Bagam, Bana, Foumban, Bali Nyonga, and Bafut. Overall, the Basel Mission operated 25 mission stations and 388 outstations in Cameroon before the outbreak of the war. The post-war Anglo-French partition of Cameroon and their recourse to anti-German mission policies led to official termination of Basel Mission activities in French Cameroon. The Paris Evangelical Mission replaced the Basel Mission on the invitation of the French Government. In the British section, the Basel Mission was allowed to resume mission work in 1925 after ten years of absence. As such, the presence of women missionaries was now limited to British Southern Cameroons as they were prohibited from operating in French Cameroon. The size of the mission field and number of mission stations and outstations under Basel Mission control significantly reduced due to the war and the partition of the territory. Just six of the 25 pre-war mission stations and 114 of 388 outstations came under the reduced mission territory of the Basel Mission.

The resumption of mission work in 1915 led to the deployment of more women missionaries to Cameroon. Missionary women who operated in mission stations that fell under French control after the war were redeployed to stations in the British section upon their return to Cameroon. From Victoria in the forest region and Bali Nyonga in the Grassfields region, attempts were made to create mission stations further inland. This led to the establishment of new stations, thus creating the need for more women missionaries. In 1927, a team of eight women missionaries (comprised of four missionary wives and four single female missionaries) were sent to Cameroon by the Home Board of the Basel Mission. Mrs. Rosli

---

the imprint of the First World War on the Basel Mission in Cameroon, read Michael Kpughe Lang, "The First World War in Cameroon: An Historical Analysis of its Implications on the Territory's Christian Religious Landscape", In Cameroon and the Great War (1914-1916), Proceedings of the 1st National Colloquium of Military History, Douala, 05-08/08/2014, Paris, L'Harmattan, 2017, pp. 241-258.

Wildi-Suter was part of the team and was posted to the Buea station alongside her husband. Her other colleagues were Bertha Glockel-Schimming, Martha Bachtold-Heiser, Therese Lutz-Elisabeth, Mathilde Autenrieth-Walker, Adelheid Hummel, Elise Schoch, and Maria Walcher. Most of these missionary women were deployed to new stations that were being established as a move intended to propagate Western ideals of domesticity. But the desire to open girls' schools yielded three strategic postings, namely the deployment of Maria Walcher to Victoria, Martha Bachtold-Heiser to Buea, and Adelheid Hummel to Bali Nyonga.[91]

From Basel Mission's reinstatement in 1925 to the granting of partial independence to the local church in 1957, nine new mission stations were opened across British Southern Cameroons. The disruption of mission work during the war era, especially the deportation of European missionaries, caused the mission agency to rethink its policy of large mission stations. There was recourse to the establishment of out-stations that were placed under the coordination of teacher-catechists.[92] The intention was to bring indigenous collaborators such as teachers and catechists into the mainstream of mission work in order to avoid a replay of the difficulties of the wartime period. The policy also came as a step in the drive towards the independence of the local church. Consequently, nine new mission stations and 484 outstations were opened from 1925 to 1957.

Owing to the creation of new mission stations but above all, because of growing interest to implement the "Christian Home" ideal, the Home Board deployed more women missionaries to British Southern Cameroons in the 1930s. The four new stations that were established in the grassfields (Mbengwi in 1930, Weh in 1932, Kishong in 1932, and Bafut in 1937) and the five new ones in the forest area, including the six that survived the war era, namely, Victoria (1887), Buea (1896), Nyasosso (1896), Bali (1903),

---

[91] Werner, *The History of the Presbyterian*, p. 66.
[92] Guy Alexander Thomas, "Why do we Need the White Man's God? African Contributions and Responses to the Formation of a Christian Movement in Cameroon, 1914-1968," PhD Thesis in History, School of Oriental and African Studies, University of London, 2001, p. 93.

Besongabang (1912), and Dikume Balue (1928) became centres where missionary wives and single female missionaries delivered practical domestic science lessons and other Western ways through which they promoted the emancipation of women in society. New arrivals such as Gertrud Lydia Angst-Gunz, Emmy Zurcher-Roggli, Verena Peyer-Binder, and Frieda Mischler engaged in a plethora of emancipation initiatives in stations where they were posted.

From the 1930s onwards, efforts were made to reorganize work among local women by materializing the creation of girls' vocational institutions. The reorganization was occasioned by the revision of Basel Mission women empowerment policy. The new approach took two dimensions: formal education in the form of girls' schools and informal education which was provided through training courses. Maria Walcher's commitment and collaborative work with missionary wives led to the creation of a proper girls' school in Victoria in 1931.[93] But her colleagues in Bali Nyonga and Buea, namely Adelheid Hummel and Martha Heiser respectively, were not successful in creating proper girls' schools in these mission stations. Because of these failures, two independent female missionaries, Anni Murer and Else Bleher, with expertise in women empowerment were sent to Southern Cameroons with the intent of intensifying work among local women. They were commissioned to work in collaboration with those on the ground in view of initiating professional training by opening vocational institutions for women. It was also their task to initiate and supervise the organization of training courses for women in mission stations across the territory. This was the context in which four other girls' vocational schools were opened in Bafut (1937)[94], Kumba (1951), Fotabe (1952), and Mankon (1961).[95]

In summary, missionary wives and single female missionaries were sent to the Cameroon mission field to spread the concept of

---

[93] Werner, *The History of the Presbyterian*, p. 67.
[94] The roots of the Bafut Girls' School are traced to 1934 when Adelheid Hummel introduced the teaching of girls in special classes at Mbengwi. When the scheme of work which privileged domestic science was developed, the school was relocated to Bafut in 1937 with boarding facilities.
[95] Werner, *The History of the Presbyterian*, p. 67.

the "Christian home" among local Christian women. The concept had a pietistic background, which had shaped their status in the internal workings of the Basel Mission. From 1886 to 1968, the women missionaries carried out controversial emancipation work among local Christian women. The majority of these women missionaries were missionary wives, with very few single female missionaries involved. This was the outcome of deep-rooted patriarchy within the system of the Basel Mission, irrespective of the knocking down of laws barring women from participation in mission work in the 1840s. The deployment of an insignificant number of single women missionaries yields the impression that patriarchy remained a defining feature of the internal workings of the Basel Mission throughout the period it operated in Cameroon.

This discrepancy notwithstanding, both categories of missionary women were sent to Cameroon to promote the Western ideals of domesticity and vocational empowerment among local Christian women. These women brought with themselves Western cultural values which determined the form of emancipation they provided to local Christian women. In most cases, female missionaries to Cameroon had a pietist background. As noted already, they were brought up in Swiss and German societies where a distinction existed between formal male and informal female roles. Their work in the spheres of domesticity and vocational training were meant for Cameroonian women who were ignorantly assumed to be lacking in modern aspects of home care, childcare, cookery, among others. The next section illustrates that emancipation work carried out by missionary women was harmful to the status of local Christian women. It was a problematic emancipation agenda informed by a female hostile Western context with no potential to produce occupational options and opportunities for local women to participate in the power structures of the Basel Mission in Cameroon. This controversial emancipation was promoted in the homes of missionaries in the mission stations and in vocational institutions (girls' schools).

Female Domesticity in Missionary Women's Homes

In the Cameroonian mission field, with its entrenched culture of women's leadership role in traditional religious institutions (as established in Chapter One), domesticity as an emancipation ideal was begun by missionary wives in their homes. In mission stations where women missionaries operated alongside their husbands, the promotion of ideals of domesticity was carried out on the verandas of the mission houses. Most mission houses had large verandas with enough space for domestic science training. The first women to receive domestic science lessons were comprised principally of domestic staff serving in the homes of missionaries. It was hoped that the female domestic staff through their exposure to the behaviour of the missionary wives were to adopt Western domestic doctrines, given that the "Christian home" ideal which had become the cornerstone of Basel Mission evangelism presented the home as the centre of women's lives and action. Clearly, the promotion of ideals of domesticity in mission houses intended to turn marriage and child-rearing as specialized fields of operation for female Cameroonian converts. With time, the wives of catechists, whose husbands were engaged by missionaries in subordinate roles as managers of out-stations, were occasionally invited to the mission houses to be taught by missionary wives. Other female Christians, especially those who did not live far from the mission station, were given access to this domestic science training.

In all mission stations, missionary wives owned sewing machines, needles, scissors, threads of varying colours, tapes, and other tools to facilitate training in sewing. They also offered lessons in hygiene, housekeeping, laundry, gardening, childcare, and Bible stories. Taken together, the purpose of this kind of curriculum was underpinned by the Christian home ideology. As aptly observed by Jonas Dah, associating women with this domestic science training was the hallmark of female education. He writes that "To produce Christian wives and Christian mothers was a chief aim of starting girls' schools."[96] Going by this objective and curriculum, it is obvious that the women missionaries did not intend to empower local women to prepare them for leadership roles in the church.

---

[96] Dah, "Missionary Motivations and Methods", p. 138.

Guided by this controversial philosophy, agenda, and curriculum, missionary wives across Cameroon engaged in work among local women. In the Mangamba Mission Station, Mrs. Bertha Glockel-Schimming usually assembled her domestic staff and other village women for training in sewing. Similar sewing lessons were offered by Mrs. Emma Maier-Schimming in the Nyasoso Station from 1909 to 1915. Mrs. Margarethe Gohring-Kalmbach was active in the Bonaberi Station where local Christians received training in sewing. These examples of how women missionaries taught local Christian women sewing happened between 1886 and 1915. But in the first two decades of Basel Mission presence in Cameroon, dressmaking classes in mission houses were concentrated in the coastal area, especially in mission stations around Douala and Victoria. The opening of mission stations in the grassfields in places such as Bali Nyonga, Bamoun, Bana, Bagam, Bandjun, and Babungo led to the diffusion of ideologies of domesticity to these places. In missionaries' homes in the Bali station, Anna Leimbacher-Brunner, Margaretha Schwarz-Vogel, and Katharina Keller-Schnetzer gathered women to whom they offered dressmaking lessons.

Apart from sewing, the domesticity curriculum in mission houses also emphasized skills like laundry, cookery, gardening, hygiene and sanitation. Missionary wives also sought to roll away certain cultural practices deemed problematic by the Basel Mission. Without exception, missionary wives promoted the necessity of monogamy and marital affection. Presenting the monogamous family unit as the norm and as the ideal of Christian marriage, missionary wives sought to mitigate marriage-related evils of patriarchy such as polygamy, concubinage, exchange of bride wealth, and wife-beating. But they were ill-informed about the nature and functioning of indigenous marriage, missing the complex ways practices associated with marriage affected the status of women in society. The overall goal was to create "good" wives and mothers, described by Melinda Adams as the Christian housewifisation of local women.[97] Informed by the "virtuous woman" ideal that was exemplified in the concept of the Christian Home, female domesticity was directed towards women's reproductive and nurturing tasks. Little wonder stress was laid on Christian marriage ideals, childrearing, husband care, and handicrafts.

To ensure that Western domesticity and marriage norms were diffused from the stations to out-stations that were managed by catechists and teachers, missionary wives occasionally invited the wives of these local agents to the mission house for short domestic science courses. It was in mission homes that catechist wives learned cookery, baby craft, hygiene, and local crafts. In 1937 for instance, Mrs. Emmy Zurcher-Roggli assembled teachers' wives in her Kishong mission station residence for domestic science and local craft training. Upon returning to the out-stations, the wives of catechists and teachers were expected to transfer this knowledge to other women in society. It thus became common to find wives of teachers and catechists organizing classes on cookery, hygiene, baby craft, housekeeping, and dressmaking in their homes. This approach led to the rapid diffusion of Western norms of domesticity across Cameroon, with an unprecedented bearing on the status of women.

The wives of missionaries, teachers, and catechists consistently used their homes as informal settings where the domesticity doctrine, which was an embodiment of Western family value systems, was transferred to indigenous Christian women. According to Dah, domestic science classes in mission houses achieved its goal of producing Christian wives and Christian mothers whose operational space scarcely went beyond the home. With the home as their sphere, very little was expected of these women in public activities. Mrs. Mathilde Autenrieth-Walker noted with pride that the women she trained at the Bonaku mission station in Douala were later happily married to teachers and catechists employed by the Basel Mission. Similarly, Mrs. Lauffer, in a boastful tone, reported that the existence of worthy Christian women in Edea was

---

[97] Melinda Adams, "Colonial Policies and Women's Participation in Public Life: The Case of British Southern Cameroons," *African Studies Quarterly*, Vol. 8, No. 2, 2006, p. 2.

the outcome of consistent work among local women. In Bakunduland, particularly in the Bombe and Banga stations, two catechist wives, Mariana Ete and Mary Basaka, played instrumental roles in transferring domesticity norms and local craft knowledge learnt from missionary wives to other women in the society. "Their homes", notes Betoto, "set the new standards of hygiene and home care that they were taught by missionaries."[98] These claims of emancipation achievements yield the thinking that the teaching of domestic science in mission homes was principally a path-way to marriage for women. Communities across the Cameroon mission field witnessed the emergence of a new class of women who were desirable as wives for the new male class comprised of teachers and catechists.

No wonder the Basel Mission is lauded in clerical and academic circles for having emancipated local women. Writing on missionary activities in Bakunduland, Betoto observes that "the coming of Christian missionaries brought awareness and liberation for women in Bakunduland who eventually contributed to the development of their society."[99] Adams corroborates this view, stressing that ideologies of domesticity unexpectedly heightened women's participation in the public sphere. To support her argument, Adams declares that "Domestic science education also provided some women with an economic livelihood as enterprising students used sewing and baking skills learned in these programs to earn an income or even open a small business."[100]

While these gains of domestic science programs in mission houses seem convincing, the stark reality is that there were only isolated cases of women who used skills from such courses to play public roles in business and administration. A good number of these women simply ended up as excellent housewives, going by clerical assessment. This was the key motivation for using missionary wives to transfer Western domesticity ideologies to local

---

[98] Joseph Ebune Betoto, "Missionary Activity in Bakunduland, Cameroon, 1873-1960: An Historical Appraisal," *Global Advanced Research Journal of History, Political Science and International Relations*, Vol. 1, No. 2, 2012, p. 053.
[99] Ibid., p. 051.
[100] Adams, "Colonial Policies and Women's Participation in Public Life," p. 6.

women. Dah is therefore right in his submission that the Basel Mission did not expect women who benefitted from domestic science training to operate beyond the confines of the Christian home.[101] This made the home to become a narrowed operational sphere for local Christian women, with public life and the executive structures of the church largely remaining the preserve of their male counterparts. In fact, the leadership structures of the Basel Mission in Cameroon remained in male hands, which made discrimination against female Christians to become the mission's defining feature. Plainly put, the limitations and controversies associated with the domestic science curriculum implemented in mission houses by missionary wives were significant. Its outcome is best described as the housewifisation of local Christian women. The opening of proper girls' vocational schools in Cameroon hinged on this same housewifisation agenda as shown in the next section.

Christian Women's Empowerment in Girls' Schools

While the mission house was the principal setting for women's emancipation, the need to create proper schools for girls was identified by the authorities of the Basel Mission in the first decade of the 20th century. But it is important to stress that from 1886 when the mission began its work in Cameroon, admission into its primary schools was opened to both boys and girls. However, the number of girls attending these schools remained insignificant owing to preference given to male children and mothers' resistance. Consequently, these primary schools came to be described as boys' schools. Besides, the curriculum that was followed in these schools was a mismatch with the women's emancipation agenda. This explains why a decision was taken in about 1910 to open special schools for girls. Such schools were already operational in mission territories such as Ghana and China. It was agreed that the curriculum in schools for girls should be a combination of formal and vocational education. The formal education curriculum was conceived to emphasize on subjects such as history, geography, mathematics, Bible studies, and German language (later English

---

[101] Dah, "Missionary Motivations and Methods", p. 138.

language). Vocational education curriculum was intended to give attention to domestic science and handicraft training.

In 1911, the Basel Mission commissioned Anna Wuhrmann, an unmarried female missionary of Swiss nationality who had trained as a teacher and nurse, to implement the girls' education policy. Upon her arrival in Cameroon, Wuhrmann worked closely with some missionary wives, especially Mrs. Margarethe Gohring-Kalmbach, who had been transferring domestic science knowledge to local women in verandas of mission houses. As early as 1906, Mrs. Gohring had experimented the creation of a proper girls' school by offering lessons in an open space in Bonaberi, Douala, to women she had assembled. Building on the Bonaberi experience, Wuhrmann was posted to the Foumban station to open a girls' school. The cooperation of the Bamoun traditional authorities, especially King Njoya, permitted this female missionary to start the pioneer girls' school in Foumban in 1911. The school functioned for three years before its closure in 1915 when Bamoun was captured by the British army during the First World War. Missionary Wuhrmann was deported to Switzerland together with other missionaries, and the school was taken over by the Paris Evangelical Mission following the Anglo-French partition of Cameroon.

Photo 1: Anna Wuhrmann with female pupils in Foumban, 1911
Source: Mission 21 Archives at Missionstrasse, Basel, Switzerland

Photo 2: Gohring-Kalmbach Margarethe with female pupils in Douala, 1906
Source: Basel Mission Archives, Basel, Switzerland, ref. 78437

The reinstatement of the Basel Mission in British Southern Cameroons in 1925 led to new efforts to revamp girls' schools. In 1927, three female missionaries with expertise in education were sent to Cameroon for the purpose of enhancing the education of girls. Two years later, these missionary wives, Maria Walcher, Adelheid Hummel, and Mathilde Walker, drew the attention of the officials of the Basel Mission in Cameroon to the problem of girls' education. In response, the male-led leadership assigned the female missionaries to open girls' schools in three key stations: Victoria, Bali Nyonga, and Buea. Posted to Victoria, Maria Walcher created a proper girls' school in Victoria in 1931.[102] In Mbengwi near Bali Nyonga, Adelheid Hummel started a girls' school in 1934. In 1937, following the creation of the Bafut mission station, the school was relocated to Bafut and renamed as the Marriage Training Centre.[103] Miss Martha Heiser toiled fruitlessly to open a school for girls in Buea, given that her efforts did not progress beyond the mere domestic science classes she organized in the mission house.

---

[102] Werner, *The History of the Presbyterian,* p. 67.
[103] Lawyer, "The Christian Women Fellowship", p. 94.

Photo 3: Wildi-Suter Rosli delivering a sewing lesson to females in Buea, 1928
Source: Mission 21 Archives at Missionstrasse, Basel, Switzerland

Though the Basel Mission was already operating girls' schools in Bafut and Victoria, the education of girls remained an important problem. There were few women missionaries with expertise in education coupled with the near absence of teachers. In an effort to surmount these challenges, two other women missionary teachers, Anni Murer and Else Bleher, were sent to Southern Cameroons to beef up the education of girls. They were instructed to envisage the opening of more schools, initiate and supervise the organization of training courses for women in mission stations across the territory, and to train local teachers. But their work was perturbed by the outbreak of the Second World War in 1939. Most Basel missionaries, including those who specialized in the education of girls, were deported by the British colonial authorities. Before their forceful deportation, women missionaries had reorganized the Victoria girls' school into a full primary school. The absence of these European women missionaries led to the temporal closure of the schools in Bafut and Victoria, which were reopened only after the war.

Photo 4: Students at Basel Mission Girls' School Victoria in 1938
Source: PCC Central Archive and Library, Buea, Cameroon

When the war ended in 1945, Britain permitted the Basel Mission to once more resume its work in Southern Cameroons. Among the new arrivals was Lina Weber who had trained as a teacher. Deployed to Southern Cameroons in 1947, Weber was charged to revamp girls' schools that were abandoned in the course of the war. From 1947 to 1968 when the Basel Mission transferred its educational facilities to the Presbyterian Church in Cameroon, preceded by the latter's partial independence in 1957, Lina Weber played a key role in the promotion of girls' education in Southern Cameroons. In 1947, she reopened the girls' school in Bafut, and ensured that training was effective in Victoria. The closure of schools during the war period caused the educational authorities of the Basel Mission to envisage the association of Cameroonian female teachers with the administration of girls' schools. Consequently, women missionaries were assisted in Victoria by Catherine Lyonga. The efforts of Lina Weber led to the development of the school in Bafut into a full primary school in 1949.[104] The fame of the school was evidenced by the hundreds of female students it attracted from communities across the grassfields region. The Victoria girls' school equally pulled Basel Mission

---

[104] Mathew Basung Gwanfogbe, *Basel Mission Education in Cameroon, 1886-1968*, Bamenda, Quality Printers, 2018, p. 130.

school girls from all over the forest region. The girls came from places such as Kumba, Mamfe, Buea, Tiko, Bakunduland, and Muyuka. In 1951, the administration of the school passed from European missionary wives to and indigenous teacher, Catherine Lyonga, who had assisted them in the development of the school. It is important to stress that Lyonga was a graduate of the school and had trained as a teacher in Nigeria.

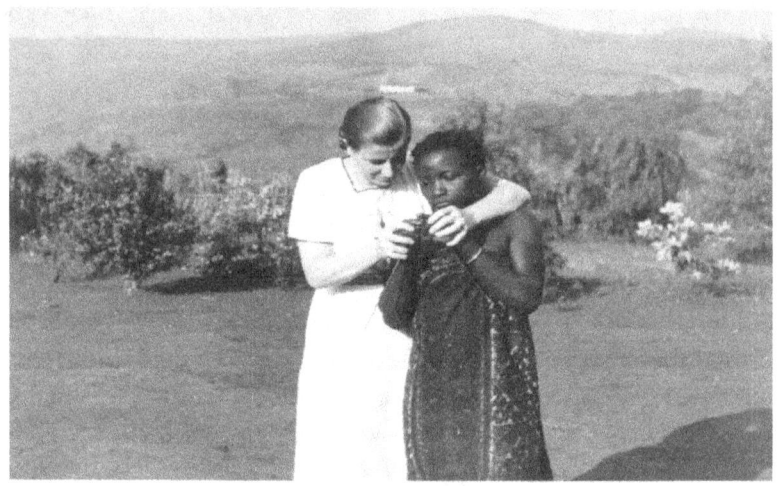

Photo 5: Zurcher-Roggli Emmy in a practical knitting lesson, 1939
Source: PCC Central Archive and Library, Buea, Cameroon

The encouraging enrolment in these two schools in Bafut and Victoria and the many girls who attended the co-educational Basel Mission schools in mission stations across the territory probably marked the apogee of girls' education by this mission agency. Between 1928 and 1951, female enrolment in girls' schools and co-educational primary schools increased from 758 to 1568. This growth was also noticeable in the number of teachers serving in girls' schools. Initially, the Basel Mission trained female teachers for its girls' schools in teacher training colleges in Nigeria and in the Catholic Girls' Training College in Kumba. Southern Cameroons' drive towards independence and fear of the conversion of Basel Mission girls into Catholicism occasioned the need for the Basel

Mission to set up its own girls' teacher training college.[105] This was the context in which Lina Weber worked in collaboration with the PCC in 1960 to obtain permission from government to set up a female teacher training college. With a financial grant from the British government for the establishment of an elementary teacher's training college, the Basel Mission created the Women's Teacher Training College (WTTC) in 1961. The school went operational at a temporary site in Bafut and was eventually transferred to Mankon in Bamenda. The college graduated its pioneer batch of 30 women with a Teachers' Grade Two Certificate in 1963. Female teachers churned out from this training college were posted to girls' schools in Bafut, Victoria, Kumba, and Fotabe.

In 1966, the Basel Mission transferred all its educational facilities to the PCC which had obtained its autonomy in 1957. It then became the responsibility of the PCC to promote girls' education. The significant developments in girls' education under the Basel Mission were the outcome of the work of women missionaries and their Cameroonian assistants. From 1911 when the first girls' school was experimented in Foumban to 1961 when the WTTC was established, female missionaries such as Anna Wuhrmann, Rosli Wildi-Suter, Bertha Glockel-Schimming, Emmy Zurcher-Roggli, Maria Walcher, Adelheid Hummel, Martha Heiser, Anni Murrer, Else Bleher, and Lina Weber worked tortuously to develop girls' education in Cameroon. The most prominent of them was Lina Weber, described by Gwanfogbe as "the architect of girls' education for the Basel Mission."[106]

Generally, the curriculum implemented in girls' schools and the lone teachers' training college for women was streamed towards grooming Cameroonian girls and women through the "Christian Home" approach. Huge attention was given to the domestic specialization of women, though emphasis was also focused on reading, writing, arithmetic, religious studies, and handicraft. In these institutions, women missionaries combined formal education with vocational training, and both were intended to produce

---

[105] Ibid., p. 132.
[106] Ibid.

virtuous Christian women and to provide employment opportunities to local women. Very controversially, these women's empowerment models had a veiled intention to reach out to new church members. Female education was a tool aimed at easing conversion to Christianity, though empowerment was quite often brandished as the intended agenda. In fact, the Basel Mission considered schools for girls as arenas for evangelizing the heathens.[107] The Basel Mission implemented similar controversial empowerment policies in other mission fields like in Ghana and China. The Basel Mission began mission work in Gold Coast (later Ghana) in 1828. Its work among local Christian women was pioneered by Catherine Ziamerman. Working collaboratively with other female missionaries, Mrs. Ziamerman educated and trained young women as prospective wives of local male clerics: pastors, catechists, and evangelists.[108] In China, the Basel Mission deployed women missionaries who educated local women on household skills.[109] These two similar case studies are parallels to the controversial emancipation of women in Cameroon by women missionaries.

Girls' schools and the training college were spaces placed under the total control of European missionaries, which permitted them to emancipate women along Western lines with little influence from the rest of the population. The schools became places where women missionaries toiled to enforce Basel Mission's civilizing mission. The new values relating to homecare, housewife, and domesticity in general were taught in these schools. While domesticity promoted the housewifisation of women, handicraft courses drove an insignificant number toward more secular activities. There is no doubt that women missionaries transformed

---

[107] Rev. Jonas Dah, a retired pastor and former Synod Clerk of the PCC, admits that God took centre stage in Basel Mission schools. In fact, preaching and teaching were carried out in these schools by both teachers and itinerant catechists. Serving as places of worship and of learning, pupils in girls' schools could not escape conversion to Christianity.

[108] Read Sill, *Encounters in Quest of Christian Womanhood*.

[109] For more on controversial emancipation of local Chinese women, read Xiang-yu, Cai, "Christianity and Gender in South-East China".

and ameliorated the lives of local Christian women in their families, careers, and participation in the local economy.

This resultant emancipation notwithstanding, I continue to argue that the formal and vocational education offered to women in girls' and mixed schools failed to empower these women for full participation in the leadership structures of the Basel Mission in Cameroon. The stark reality is that after many years of controversial emancipation, leadership in the Basel Mission in Cameroon remained in the hands of men, with women missionaries and the Cameroonians they empowered taking only a peripheral position in the governance of the church. The next chapter examines the nature of transformation experienced within the Basel Mission church as an outcome of their emancipation. It will argue that patterns of discrimination against women persisted in the system of the Basel Mission church in Cameroon. Plainly put, emancipated women had no decision power in the male-dominated hierarchy of the church.

Chapter 4

Discrimination Against Women in Leadership Structures of the Basel Mission Church

The institutionalization of the Basel Mission Church in Cameroon was the handiwork of European missionaries with patriarchal beliefs acquired during their formation in Basel. The Basel Mission Church in Cameroon was a clerical institution with an operational system anchored on patriarchal norms. It was earlier noted that the Basel Mission sent missionaries to Cameroon at a time when women had been pushed to the margins of its power and leadership. From 1886 when the pioneer missionaries were deployed to 1957, measures were consistently taken to establish a local church. In the slow process of planting a church in Cameroon, the Basel Mission, just like other mission bodies, offered a second-class citizenship status to its female members. The latter, despite their empowerment in formal and vocational schools, were kept in a narrowly defined space, with little or no participation in the leadership structures of the church. The main contention of this chapter is that the controversial emancipation of Christian women based on the Western Christian Home ideal, with focus on domesticity, marriage, childcare, and handicrafts, yielded a pattern of predominantly male leadership in the structures of the Basel Mission. The chapter brings to light empirical evidence to illustrate the patterns of discrimination against women in the executive structures of the Basel Mission in Cameroon. In the first section I present the organizational set up of the Basel Mission Church in Cameroon; then I will examine the extent to which local Christian women were associated with the leadership of the church in these structures. I shall examine the place of women in the social and economic activities of the Basel Mission such as medical work, education, and the economy. In the concluding section, I shall analyse women's role in the process of transition from the Basel Mission to the Presbyterian Church in Cameroon in view of explaining why the new autonomous church inherited the patriarchal beliefs of its founding mission.

Organizational Structure of the Basel Mission Church in Cameroon

The organizational structure of the Basel Mission Church in Cameroon evolved with time and circumstances. From 1886 to the outbreak of the First World War, Douala served as the headquarters of the Basel Mission from where the rest of the church was governed. During this period, the church was organized into ascending organs: the out-stations, stations, and synod. Out-stations were placed under catechists (most of whom doubled as teachers) who carried out local evangelism, prepared catechumens for Baptism, and ensured that converts were committed followers of Christ. A number of out-stations constituted a mission station. The latter was placed under a European missionary. Serving as a place where one or more missionaries were resident, the station comprised a church building, school, and missionaries' residents. Communication between the missionaries in the stations and catechists in out-stations was made possible through evangelists who were regularly sent out to supervise out-stations. This made the evangelist an itinerant worker of the church as he was constantly on the move visiting out-stations and reporting back to the European missionaries. It was the duty of the evangelists to ensure that catechists did their work properly, especially the preparation of candidates for Baptism. Occasionally, perhaps once a year, the European missionary made a tour of out-stations found in his station. In 1914 when the work of the Basel Mission was interrupted by the First World War, 46 male missionaries, 31 missionary wives and six specially trained female missionaries operated 16 stations and 202 out-stations in Cameroon. Within the inner power structure of the mission station, there existed a distribution of roles with European missionaries as bosses and their local assistants (catechists and evangelists) as subordinates.

The central organ of the church before the First World War was the General Conference which was convened twice a year and was chaired by the Field Secretary of the Basel Mission. The latter doubled as leader of the team of missionaries working in the territory. The General Conference was attended by the 46 male missionaries and the six female missionaries, most of whom were nurses and teachers. It was the responsibility of the General Conference to take key decisions on the evangelical, medical, educational and other activities of the Basel Mission in Cameroon. Uniformity in the mission work in Cameroon was ensured by this supreme organ through its decisions. It consulted the Home Board on pertinent issues, while at the same time was empowered to take and implement its decisions. Sadly, this institution resolved to limit the ordained ministry to men despite the fact that the Basel Mission had started ordaining women in its seminaries in Switzerland and Germany. By fashioning male-friendly policies for implementation in Cameroon, the Conference contributed in making the leadership structures the preserve of men.

The resumption of Basel Mission activities in British Southern Cameroons in 1925 yielded a new organizational structure. In 1935, the first official constitution of the Basel Mission Church in Cameroon was drafted and adopted. The constitution was not only intended to lay down the guiding principles of the church, but also geared towards integrating and linking the numerous Basel Mission stations and churches with one another. The constitution changed the organization of the mission church considerably. The new structure of the Church in ascending order was comprised of Local Congregations, Stations, Districts and the whole Church.[110] The congregations were the smallest units of the church whose members were the local Christians. The governing body of the congregation was the Congregational Meeting chaired by the catechist, with membership limited to adult communicant Christians. The executive body of the Congregational Meeting was the Session which was presided over by the catechist. Its membership consisted of duly elected elders. The stations, which were renamed as presbyteries, consisted of a number of congregations. The administering body of the presbytery was the Presbytery Synod whose membership comprised three elders from

---

[110] Dah, "The Vision and Challenges", p. 34.

every local congregation, catechists, evangelists, and ordained ministers, and one teacher from each mission school. The Presbyterial Synod Committee, comprised of nine members, was the executive organ of the Presbytery Synod. During the Basel Mission era, there were thirteen of such stations/presbyteries organized into the Grassfields and Forest districts. Hence, each district was made up of presbyteries, with the District Synod functioning as the administrative organ. Convened once a year, the District Synod was attended by ordained ministers, three unordained church workers, four elders, one teacher from each presbytery, and the supervisor of schools. The District Synod Committee was the executive organ of the District Synod whose eleven members met twice a year. The Forest and Grassfields Districts together with their stations or presbyteries and congregations combined to form the Basel Mission Church in Southern Cameroons. Considered as an equivalent of the General Conference, the Synod was the central governing body of the church and consisted of ex-officio members, the two secretaries of the District Synods, the Field Secretary of the Basel Mission, the Supervisor of Schools, and elected members from either district (seven elders, twelve ordained ministers, three evangelists, two catechists, and one teacher). This supreme organ had a Chairman, Vice-Chairman and a Secretary who together with representatives of the districts constituted the General Synod Committee.[111]

The various administrative organs of the Basel Mission Church in Southern Cameroons discussed above were structures where leadership in the church rested. From the supreme organ, Synod, down to the Session of the Congregation, leadership was in the hands of various members of the church. This complex bureaucracy has been laid out for the purpose of understanding the extent to which female members of this church were associated with its governance. These structures were established to take actions aimed at enabling the Basel Mission to achieve its missiological agenda in Cameroon. An objective examination of the workings of these

---

[111] Dah, J. N., "Missionary Motivations and Methods: A Critical Examination of the Basel Mission in Cameroon 1886-1914", PhD Thesis in Theology, University of Basel, 1983, p. 254.

organs should reveal the place that was accorded to women. This is important because these administrative structures coordinated the various activities of the church in the spheres of evangelism, educational mission, and medical mission. The remaining sections of this chapter will demonstrate how women, because of entrenched patriarchy and controversial empowerment, were marginalized in these leadership structures. There was evidence of such marginalization in the administrative organs of the church, with sectors like evangelism, education, and health being the preserve of men.

Bias Against Women in Ministry

The chief goal of the Basel Mission in Cameroon was evangelization for Christ. Its missionaries were deployed to plant evangelical Christianity among the heathen and to build viable congregations. From 1886 to 1957, foreign missionaries and their local collaborators (evangelists, catechists, and pastors) pursued this goal of mission. The various congregations, mission stations, and church districts that resulted from this mission work came with leadership opportunities in the evangelism ministry. These evangelical structures had to be administered to enable the Basel Mission build a vibrant church in Cameroon. This section examines the extent to which women, whose status Basel missionaries wanted to improve, were associated with leadership in the evangelism ministry. Did the promotion of women's education in Cameroon lead to their participation in the evangelism ministry of the Basel Mission? So, I investigate the role empowered women played in the conversion of sinners and the administration of the Basel Mission Church in Cameroon. I intend to demonstrate that though the Basel Mission had opened its ordained ministry to women, its evangelism ministry in Cameroon remained the preserve of men. The church in Cameroon was resistant to accepting local women in roles of leadership.

The refusal to engage women as evangelists, catechists, and pastors by the male-dominated leadership of the Basel Mission Church in Cameroon placed empowered women at the margins of leadership in ministry. Women were barred from participating in the ordained ministry, and could not be trained and engaged as catechists, evangelists, and pastors, despite the fact that foreign female missionaries worked in the territory. The theological institutions that were created to train ministry staff admitted only male candidates. Women, their level of education notwithstanding, were consistently excluded from theological training. Missionaries to Cameroon, contrary to the knocking down of laws barring women from participation in ministry professions by the Basel Mission Committee, enforced a custom limiting access to these professions to men.

The catechist profession was opened only to men throughout the era of the Basel Mission in Cameroon. Before the First World War, the training of catechists took the form of refresher and special training courses in centres that were established in Buea, Nyasoso, Bali, Bome, and Bando.[112] The poor performance of catechists in congregations placed under their care led to the opening of a proper seminary in Nyasoso. Training lasted for three years and students came from both the Forest and Grassfields Districts of the church. The pioneer principal of the seminary, Rev. E. Staub, ensured that the law excluding women from the unordained catechist ministry was strictly respected. There was recourse to this same policy in the new Catechist Training School opened in Bali in 1936. The school was transferred to Bafut in 1940 where it continued with its policy of training only men as catechists.

For three decades, the training institutions in Nyasoso and Bafut produced the hundreds of catechists that were engaged by the Basel Mission. In 1957, the Basel Mission Church in Cameroon had a total of 434 male catechists who were placed at the helm of congregations across Southern Cameroons. This Swiss-based mission agency ended its evangelism ministry in the territory in November 1957 without producing female catechists. Women who qualified for admission into catechist training institutions were never given the opportunity to participate in this unordained ministry. Expectedly, the catechist profession became an all-male affair, with women completely excluded. As unordained ministers,

---

[112] Werner, *The History of the Presbyterian*, p. 90.

catechists were associated with the leadership of the mission church, though in lower ranks. They were entrusted with pastoral work in one or more congregations, and were expected to preach the word of God, prepare candidates for Baptism, preside over prayer meetings, carry out Sunday School work, among other tasks. To put it another way, catechists were leaders of the congregations, with ministerial and administrative functions. Women were excluded from this leadership role in the church, which was a source of employment for the privileged men. Catechists had access to income as they were placed on the pay roll of the church. The catechist profession was also a launching path to the ordained ministry given that being a catechist was one of the conditions for selection as a candidate for the ordained ministry. These benefits caused resistance to women in the catechist profession to increase. For all empowered female members of the church, especially those who graduated from girls' schools and mixed institutions, acceptance into the unordained ministry as catechists was neither an option nor a dream.

Women's marginalization was even more pronounced in the unordained evangelist ministry. The training of evangelists was opened only to male members of the church. It was a theological course of 16 months' duration in Nyasoso. Started by Rev. H. Bachtold, the training commenced in 1946 and continued up to 1957. Before terminating its evangelism ministry in Cameroon, the Basel Mission had trained 43 evangelists who were entrusted with work in pastoral areas. They played leading roles in the teamwork of the evangelistic activities in areas placed under their jurisdiction. They worked in close collaboration with ordained ministers by assisting them to conduct preparatory talks for Holy Communion and to visit congregations placed under catechists. Simply put, the evangelist was more of an itinerant unordained minister with duties not very much different from those performed by an ordained minister. The exclusion of women from this profession made it impossible for them to use it as a pathway to ministerial practice.

Clearly, the unordained ministry of the Basel Mission Church in Cameroon was not opened to women. All the catechists and evangelists who constituted this ministry were men, with the missionaries consistently barring women from joining these professions. The Basel Missionaries therefore planted a more exclusive Christ-centred Church in Southern Cameroons, with women discriminated upon in the unordained ministry. This discrimination against women, despite the fact that they qualified for admission into training schools, made them never to serve as evangelists and catechists. It then appeared as if only men were gifted for service in these positions. Men such as Aaron Su, Jacob Shu, Daniel Foningong, John Mosi, Daniel Lyonga, Emil Molindo, John Ashili, and Elisa Petha gained leadership roles in the mission church either as catechists or evangelists. Some of them had studied in mixed schools with women who had better academic records. But bias against women in the unordained ministry turned these men into bosses. A false impression was given that women were not gifted for service in these professions. Miles maintains that Western mission agencies had a negative bearing on women's status. She notes particularly that "European colonial missionaries discounted African women's religious leadership, relegated them to helper positions, and lowered women's status."[113] By excluding women from its catechist and evangelist professions which came with opportunities for participation in the power structure of the church, the Basel Mission tacitly endorsed Steven Goldberg's controversial claim that men's gushing testosterone gives them an aggression advantage which enables them to monopolise power in all high-prestige non-child-related positions in the social order.[114]

Entrenched patriarchy in the Basel Mission system in Cameroon also led to women's total exclusion from the ordained ministry. They were not permitted to pursue theological training to become ordained denominational clergy. Only men had access to the ordained ministry, irrespective of the fact that the Basel Mission Home Board had ordained and deployed female missionaries to Cameroon. In 1957, there were 53 ordained ministers in Southern

---

[113] Miles, Carrie A., "The Church Versus the Spirit: The Impact of Christianity on the Treatment of Women in Africa," Paper presented at the SSSR/ASREC, 2007, p. 1.
[114] Stevens Goldberg, *The Inevitability of Patriarchy*, New York, William Morrow & Company, 1973.

Cameroons (42 indigenous pastors and 11 foreign missionaries) engaged by the Basel Mission. Most of the indigenous pastors began as unordained ministers (catechists and evangelists) before pursuing training as pastors. The barring of women from the unordained ministry thus laid the foundation for the male domination of the ordained ministry. Evangelists and catechists like Daniel Foningong, John Mossi, John Ashili, Aaron Su, Jacob Shu, Elisa Petha, Modi Essoka, Gustav Bolanga, Elisa Ndifon, Thomas Seta, Jonah Fomukong, Hans Mongo, Manfred Nkembe, and Otto Ese were trained and ordained as pastors. Of the 42 indigenous pastors the Church had in 1957, none was a woman.[115] But three out of the 11 foreign missionaries were women who had been ordained in Basel and sent to Cameroon. Evidently, local women who had wishes of dedicating their lives to the Christian ministry were barred from pursuing these dreams. Accruing from this prohibition and bias was the absence of women in leadership ministry.

Indeed, the prohibition of local women from becoming unordained and ordained ministers of the Basel Mission Church served as a basis for their marginalization in the clerical leadership structures of the church. It should be stressed that unordained and ordained ministers were those members of the Church set apart for the shepherding of the flock. They exercised Christian leadership from which women were totally excluded. The men who became catechists, evangelists and pastors were given leadership responsibilities in congregations, presbyteries, church districts, and in the central administration of the church. They had influence, responsibility and hierarchical authority, given that they carried a clerical function in terms of representing people to God and God to people. Sadly, women lacked this influence and clerical authority as they were not given the opportunity to minister to the people and to lead the church. Local Christian women in Ghana also faced exclusion from the ordained and unordained ministries of the Basel Mission. With no opportunity to train as pastors, catechists and evangelists, local Ghanaian women used their domestic science

---

[115] Werner, *The History of the Presbyterian*, p. 92.

skills to become pastors' wives. So, the Basel Mission policy which barred women from participation in the ordained ministry was strictly implemented in all its mission fields.

Again, because of patriarchy, women had a much-lowered status in the ministry leadership structures of the Basel Mission. As a mission agency at the mercy of Western gender beliefs and practices, the Basel Mission enforced boundaries between male and female roles in ways that were harmful to the status of women in the evangelism ministry. No wonder church planting, pastoral and leadership responsibilities were reserved for men. Throughout the Basel Mission era, the defining features of the ministry were male leadership and unquestioned female dependency. Rather, domestically empowered women, upon whom leadership limitations were placed, were made to serve as domestic staff in mission stations and in the homes of pastors. Graduates from girls' schools were carefully prepared to become wives of catechists, evangelists and pastors. There was an unwritten marriage policy requiring that ordained and unordained ministers should marry only women with domestic science training. The church ministers suggested their marriage partners, and often that choice fell on graduates from girls' schools. Foreign missionaries ensured that their indigenous ministers got married to loyal women with a firm domestic science background.

Contrarily, while wives of foreign missionaries, whose number stood at 17 in 1957, possessed capabilities suitable for mission, wives of indigenous ministers had only domesticity capabilities as they were not expected to perform their share of the mission's work. This amounted to differential treatment between wives of foreign missionaries and those of indigenous ministers. Missionary wives enjoyed the status of missionaries while local women married to catechists, evangelists, and pastors hardly functioned beyond their homes. They were ideal wives with a subordinate status. As wives, local Christian women became servants to their husbands and children instead of serving the church in clerical leadership roles. Clerical leadership roles were reserved for the ordained and unordained ministers. Women were, therefore, excluded from congregational meetings, station or presbytery synod meetings, district synod meetings, and General Synod meetings. Even the foreign female missionaries who attended these meetings had very little say on issues that were discussed. The General Synod in particular was an all-male institution in the 1950s. For instance, the Grassfield Synod met on 13 April 1950 to constitute its team of delegates to attend a General Synod Meeting at Buea on 5 May 1950. There was no woman among the ten persons who were selected to attend the meeting.[116] It was during these gatherings that key decisions and actions relating to the work of the Basel Mission in Cameroon were taken. In most cases, attendance in some of these meetings was limited to the ordained and unordained ministers. Women were not therefore associated with administrative structures that coordinated the various activities of the church in the spheres of evangelism, education mission, and medical mission.

Photo 6: All-male General Synod Meeting of the Basel Mission Church in Cameroon. Source: PCC Central Archive and Library, Buea, Cameroon

This discrimination and exclusion from the ministry notwithstanding, women were active in the propagation of the gospel in communities across Southern Cameroons. They displayed profound commitment to Christian faith by constituting and

---

[116] PCCCAB, File No. 22, Grassfields Synod Meetings, 1948-1958.

leading informal prayer group meetings. Described in Basel Mission reports as "community mothers", these women, according to Guy Alexander Thomas, gave a helping hand to catechists in carrying out small-scale evangelization in their communities. Thomas further notes that "The Christian community grew out of such initiatives as chains from families to prayer groups, catechumen classes and congregations to form the larger Christian movement."[117] Women such as Elizabeth Mbonifor, Ruth Ndando, Sophie Limunga Ndando, Ida Mallett, and Catherine Musoko preached the word of God and led prayer meetings in their communities.[118]

Women in Education Leadership

Discrimination against women in Christian leadership went beyond the ordained and unordained ministries. Hardly did the Basel Mission associate women with its non-ministry structures of power within the church in Southern Cameroons. Leadership in the educational work of the Basel Mission resided in the hands of men, and this served as evidence that the Basel Mission lacked a holistic and inclusive approach to church leadership. Leadership in the vernacular, primary, vocational, and secondary educational institutions that were set up by the Basel Mission failed to reflect equality and equity for all gender identities. Women lagged behind as their participation in educational governance was not prioritized by the male-dominated church. This biased use of power structures was a defining feature of the entire Basel Mission era in Southern Cameroons.

Irrespective of the fact that women had received vocational training in girls' schools and the fact that some had graduated from mixed schools, only a few of them were associated with the administration of these institutions. This was partly because only a few of these women were given the opportunity to gain admission into teacher training institutions. In 1945, for instance, all the 68

---

[117] Guy Alexander Thomas, "Why do we Need the White Man's God? African Contributions and Responses to the Formation of a Christian Movement in Cameroon, 1914-1968," PhD Thesis in History, School of Oriental and African Studies, University of London, 2001, p. 213.
[118] PCCCAB, File No. 723, Minutes of the General Synod, 1948-1957.

primary schools that were operated by the Basel Mission had male headmasters who had graduated from teacher training institutions. In that same year, all 200 indigenous teachers that were employed by the mission were male. This marginalization of women in teaching and administration in Basel Mission primary schools resulted from the barring of women from the loan mission teacher training centre in Nyasoso. Created in 1944, the Elementary Teachers Training Centre (ETTC), which was transferred to Bali in 1947 and finally to Batibo in 1949, received only male candidates for training.[119] This policy of discrimination against women in the ETTC was the product of patriarchal beliefs in the Basel Mission. While there existed mixed or co-educational primary schools for girls and boys, the teacher training institution functioned as a training college for male teachers. Besides, the mission operated girls' schools in Victoria, Bafut, Kumba, Bali, and other parts of the territory, but delayed efforts in establishing a female teacher training college. Little wonder the teaching profession in the mission educational system was the province of men throughout the 1930s and 1940s. The entire Basel Mission educational system was administered by men, with women totally left out. As a patriarchal mission agency, the Basel Mission did not raise the level of women in education leadership. Decision-making was in male hands, with women either absent or assigned subordinate roles.

Given the lack of female teacher training institutions, the Basel Mission chose to train its female teachers in Nigeria. This approach did not solve the problem of lack of female teachers as many parents hesitated sending their children to far away Nigeria. The creation of a Roman Catholic Girls' Teacher Training College in Kumba in 1951 would have solved this problem if not of fear of conversion of Basel Mission girls into Catholicism. Consequently, only an insignificant number of female Basel Mission teachers were trained in Nigeria and in the Catholic institution. Though insignificant, the training of indigenous female teachers abroad and in the Roman Catholic college in Kumba came with rare

---

[119] Gwanfogbe, *Basel Mission Education*, p. 126.

opportunities for the few privileged women to serve as teachers and administrators in Basel Mission schools.

The breakthrough was pioneered in 1951 by Catherine Musoko Lyonga at the Victoria Girls' School. Fathered in 1926 by a Cameroonian Basel Mission Catechist, Catherine Lyonga attended Basel Mission Elementary School in Nyasosso in 1933 and later proceeded to the Basel Mission Higher Elementary School in Esossong. She obtained a Standard VI certificate in 1941 and continued at Quality Girls School in Nigeria where she trained as a Grade III teacher on government scholarship. She later returned to Southern Cameroons as the first trained female teacher. Catherine Lyonga taught for a few years as the lone indigenous teacher in Basel Mission Girls' School in Victoria, and distinguished herself by becoming the pioneer indigenous headmistress when the European missionary ladies' administration of the Girls School in Victoria came to an end.[120] Under the administrative leadership of Catherine Lyonga, enrolment in the Girls School increased. She also worked closely with expatriate missionary teachers to knock down barriers against women in education leadership.

Similar examples, though with limited access to Basel Mission education leadership, were Ida Mallett, Elizabeth Mbonifor, and Ruth Ndando. After obtaining her Standard VI certificate from Basel Mission Higher Elementary School in Kumba in 1942, Ida Mallett was trained as a Grade III teacher at the Teacher Training College in Shagamu, Nigeria. She became the lone female teacher at the Basel Mission Higher Elementary School in Kumba which was under male administrative leadership. Born in 1934, Elizabeth Mbonifor returned from Nigeria with a Grade III teacher certificate and was not lucky to join the teaching corps of the Basel Mission possibly due to patriarchy. She was absorbed by the Colonial government and taught in government schools in the late 1950s, while maintaining close ties with Christian women's activities in the Basel Mission and PCC. In a closely similar way, Ruth Ndando's Standard VI certificate obtained in 1951 from the Basel Mission Girls School in Victoria failed to result in participation in mission

---

[120] Thomas, "Why do we Need the White Man's God", p. 213.

education leadership. Rather, she served as a domestic science demonstrator for the Cameroon Development Corporation (CDC) after which she became a council worker and trade unionist. Ndando's case represents a clear example of a woman who was educationally empowered and discriminated against in leadership by the Basel Mission. This explains why teaching and leadership in Basel Mission educational facilities were dominated by men, despite the availability of female holders of standard VI and Grade III Teacher certificates.

It was thanks to initiatives taken by these educated female Basel Mission Christians in collaboration with foreign female missionary teachers that a Women's Teacher Training College (WTTC) was opened in Mankon in 1960. The school, according to Gwanfogbe, "helped in supplying the trained female teachers that the mission and the Church needed at independence."[121] Though the existence of this teacher training institution led to an increase in the number of female teachers in Basel Mission schools, male dominance in terms of numbers was also on the rise. Evidence suggests that about 99 percent of the 123 Basel Mission primary schools in 1966 were administered by headmasters, with an insignificant number under headmistresses. The mission had therefore succeeded in training mostly male Cameroonians to whom education leadership in schools was progressively transferred. Even more surprising is the fact that administrative leadership in the WTTC Mankon was transferred from female missionary teacher, Lina Weber, to an indigenous male teacher, Mfobe Fusi. This was the height of women's discrimination in education leadership as a male teacher played an executive role in a female teacher training college. This marginalization of women in education leadership was even more pronounced in the lone secondary school that was operated by the Basel Mission. Created in 1949 by the Basel Mission and eventually jointly operated with the North American Baptist Mission, the Cameroon Protestant College (CPC) Bali, as the college came to be known in 1957, had an all-male pioneer batch of students and

---

[121] Gwanfogbe, *Basel Mission Education*, p. 133.

teachers.[122] In fact, admissions into CPC Bali in the first two decades of its existence were reserved for boys. The institution received its pioneer female students only in 1972.[123] This explains why ex-students of this prestigious secondary school constituted themselves into the gender insensitive Bali Old Boys Association (BOBA). The latter has survived to this day irrespective of the fact that its membership is now comprised of former male and female students. This was not good for women's status given that there was an increase in the number of girls graduating from primary schools with the Standard VI certificate. Besides, some of the few indigenous female teachers who had graduated from teacher training institutions in Nigeria, especially Catherine Musoko Lyonga, might have qualified to teach in CPC Bali. But the patriarchy which had eaten deep into the educational system of the Basel Mission could not allow such leadership strides to be made by women. Pioneer students and indigenous teachers (all-male) in this institution gained from their experiences in CPC to emerge as education leaders in the PCC. Examples include Samuel Mbong Eseh who became principal of Basel Mission College in Besongabang and A. T. M. Mofor who moved from CPC as a Geography teacher to Basel Mission College in Besongabang as principal.[124]

Biases against women in education leadership were even more pronounced in the remaining education administration structures set up by the Basel Mission. There existed a hierarchical education administration system in the Basel Mission, from the Education Board to the administrators of primary schools. The entire educational system was under an Education Secretary, who throughout the Basel Mission era was an expatriate male missionary teacher. This position was occupied in the 1940s and 1950s by Rev. Raflaab. The latter led efforts in maintaining women at the fringes

---

[122] From 1949 to 1957, the lone mission secondary education institution went by the name Basel Mission College.

[123] The masculinization of admissions into CPC Bali during the first two decades of its existence was promoted by its white administrators: D. H. O'Neil, 1948-1957 and Dr. Peter Rudin, 1957-1966.

[124] Gwanfogbe, *Basel Mission Education*, p. 141.

of education leadership. The Education Secretary was aided by two Supervisors of schools responsible for education matters in the Grassfields and Forest districts of the Basel Mission Church respectively. The entire education system had 14 Managers of schools shared equitably between the two church districts. Primary schools were headed by headmasters while secondary schools were under principals. The overall governing body was the Education Board and its Executive Committee. In 1949, two subordinate education committees were created to oversee education matters in the Grassfields and Forest districts respectively.

The stark reality is that leadership in all these hierarchical education structures was hugely dominated by men. The position of Education Secretary remained in the hands of men, with Eugene Ekiti becoming the first Cameroonian to hold the position in 1966 when all educational facilities were transferred from the Basel Mission to the PCC. The Education Board was largely dominated by men, with its few female members being foreign female missionary teachers like Lina Weber. The male-dominated Board took education decisions, and did very little to check patriarchy in education leadership. In fact, it was a gender insensitive Education Board which tacitly endorsed the marginalization of women. The total absence of Cameroonian women in the Education Board could be explained by their marginalization in subordinate education administration bodies and positions. It should be stressed that membership in the Board was opened to Supervisors and Managers of schools in the two districts as well as to some members of the District Education Committees.

But women were very much underrepresented or even absent in these decentralized education leadership positions and committees. Throughout the era of the Basel Mission, the position of Supervisor of schools in both the Grassfields and Forest Districts was never held by a woman. Appointments to the position were made by the Education Secretary on the recommendation of the Education Board. Eugene Ekiti was the first Cameroonian to occupy the position of Supervisor of Schools in the Grassfields District. Appointed in 1959, Ekiti's experience in this position prepared him for appointment as Education Secretary in 1966. Earlier in 1954, other education administration positions such as that of Visiting Teachers for the Forest and Grassfields Districts were placed under J. T. Ebai and J. F. Mancho respectively. Deliberations about their appointment at the General Synod Meeting of 6 April 1954 revealed the gender insensitivity of the Supervisor of Schools. He introduced to the Synod the question of appointing two visiting teachers, and suggested the names of two men who had just returned from their training abroad.[125] By 1960, all 14 Managers of schools in both districts were male Cameroonians, with women completely sidelined. Women were also underrepresented in the two District Education Committees. The latter, whose members were appointed by the Education Secretary, were responsible for education matters in the two church districts.

It emerges from the foregoing discussion that women who graduated from girls and mixed schools were underrepresented in teaching and leadership within the Basel Mission education system. Most classrooms were presided over by men as opportunities for women to train as teachers were limited. Even more troubling was the monopolization of education leadership roles by men as patriarchal barriers kept women out. Surprisingly, the desire by the Basel Mission to transfer schools to the PCC was turned down on grounds that there was a shortage of teachers and administrative staff. Yet, women having the qualification to teach and to serve as school administrators were not given the opportunity to do so. Women were therefore deprived of the teaching and education financial benefits which would have improved their wellbeing. Such masculinization of teaching and school administration stands as evidence that the Basel Mission was caught in an entrenched patriarchal culture. Educated female Christians stayed within their culturally defined gender-role boundaries, with many hardly functioning beyond their homes. In 1966, the Basel Mission completed the transfer of its educational facilities (123 primary schools, three secondary schools, three teacher training colleges, a bookshop and a printing press) to an all-male PCC education

---

[125] PCCCAB, File No. 596, Minutes of General Synod Meeting at Buea, April 1954.

administration. The highest administrative rank attained by a woman was Headmistress. The underrepresentation of women in leadership roles was also a defining feature of the Basel Mission healthcare system in Southern Cameroons.

Barriers to Women in Healthcare Leadership

Basel Mission healthcare work began in the form of dispensaries before progressing to general primary healthcare hospitals. In the 1930s, maternity homes for maternal and childcare were opened in Nyasoso and Buea. Later in 1955, this missionary society established its pioneer hospital at Manyemen.[126] The Manyemen Hospital placed emphasis on primary healthcare, offering various diagnostic and curative services to the population. The hospital was nationally famous given the good reputation it enjoyed. This explains why patients took on long and exhausting travels to reach the hospital with a view to benefitting from its curative services. Its staff which was initially headed by Doctor E. Ode was competent and did not suffer from inadequate equipment.[127] The medical doctor, who was the first to be deployed in Southern Cameroons by the Basel Mission, was assisted by midwives in the likes of E. Scherrer, M. Honegger, and E. Wagner. Earlier in 1954, the Basel Mission opened a leprosy settlement at Manyemen in an effort to roll back the high prevalence of leprosy. Overall, the healthcare system of the Basel Mission comprised of one general hospital, health centres, maternity homes, and a leprosarium. In this section, I argue that women were underrepresented in Basel Mission's healthcare leadership.

Women were underrepresented in Basel Mission healthcare leadership, even though they represented the vast majority of the specialized healthcare workforce. The Health Board which was responsible for health matters was dominated by men. In 1968 when the Basel Mission transferred its medical facilities to the PCC,

---

[126] Christian Asongwe, "Healthcare Delivery in British Southern Cameroons, 1922-1961: A Historical Investigation", PhD Thesis in History, The University of Yaounde I, 2018.
[127] PCCCAB, File No. 1613, Minutes of the Manyemen Hospital Staff Meeting, 7 February 1958.

there were seven women in the Board out of a total of 25 members. These female members, most of whom were foreign missionary nurses, represented mission maternities, dispensaries, and the General Hospital in Manyemen. The Medical Board meeting of 18 September 1968 was attended by missionary nurses like Dr. Emilia Ode, H. Gerber, Lore Gabelmann, L. Meyer, U. Petzsch, H. Rubli, and B. Forbang. Dr. Emilia Ode presided over the Medical Board and was instrumental in ensuring that more women were active in it.[128] But B. Forbang, a nurse trained in Nigeria, was the lone female Cameroonian member in the Medical Board.[129] Indigenous female nurses and midwives like Perpetua Abraham, Grace Chemfor Shu, Monica Chombeng Shu, Lucy Bayongson Sone, and Prisca Awanda were excluded from this supreme healthcare administrative body. This is evidence that female Cameroonian medical staff were marginalized in the Board. This underrepresentation of local women in such a top healthcare leadership structure, which was chaired by a female European Missionary Doctor, was not only due to patriarchy, but probably because of the racial divide between European and indigenous female healthcare workforce.

The marginalization of indigenous female healthcare staff by their European colleagues was even more noticeable in the mission hospitals and maternal and child welfare centres. Leadership in the General Hospital and Leprosarium at Manyemen was largely in the hands of white female and male administrators. For instance, Dr. Frommherz Symark, a German, was appointed by the Basel Mission as Manager of the Leprosy Settlement at Manyemen on 9 January 1955. Dr. Symark presided over the Leprosy Committee which was the supreme governing organ of the settlement. The Leprosy Committee's all-male membership comprised of the Secretary of the Basel Mission, two missionaries appointed by the Basel Mission, two representatives of the General Synod, three representatives from Cameroon Native Authorities (each from Kumba, Mamfe and Victoria Divisions), and one representative of the Staff Meeting. Women were not therefore associated with this Committee which

---

[128] PCCCAB, File No. 1616, Minutes of Medical Board meeting at Bamenda on 18 September 1968, p. 6.
[129] Ibid.

was responsible for issues relating to the running of the Leprosarium. However, there were indigenous women in lower administrative roles given their significant representation in the Staff Meeting which handled all internal affairs of the settlement. It ensured the coordination of the work of the various departments and served as a forum for the discussion of issues of common interest. The Staff Meeting saw into it that rulings and instructions of the Leprosy Committee were carried out. It decided on questions of appointment, promotion, disciplinary cases and termination of appointment of junior staff. On its part, the Settlement Council on which all sections of the patients were represented administered the patients' community. The Council met twice monthly. It elected a chairperson from among its members, who represented its interest in the Staff Meeting. The Settlement Council consisted of nine members with the duty of discussing all matters relating to the wellbeing of patients.

Indeed, indigenous women made insignificant progress in attaining administrative positions in the Basel Mission healthcare system. The latter was largely under the headship of white missionary nurses as evidence from the Medical Board and the Leprosarium in Manyemen has shown. Throughout the Basel Mission medical mission era which ended in 1968, the Cameroonization of healthcare leadership was starkly slow, with some white healthcare administrators like Dr. Emilia Ode and Lore Gabelmann remaining at the helm of these facilities up to the 1970s. Even maternal and child welfare centres in Bafut, Nyasoso, Buea, and Acha-Tugi remained under the control of white missionary nurses. Their Cameroonian colleagues, some of whom have been mentioned above, remained in subordinate roles even though they had accomplished healthcare work in hospitals, maternity homes and dispensaries in different localities across the territory. These women were hopeful that the transfer of medical work to the PCC in 1968 would come with leadership opportunities for them. This was because the Basel Mission trained mostly women as indigenous healthcare workers. But the male-dominated leadership of the Church decided to delay the Cameroonization of healthcare leadership despite PCC's takeover of the services in

1968. During the Medical Board meeting organized by the Basel Mission in 1968, PCCs' Moderator, Right Reverend Jeremiah Chi Kangsen, "requested that not all posts in the healthcare administration should be Cameroonized."[130] Rev. Kangsen urged white healthcare administrators who were planning to leave for good to remain in Cameroon, arguing that there were no local medical personnel to fill the gap. In the late 1970s when most of the white healthcare administrators finally left for good, as I will demonstrate later in the book, their replacements were mostly male Cameroonians. This suggests that the patriarchal church leadership delayed the transfer of healthcare leadership to Cameroonians because there was an insignificant number of male indigenous medical work force. Small wonder PCC's healthcare facilities were largely administered by men whose numbers have been increased through male-focused training. Even more detrimental to women's leadership status was the masculinization of the transition from the Basel Mission to the PCC in 1957.

Women Marginalized in the Transition from Basel Mission to PCC

The marginalization of women in the evangelism ministry, education, and healthcare sector enabled male members of the Basel Mission Church in Southern Cameroons to feature prominently in the transition to the Presbyterian Church in Cameroon. The transition, which coursed for about two decades, was intended to fulfil the missionary goal of creating an indigenous church under African leadership. My concern in this final section is to demonstrate that the Basel Mission gave birth to an independent or self-governing Presbyterian Church under male leadership. Propelled by the nationalist consciousness in Southern Cameroons, which had yielded requests for autonomy within the Church, Basel missionaries initiated a handing-over procedure.[131] As indigenous

---

[130] PCCCAB, File No. 1616, Minutes of Medical Board meeting at Buea on June 1969, p. 5.

[131] For detailed information on the connection between the nationalist struggle in Southern Cameroons and demands for autonomy in the Church, read Thomas, "Why do we Need the White Man God?", pp. 197-201.

Basel Mission agents (mostly pastors, evangelists, catechists, and teachers) began questioning white missionary supremacy, selfhood of the Basel Mission Church was prioritized and accelerated. The path to an independent Church was marked by the transfer of the leadership of the elaborate administrative bureaucracy from Europeans to Africans. In this process of devolving leadership responsibility to Africans, the Basel Mission felt that the new leaders of the independent Church should be members of the ordained ministry. And considering that women were barred from the ordained ministry as emphasized already, an autonomous local church exclusively under African male hegemony was in gestation.

From 1949 to 1957, executive posts in the central administration of the Basel Mission Church were transferred to pastors, all of whom were male. This was the outcome of talks and meetings between European missionaries and indigenous pastors with which women were scarcely associated. In an all-male General Synod meeting in October 1950, Rev. Peter Essoka Diso was elected Chairman of the General Synod, being the first Cameroonian to occupy the post. The post of Chairman of this supreme governing body of the Basel Mission Church, it should be stressed, was eventually transformed into the post of Moderator. With the General Synod presided over by a Cameroonian, steps were taken to revise the constitution of the Basel Mission Church as an effort towards selfhood. The new constitution, prepared by a Church Constitution Revision Committee composed of both European and Cameroonian priests, was adopted by another all-male General Synod which held in Bali on 13 November 1957.[132] By the adoption of the new Church Constitution, the Basel Mission Church became an autonomous church known as Presbyterian Church in the Cameroons. The central administration of the independent church, otherwise referred to as the Synod Office which is presently seated in Buea, was made up of General Synod officials: Chairman (later Moderator), Secretary (later Synod Clerk), Vice Chairman, and Supervisor of Schools (formerly Education Secretary).

---

[132] Dah, Jonas, "The Vision and Challenges of an Autonomous Church". In Jonas N. Dah ed. *Presbyterian Church in Cameroon: 50 Years of Selfhood* (Limbe: Presprint, 2007), p. 35.

Later in 1958, an Elective General Synod meeting, chaired by Rev. Peter Essoka, held in Bali to select the pioneer four top administrators of the independent church. This led to the election of Rev. Abraham Ngole as the first Cameroonian Chairman/Moderator of the independent PCC. The three other posts remained in the hands of European missionaries, given that the transfer of administrative leadership to Cameroonians was a gradual process. In 1959, Rev. Aaron Su and J. F. Mancho became pioneer Cameroonian Secretary General (Synod Clerk) and Vice Chairman of PCC's General Synod respectively. In 1966, the post of Supervisor of Schools was occupied by the first Cameroonian, Eugene A. Ekiti. With women side-lined in the course of events that led to the birth of the PCC, the Basel Mission left behind an independent church whose key leadership positions were in the hands of men. Women were not therefore represented in the elaborate bureaucracy called the Synod Office. It had extraordinary power and influence, with the Moderator and close collaborators empowered to take actions affecting the entire Church, even though women traditionally outnumbered men.

Overall, there was consistent discrimination against women in the leadership structures of the Basel Mission Church in Southern Cameroons. Women were totally excluded from the ordained and unordained ministries, with clerical functions such as pastors, catechists, and evangelists accessible only to men. This caused women to be underrepresented in the Church's hierarchical administrative structures from the Congregational Meetings all through to the General Synod. Education leadership, despite the availability of educated women, especially trained teachers, was heavily dominated by men in positions such as headmasters, visiting teachers, managers of schools, education secretary, and members of the Education Board. Though healthcare leadership was largely in the hands of women, Cameroonian female nurses and midwives were consistently subjected to the hegemony of European female missionary medics. In fact, women's desire to play a greater role in the leadership of the Basel Mission Church was stalled by the patriarchal beliefs of the European missionaries, be them male or female. The extent of such bias against female Christians should hardly be surprising, for their education or empowerment in mixed and girls' schools was not intended to associate them with the leadership of the Church. They were empowered to play a primary role in the domestic sphere. The emancipation they received secured them a new status often defined in terms of dressing, cooking, and childcare, not participation in Church leadership. While these biases went almost unchallenged throughout the Basel Mission era, recourse to a similar policy by the independent PCC, probably under continuing foreign missionaries' influence, met with resistance from some women who became conscious of how they were kept subservient to male hegemony. This amounted to efforts to associate women with leadership in the PCC even though its hierarchy remained male-dominated as analysed in part two of this book.

Part II

Women in Presbyterian Church in Cameroon Power Structure

Chapter 5

Women's Work in the PCC: Empowerment for Leadership?

The PCC inherited a patriarchal culture from the Basel Mission, with its male members, especially the pioneer all-male leadership, aiming to reserve to themselves the power and authority for decisions and administration of the independent church. In the first two decades of independence, female Christians remained powerless as there was continuing recourse to patriarchal practices. Male members of the young Church assumed the power bestowed on them by the founding mission agency, and sought to legitimize the exclusion of women from the Church's leadership, notwithstanding that there were more women than men in the Church. So, the cultivation of leadership by a single sex (male) became a masked agenda of the PCC.[133] The latter's all-male leaders were ignoring the fact that every member of the Church, whether male or female, was gifted to serve if he/she was empowered to do so. Little wonder the "Christian Home" ideology was promoted as a hallmark of women's emancipation and empowerment. As such, the domesticity agenda of the Basel Mission was continued by the PCC through some of the activities of the Christian Women Fellowship (CWF) in ways that further placed women on the path to housewifization, not full participation in leadership. The barring of women from the ordained ministry was also upheld by the new Church, as theological education and ordination were accessed only by men. The pursuance of these gender insensitive policies yielded an exaggeratingly male-dominated leadership in congregations, presbyteries, and central administration of the Church. Leadership

---

[133] In other mission fields such as in Ghana and South East China, the Basel Mission gradually transferred leadership to an all-male clerical corp. The Presbyterian Church of Ghana (PCG) which emerged from Basel Mission's ecclesiastical mould inherited the laws barring women from the ordained ministry. Just like the PCC, the PCG became a church in male hands, and efforts were made not to reverse the situation.

in education, healthcare, and economic structures of the Church were also largely in male hands. The PCC, as noted already, had an ascending hierarchical organizational chart comprised of Congregations, Presbyteries and the Synod. In the Presbyterian system, therefore, governance was exercised by the Christians through representatives whom they elected and who were called presbyters or elders. They held to the unity of the church, and the institution was administered through a series of ascending administrative units and institutions. Although leadership in the church was shared between the ministers and laity, key positions such as Moderator, Synod Clerk, Presbytery Secretaries, and Presbytery Treasurers remained the province of the ordained ministers, who unfortunately were all male.

While an all-male leadership was becoming the norm in the PCC, growing Christian feminism resulted in internal resistance to the powerlessness of women. Since the 1970s, the PCC has been caught in a sustained struggle of empowering women and accepting them in leadership positions from the congregations all through to the Synod Office. Trapped in these controversies over women's right to leadership, the PCC authorities were obliged to take concrete measures aimed at eliminating decades of arbitrary rules against women in the church's power structure. This advocacy, though timid, yielded a policy of gender justice in the early 1970s. And though slow and halting, the attempt to try and provide women with more access to leadership was running its course. This chapter of the book is therefore devoted to the treatment of women's work in the PCC in view of appreciating its bearing on women's participation in the church's leadership structures. In the opening section, attention is given to women's empowerment through the activities of the CWF under the coordination of the Women's Work Department. It examines the operation mechanism and activities of the CWF, arguing that the church group has not been able to roll away patriarchy in the power structures of the church. In section two, I examine PCC's empowerment of women in the context of the Ecumenical Decade of the Churches in Solidarity with women launched in 1988 by the World Council of Churches (WCC). In the final section, the role of the Women's Education and

Empowerment Programme (WEEP) in the empowerment of women for leadership is analysed. Overall, the chapter seeks to demonstrate that, despite women's empowerment initiatives through the CWF, the Ecumenical Decade of the Churches in Solidarity with Women (1988-1998), and the WEEP, interactions between men and women in the PCC coursed within an imbalance of power, with women largely remaining subservient to male leadership hegemony. Indeed, the progress made in associating women with leadership through women's work was meagre, and represented only a slight shift from the all-male Basel Mission power structure.

Christian Women's Fellowship and Women's Empowerment for Leadership

Many adherents of the PCC hail church women groups like the CWF for the opportunities it has offered women to participate in the leadership structures of the church. But the continuing marginalization of women in the power structure of the PCC necessitates an assessment of the imprint of this movement on women's leadership status in the church. Hence, this section examines the historical roots, operation mechanism and activities of the CWF as a leeway to ascertain the extent to which it empowered the female laity for leadership.

Genesis and Operation Mechanism of CWF

In 1961, the Christian Women Fellowship (CWF) was created as a means by which female Presbyterians could achieve economic, social, and religious empowerment.[134] It emerged from women's work in Cameroon under female Basel Missionaries such as Maria Walcher, Elisabeth Buhler, Waltraud Haas, Maria Schlenker, and Rose Mary Peter-Bayer. In the late 1950s, Maria Schlenker and Rose Marie Peter-Bayer saw the need to create an association in charge of women's work in the PCC. Based on the consent of the other female missionaries and some local Christian women, the matter was presented to the General Synod of the PCC in 1961 by Maria

---

[134] Lawyer, "The Christian Women Fellowship", p. 29.

Schlenker. After examining the proposal, the General Synod unanimously endorsed the creation of the association and placed it under the Women's Work Department. The movement, according to Victorine Qui Wetuh, brought together female members of the PCC in congregations spread across the national territory.

With its branches established in presbyteries and congregations across the national territory, the CWF engaged in various women empowerment activities that made women not only to aspire to their traditional roles of wife, mother, and homemaker, but to function in congregations as singers, with little administrative functions in the church's hierarchy. The mission of this female Christian movement, as Lawyer notes, was "to lead the Christian women and girls (of 18 years and above) of the PCC to a fuller understanding of their faith and to enable them serve the Lord with joy in their homes, congregations, community and nation as a whole".[135] To put it more succinctly, the CWF, apart from its Christian Home oriented goals, was intended to build women spiritually. Overall, the movement was aimed at improving the status of women by strengthening them spiritually, socially, and economically.

The foregoing mission of the CWF which waived any effort towards associating women with the ordained ministry and church leadership had to be attained through work done in women's work institutions and CWF groups spread across presbyteries and congregations. It was catered for by the Women's Work Department (WWD) which was the main organ charged with the coordination of women's work. The WWD had a steady staff in the offices and over a hundred voluntary and part-time workers at the grassroots. Seated in Bamenda, the department was coordinated by a National Office at the helm of which was the National Secretary of Women's Work. The pioneer National Secretary was the movement's founder, Maria Schlenker, a female Basel Missionary.[136]

---

[135] Ibid.
[136] Born in Heidenheim, Germany, Maria Schlenker trained as a catechist and was sent to Cameroon for mission work by the Home Board of the Basel Mission. After promoting women's work for twelve years, Schlenker returned to Germany in 1972. After working for two years at the Mission and Ecumenical

Under Schlenker's leadership, women's work was organized and expanded. Together with Waltraud Haas and Anna Frank, she trained local women and set up the WWD. In 1972, Schlenker returned to Germany after twelve years in Cameroon, and leadership of the movement was transferred to Cameroonian leader, Grace Akwe Eneme. After Eneme's tenure, the post of National Secretary was successively occupied by Elizabeth Gana, Ngeh Beatrice, and Rev. Mary Salle. The National Office was responsible for the production of study material for the groups, alongside the education and training of members. This explains why Women's Work Helpers (WWHs) were attached to the National Office. The WWD was responsible to the Synod of the PCC through the Committee of the Ministry. The latter supervised the functioning of the department and reported to the Synod. The WWD operated under three provinces, each coordinated by the Provincial Office for Women's Work. The Provincial Office was headed by a Provincial Secretary who was a full-time employee of the PCC. The three Provincial Offices were in Bamenda, Kumba, and Douala, with each having a Christian women centre. The activities of the CWF in the various presbyteries of the church were supervised by the Provincial Office. The CWF at the Presbytery level comprised of all congregational groups and zonal set ups coordinated by a Presbytery Executive presided over by a President. Just below the Presbytery were the CWF Zones comprised of groups within a specified area coordinated by a Zonal Executive that was answerable to the Presbytery Executive. At the lowest level were CWF groups in all PCC's congregations at home and abroad. In 2011 when the Golden Jubilee of the CWF was celebrated, there were over 1,000 CWF groups with over 47,000 members worldwide.

Probably in an effort to ensure that the PCC was not departing from the domestic women empowerment policy, the Basel Mission

---

Service in Ulm, she travelled to Sudan in 1975 on the invitation of the Presbyterian Church in Sudan. Schlenker initiated women's work in South Sudan, and returned to Germany in 1985 when the civil war began. Later in 1992, Schlenker was awarded the Federal Cross of Merit in recognition of her work among women in Cameroon and Sudan.

sent female fraternal workers such as Sr. Rose Mary Peter, Maria Schlenker, Sr. Marie Ringli and Miss Anna Frank to coordinate the activities of female Presbyterians. These were the foreign female missionaries whose women's work initiatives in Cameroon had culminated in the birth of the CWF in 1961. But these female fraternal workers worked in close collaboration with Cameroonian women such as Elizabeth Gana, Roseline Tanga, Margaret Morikang, Rachel Song, Frieda Maliva, Ophelia Ndifor, Catherine Chofor, Naomi Tamufor, Catherine Ntumngia, Regina Anjeh, Anna Ngwa Yingfuh and others. In the first three decades of its existence, the activities of the CWF under the coordination of the WWD remained in the path of domesticity as analysed in the next section.

Nexus between CWF Activities and Empowerment of Women for Leadership

Members of the CWF engaged in a plethora of activities intended to achieve the mission of the movement. In this section, these activities are discussed in view of appreciating the extent to which they empowered women for leadership in the church. The activities of the movement ranged from spiritual growth through Bible study, singing, needlework, cookery, crop farming, livestock development, general hygiene, to many other income generating initiatives.[137] Most of these activities were carried out at the congregational level, to which should be added women's participation in the fellowship of the Least Coin (an international monthly prayer) and the celebration of the International World Day of Prayer. In an effort to ensure that these activities were effective, evaluation meetings and conferences were routinely organized at the congregational, zonal, presbytery, regional, and national levels. These empowerment activities were promoted in the entire PCC system through seminars and leadership courses that were organized by the WWD in association with the CWF at national, presbytery, zonal, parish and congregational levels. Apart from providing female Presbyterians with an entrepreneurial prowess

---

[137] For a detailed discussion of CWF activities up to the late 1980s, read Lawyer, "The Christian Women Fellowship", pp. 31-36.

intended to serve as a launching path to self-reliance through self-employment, the empowerment agenda also gave women the best training as mothers, with a capacity to build their children's personality. Clearly, PCC's pursuance of the domesticity policy which largely focused on heralding the "Christian Home" enabled women to function properly as Christian housewives and imparted in them an entrepreneurial spirit which served as a basis for their engagement in the local economy. Charles Fonchingong observes that CWF members were drilled in micro projects such as livestock production, gardening, marketing skills, tailoring, and weaving, which no doubt amounted to economic empowerment in the wider society.[138]

With this Basel Mission-PCC domesticity empowerment partnership running its course, CWF activities in most of its forms swiftly revealed that the old tradition of training girls and women to fit well into the so called "Christian Home" was still a norm within the PCC system. The women's empowerment activities that were carried out by the WWD through the CWF produced domestically-specialized women who were marginalized in the life of the church. A significant number of the over 47,000 members of the CWF became specialized in childbearing and in those productive activities that could be undertaken concurrently with pregnancy, nursing, or childcare. This domestic specialization which is described by some scholars as the "housewifization of women" made the home the operational zone of Christian women. The continuing male dominance over women in the power structure of the PCC persisted, though Cameroonian leaders of the CWF claimed that women's work was beneficial to the status of women in society and the church. Elizabeth Gana, one-time National Secretary of Women's Work in the PCC, held the view that the movement empowered women for active participation in the church. She observed that "Thanks to the open-minded policy of the PCC,

---

[138] Charles Che Fonchingong, "Religiosity and Existentialist Approach to Poverty in North-West Cameroon", *International Journal of Religion and Society*, Vol. 4, No. 3, 2013, p. 170.

women and girls have the opportunity to excel in all fields today."[139] Similarly, Grace Eneme, who had also served as National Secretary for Women's Work, was very positive about the gains of the CWF. Speaking on the occasion of the celebration of PCC's Silver Jubilee in 1982, she observed that:

> Despite the fact that the CWF members have weekly intensive Bible studies apart from the normal Sunday Service in the congregation one wonders how far they have made the lessons part of their daily experience. Many women are still governed by fear and superstition which impede their spiritual growth. From the missionary era to the present-day women, have been well taught how to take care of their children, home, and how to be a devoted, dutiful wife in addition to the normal traditional training towards womanhood.[140]

On 27 November 1986 the Silver Jubilee of the CWF was celebrated. During the occasion, PCC's Moderator Rt. Rev. Henry Anye Awasom acknowledged CWF's role in the empowerment of women for full participation in the church and society as a whole. He emphasized that the CWF had gained recognition for its active role in providing leadership and fellowship to women of the PCC. He described the movement as one of the pillars of the church, and credited it with such merits as providing sound Biblical teaching, promoting a sense of community, and equipping women with education and practical skills needed to better serve their families, church, and communities.

Grace Eneme and Rt. Rev. Awasom seem to have contrary views on the achievements of the CWF. While Grace Eneme argues that women's work in the PCC through the activities of the CWF produced domestically specialized women, Rt. Rev. Awasom insists that its activities have helped in associating women with the church's power structure. Awasom's view, which represents a

---

[139] Elizabeth Gana, "History of CWF as a Development Agent", In Gana Elizabeth, ed., *Christian Women Move on in Hope and Hope in Christ*, Limbe, Presbook Print, 2001, p. 63.

[140] Grace Eneme, "Women's Work Department", In Nyansako-Ni-Nku, ed., *Journey in Faith: The Story of the Presbyterian Church in Cameroon*, 1982, p. 149.

positive assessment of the CWF from a leadership empowerment perspective, is also shared by other scholars who present the movement as having succeeded in enabling more women to participate in the power structure of the church in clerical and lay positions. Victorine Qui Wetuh describes the CWF as a "movement for women's empowerment for participation in leadership in the PCC."[141] However, the truism is that the tendency of the male-dominated leadership to side-line domestically-specialized women rather became more institutionalized in the PCC. While members of CWF were taught that they were equal, free and armed with potentials to take up independent responsibilities in the church and society, no concrete measures were taken by the leaders of the movement to challenge PCC's patriarchal governance system. So, in spite this acclaimed success, partly justified by the increase in the membership of the CWF and the increase in the number of domestically specialized women yielded by the Christian Home empowerment policy, it is obvious that the CWF lacked the potential to empower women for leadership in the church.

This failure to openly challenge patriarchal leadership notwithstanding, CWF's evangelical activities offered women opportunities to contribute to the spiritual and numerical growth of the PCC. CWF members were pillars of congregations where they committed themselves to church activities. The CWF, no doubt, has opened up new opportunities for women to take interest in congregational leadership as elders, members of Session and to be elected as chairpersons in congregations and presbyteries. Women eldership, which will be insightfully discussed in a separate chapter, has gained prominence in the PCC, with most female elders belonging to the CWF. The work of pastors in all PCC congregations, according to Simon Mbamoh, is facilitated by female elders.[142] Without offering any resistance, CWF members accepted their task as unpaid elders in local congregations. Dressed in white

---

[141] Wetuh, V. Q., "From a Local Church Group to a Movement for Women's Empowerment and Societal Transformation; A Case Study of the CWF of the Presbyterian Church in Likomba-Tiko, Cameroon", Master's Thesis in Theology, MF Norwegian School of Theology, 2017, p. 57.

[142] Interview with Simon Mbamoh, Bambili, 28 December 2019.

robes, women elders perform numerous tasks like collection of offerings, sharing of communion to congregants, and ensuring order during church services. As already noted, some CWF members were able to tap from the activities of the group to challenge men in elections to local leadership positions in congregations and presbyteries, especially the post of Chairperson, which had become the preserve of men as was the case in the Basel Mission era.

In the Molyko Congregation for instance, Dr. Hannah Etonde Mbua was elected Congregational Chairperson in March 2019 in a hotly contested transparent election. Born in 1978, Elder Etonde Mbua was the pioneer female South West Regional Delegate for Secondary Education. She was a devout Presbyterian Christian who believed strongly in the giftedness of women to participate in the power structure of the church and in the wider society. As recognition of her valuable contributions to nation-building, Elder Etonde Mbua was decorated by the state of Cameroon with the Knight of the National Order of Valour medal. It is important to stress that Elder Etonde's election as Congregational Chairperson was facilitated by her role as a politician, educationist and her membership in the Christian Women Fellowship.[143] She led a group of 25 elders and contributed in her own way in the smooth functioning of the Molyko Congregation.

This pushes me to disagree with Linda Lawyer's celebratory submission that, through the CWF, the PCC was able to bring women on board its leadership. Rather, the stark reality is that the gender policy of the PCC during its first decades of autonomy was intended to empower women to challenge patriarchy in the wider society, while accepting male domination of leadership in the church as an unchallengeable divine principle. Little wonder women were completely excluded from theological education and the ordained ministry of the PCC. More revealing is the fact that the first constitutions of the church conditioned that only the ordained could occupy key administrative positions in the church such as

---

[143] For more insight on Elder Etonde Mbua's election as Congregational Chairperson, read Cameroon-Info-Net, 3 April 2019.

moderator, synod clerk, and presbytery secretary. Interestingly enough, the emergence of Christian feminism resulted in controversies over women's right to leadership in Christian organizations, necessitating the revision of the problematic Basel Mission-inherited gender policy. This led to a redefinition of the work of the CWF which was tailored to reflect the World Council of Churches' Ecumenical Decade of Churches in Solidary with Women launched in 1988.

Reforms in the Context of the Ecumenical Decade of Churches in Solidarity with Women, 1988-1998

Established in 1948, the World Council of Churches (WCC) took measures from the 1980s to improve the status of women in its member churches. This ecumenical organization had noticed that the power structures of Protestant churches were dominated by male Christians and resolved to work towards bringing women on board. This was evidence that domesticity had failed to associate women with leadership in these churches. In 1973, the General Assembly of the WCC adopted Resolution No. 8525 on the Leadership of Women in the Church. This was followed by a 1985 resolution stating that the Christian Church (Disciples of Christ) supported and recognized women as full partners in church and society. These reforms, no doubt, were motivated by the United Nation's Decade for Women, 1975-1985. It was noticed in 1985 that the United Nation's Decade had no influence on churches. In an effort to take practical measures to empower women for leadership in church and society, the WCC launched the Ecumenical Decade of Churches in Solidary with Women, 1988-1998. Its key aim was to work towards the full participation of women in church decision-making bodies and to incorporate women's issues, concerns, and commitments into study and action in the areas of justice, peace, and the integrity of creation. In its 1989 General Assembly meeting in Indiana, the WCC adopted Resolution No. 8936 concerning churches' participation in the ecumenical decade. All member churches of the WCC were called upon to fully participate in the ecumenical decade by taking concrete actions for women's participation in leadership structures.

As member of the WCC, the PCC was expected to take measures geared towards achieving the aims of the Ecumenical Decade. This was an opportunity for the PCC to reject patriarchy and to empower women for leadership. Undoing patriarchy required that something beyond domesticity be done within the church, given that the lack of proper empowerment of women was evident. Remaining structural odds were still limiting women's access to executive and decision-making structures of the PCC. For the first time in its history, the PCC began taking some practical measures to roll away women's subordination to male leadership. So, Catherine Muke Chofor from the WWD was appointed as Coordinator of the Ecumenical Decade Program in the PCC. It was her duty to ensure that appropriate actions were taken to associate women with decision-making in the church through a plethora of activities. Catherine Chofor was expected to motivate many women to take part in the programs and activities of the decade. During the ceremony launching the Decade in 1989 which was attended by more than 200 women, the Coordinator and officials of programs encouraged women to fully participate in the earmarked activities, stressing that it was an opportunity for them to rollaway patriarchy in the church and society.

During the Ecumenical Decade, the Coordinator and officials of programs ensured that activities were implemented in PCC presbyteries and congregations across Cameroon. For ten years, officials and resource persons organized campaigns, conferences, and training seminars in leadership and income-generating activities. Apart from targeting women, Chofor and her team involved men in the hope of changing their attitude towards women. The decade provided the PCC an opportunity to recognize that solidarity with women in the church is vital for growth. This explains why the actions that were taken aimed at bringing about more equality in the church. In 1993, a team from the WCC visited Cameroon for a mid-term evaluation of the Decade. It emerged from the evaluation that the PCC, despite initial hesitation, was engaged in an aura of activities earmarked for the Decade.

When the Decade ended in 1998, the church's leadership jubilated that it was very successful in empowering women during the decade. The programme did cause the leadership of the PCC to take women more seriously. In the church's congregations, women were permitted to read the Gospel during the liturgy and could bless children after baptism. In the Likomba Congregation for instance, Victorine Qui Wetuh served as a lay preacher and led church services. So, gone were the days when women could only serve as leaders of the CWF movement. In fact, it was realized during the Decade that churches could not prosper without the full participation of women. This explains why it was during the Decade that concrete actions were taken to undo laws barring women from the ordained ministry. The number of female pastors increased from 2 to 18. These female pastors played important roles in their congregations irrespective of the fact that only a few were able to participate in the church's power structures as will be detailed in Chapter Six.

There was evidence that the programme had empowered some women, arming them with a daring attitude to challenge men in elective positions at the local level of the church's power structure. A few of these women became chairpersons in congregations and presbyteries. In the Ntahmulung Congregation in Bamenda, Elder Jacky Kisub was elected to the position of Chairperson after defeating male candidates. At the Presbytery level, Esther Tegha served for more than ten years as Chairperson of the Menchum Presbytery with headquarters in Wum. Other women who were elected to the position of Presbytery Chairperson included Enanga Ndandoh Ruth of Fako North Presbytery and Helen Anyangwe of the Mezam Presbytery. But these were very isolated cases given that although the church had trained women through seminars and workshops, there was huge hesitation to give them leadership positions. For instance, positions such as moderator, synod clerk and secretaries and treasurers in presbyteries remained under the full control of men. It is obvious that the programme lacked the capacity to dismantle what Atem describes as ecclesial marginalization of women within the PCC's structure. As a matter of fact, the evaluation of the Ecumenical Decade in 2002 revealed the stark reality that the gains from such an empowerment agenda were insignificant given that there were only a few examples of women engaged in the power structure of the PCC. Women's contributions were still side-lined to the margins by the male leaders who, for whatever reason, found women including female pastors unfit to participate in the higher echelons of the church's power structure.

Given that the church leadership was still widely male dominated after the implementation of the above programme, the gender issue was again the subject of a fierce debate at the highest level of PCC's power structure. The leadership of the church crafted a strategic plan for its ministry and mission beyond the year 2000. Christened as *Agenda 2000 and beyond Programme*, the new strategic plan, just like was the case in 1971 when there was a rethinking of the gender policy of the founding mission, acknowledged the persistence of ecclesial patriarchy and its demotion of women's status. It was in the light of this recognition of consistent women's marginalization in the PCC that the gender issue was examined at the 40th Synod Meeting in 2003. The Synod adopted an entirely new gender policy aimed according more space to female adherents of the church. Among other things, the gender policy required that the church should ensure the education and training of its Christians with an emphasis on the women folk. The PCC also resolved to sensitize its Christians on the potentials of women. Most importantly, the new policy required that measures be taken to eliminate women's discrimination in the spheres of employment and appointments to leadership positions in the church.[144] In fact, the chief goal was to heighten women's association with the power structure of the church, not only through ordinations and appointments that were the sole prerogative of the male-powered central administration, but to explore other options. It was in pursuance of this gender policy that the PCC designed the Women's Education and the Empowerment of Women Programme (WEEP) in 2005 for the empowerment of its female faithful.

Women Education and Empowerment Programme

---

[144] Bettina, "Gender Justice," p. 198.

Coming on the heels of the failure of the Ecumenical Decade and the adoption of a new gender policy, the Women's Education and Empowerment Programme (WEEP) was a new approach to the empowerment of women within the PCC. Its main goal was to enable women "discover and recognize the talents and quality of power embedded in them". With technical and financial assistance from Bread for the World, a German-based Christian aid agency, WEEP's coordinators implemented the project in collaboration with a local Common Initiative Group called Nkong Hill Top Association for Development (NAVDEV).[145] Coordinators of the programme had a passion for women's emancipation and were committed to break the chains of ignorance and having victims of marginalization speak out. The programme's motto was "Empowering women for sustainable development."[146] To put it another way, the programme's goal was to empower women through sustainable economic and leadership programmes and enhance women's knowledge for self-development and participation in the power structures of the church and society. Started in 2005, the programme had a main office at the Synod Office of the PCC in Buea, and its Coordinator was Rev. Mary Wose. The overall mission of the Women's Education and Empowerment Programme was to empower and situate women at the forefront of decision making and socio-economic development. In specific terms, the programme was intended to increase the literacy rates of women and girls in order to better their status, to enhance women's participation in decision making processes and finally to increase men's awareness on gender and development.[147] Did this mission of WEEP imply that the PCC would, for the first time, commit itself to the association of women with its executive structure? A close examination of the programme's activities reveals

---

[145] V. Q. Wetuh, "From a Local Church Group to a Movement for Women's Empowerment and Societal Transformation; A Case Study of the CWF of the Presbyterian Church in Likomba-Tiko, Cameroon", Master's Thesis in Theology, MF Norwegian School of Theology, 2017, p. 25.
[146] Interview with Beryl Esino, aged 43, Project coordinator, 25-02-2017, Buea.
[147] Presbyterian Church in Cameroon (PCC), Women's Education and Empowerment Program (WEEP), Gender and Human Rights Manuel for Grassroots Population, First Edition, January 2017, p.1

that women's empowerment for leadership was yet to be taken seriously by this Protestant Church.

Activities of WEEP

In an effort to attain the mission of the WEEP, its Coordinator and immediate collaborators engaged in the organization of capacity building and training seminars on gender issues, women's participation in governance, women's rights, girl child education, economic empowerment, among others. Initially limited to the Fako Division in the South West Region of Cameroon, the programme's activities were intended to be streamed towards bridging gender gaps within the church and in the wider society. Since 2005, WEEP runs capacity-building sessions on a broad range of topics with various categories of women groups.

It was in the Fako Division that the first capacity building seminars were organized. In collaboration with NAVDEV, WEEP officials organized seminars aimed at increasing women's participation in leadership in the church and in the wider society. The seminars which took place in Buea and Limbe were aimed at addressing the legacy of gender bias and imbalance in the leadership structures of the church and society at large. It was hoped that more women would be empowered and given access to leadership. This explains why the seminars brought together lay Christian women to learn and share experiences on approaches to women's leadership. In July 2007 for instance, WEEP organized a training workshop on women's leadership and local governance in Buea. Facilitators at the workshop addressed several dimensions of barriers to women's participation in leadership. They revealed the features of a good woman leadership, and stressed that women aspiring to hold leadership positions need to be knowledgeable, unbiased, flexible, brave, respectful, and endowed with communication skills. The over thirty participants at the workshop shared their experiences through presentations, participatory activities and group discussions. It emerged from the workshop that women's empowerment was the first step towards full participation in leadership. So, the empowerment workshop built the personal capacities of women as a steppingstone for their involvement in leadership. The church and wider society were urged to provide an enabling environment for the actualization of women's leadership potentials.

Some women shared their experiences on the knowledge gained through the leadership seminars organized by WEEP. For instance, one participant at the WEEP seminar observed that:

> I have benefited much from the WEEP empowerment programme. I was one of the many participants of the workshop on women's leadership and local governance. As president of a group, I now better understand how to deal with leadership matters. I learned management skills, public speaking at the workshop organised by WEEP.[148]

The training on governance and leadership had changed her perspective on leadership. She was happy and determined to implement what she had learned from the training to better her group. Another woman said the following on the issue of human rights:

> I attended several of the seminars and workshops organized by WEEP. They have improved my knowledge of human rights issues. As a politician, I learned how to talk well in public and how to better manage my business. In fact, the training got from WEEP workshops changed me completely. [149]

It is worth stressing that from 2012, WEEP's activities were extended to the Meme Division still in the South West Region of Cameroon. The capacity building seminars that were organized in the town of Kumba targeted mostly female members of political parties, especially councillors in local councils across the division. In November 2013, for instance, a capacity building seminar was organized at the Presbyterian Church Centre Kumba by officials of

---

[148] Fanny Ndive, Head teacher/ Zonal president CWF Buea in Smiling Women. Measuring gender gaps 2007: A Newsletter by WEEP of the Presbyterian Church in Cameroon, number 1 edition, October, 2008, p.7.

[149] Gladys Agbor, councillor-Idenau council reported in Smiling Women: A Newsletter by WEEP of the Presbyterian Church in Cameroon, number 1 edition, October, 2008, p.10.

the Women's Education and Empowerment Programme. The seminar was attended by thirty female councillors drawn from the five local councils in Meme Division. Its objective was to educate female councillors on gender mainstreaming, leadership, and good governance in relation to council budgeting. It was hoped that knowledge on gender mainstreaming could help women to press for council projects and budgets that take into consideration the needs of the youth and women who were most often not prioritized. The participants eventually constituted themselves into the Association of Meme Female Counsellors (AMFCO) whose role was to promote the participation of women in municipal and parliamentary elections. This initiative enabled female politicians in Meme to contest for top political positions. For example, five women contested for the position of Mayor and three for the position of parliamentarian but did not make it.[150] A total of 178 female politicians were trained directly on strengthening Women's Strategies for Political Leadership in Municipal and Legislative Governance in Meme Division and also coaching for six Female Mayors. These measures also helped women in politics to pursue the goals within their council areas, with 30 percent of the lists comprised of women.[151]

The leadership empowerment seminars and conferences had a bearing on the association of women with power structures in the church and society at large. In Fako Division, the number of women's representation in church group leadership rose from 63 to 134, making a 55.9% increase. Women's representation in traditional council rose from 14 to 24 persons, constituting a 44.3% increase. In the political domain, 14 women were elected as municipal councillors and one more woman became a parliamentarian to add to the existing one. During the 2011 municipal and parliamentary elections, a total of 775 women were enrolled in the electoral registers owing to empowerment initiatives of the WEEP.[152] Furthermore, the project changed and touch lives

---

[150] Interview with Mary Wose, WEEP Coordinator, Buea, 20 February 2019.
[151] Idem.
[152] Womens and Empowerment Programe(WEEP), Gender and Human Rights Manuel for Grassroots Population, p. 3.

in a plethora of ways. For example, the grassroots training on Gender and Women's Right in 81 communities reached over 27.523 women. Women were able to assert themselves and gained more knowledge on gender issues which fostered collaboration between men and women in communities.[153]

In addition to empowering women for leadership, officials of the Women's Education and Empowerment Programme took measures to roll away the numerous challenges encountered by women whose marriages were not legally recognized. Many women were living with their partners without legal rights and protection of marriage. Some women were dispossessed of their property after the demise of their partners. To end this injustice on women and to empower them for leadership in the home setting, WEEP facilitated the acquisition of marriage certificates for 30 couples in Fako and Meme divisions in May 2011. This happened during a Mass Marriage Ceremony at the Konye Council Hall. Couples came from Konye, Ikiliwindi, Diongo and Mbakwa Supe.[154] This earned women, especially widows, greater access in the law courts to claim and inherit properties of their late husbands. Also, the marriage certificates enabled the women to gain recognition in their communities. Children born in such unions were given a sense of belonging and security within their families.[155]

In order to further address the problem of gender bias at the grassroots level, about 62 traditional rulers and chiefs (59 men and three women) received training on gender, access and control over natural resources in Fako, Konye and Mbonge administrative units. This facilitated collaboration between the chiefs and the women through their inclusion in resource management at the local level.[156] This meeting strengthened the knowledge gained by the women as they later demonstrated stronger commitment in advocacy.[157] Moreover, WEEP trained 1500 women and girls on income

---

[153] Interview with Gladys Agbor, Councillor, Limbe, 20 February 2017.
[154] Smiling Women. WEEP Helps Legalize Marriages: A Newsletter by WEEP of the Presbyterian Church in Cameroon, (October), number 3 edition, 2012.
[155] Ibid.
[156] Interview with Ndifor Patience, aged 49 years, SIRDEP Coordinator, 25/2/2017, Buea.
[157] idem

generating activities in the South West Region. A total of 875 women were involved in soap making while 625 women were involved in cake baking and icing. As such women's economic power increased as they supported their husbands to sponsor their children in schools and catered for their home. Two thousand copies of the WEEP Newsletter were produced and distributed. This earned the project a wider publicity and readership in most communities within Fako and Meme areas.[158]

Critique of WEEP

This laudable programme, as its central objective reveals, was bedevilled from inception. Instead of first of all ensuring that the talents and quality of leadership inbuilt in women were enhanced and exploited for the better stewardship of the church, efforts were rather made to empower women for political, economic and social roles in the wider Cameroonian society. This approach, I believe, was hypocritical, because the PCC with its entrenched tradition of patriarchy which had harmed women's status was trying to educate the wider society on matters of women's empowerment. In fact, it was the church, the government, the street and the entire society that marginalized women in Cameroon. The PCC, under the new programme, would have shaken things up. Logically concrete and workable measures would have been taken to roll back the patriarchy in the power structure of the church before focusing on the wider society. This hypocrisy could be described as "the pot calling the kettle black" or better still a church that had placed women on the fringes of power calling for their empowerment in society.

Clearly, the financial resources that were provided by Bread for the World for the implementation of this programme were used in carrying out activities that were not intended to directly battle the patriarchy in the PCC. Although the WEEP, which was experimented in the Fako Division in the South West Region, yielded some empowerment benefits such as increased female

---

[158] Interview with Ikome Vivian, aged 48 years, WEEP Board Member, 20/2/2017, Buea.

representation in church congregational group leadership, this achievement, I argue, was limited to the base of PCC's power hierarchy. The programme, in the light of its meagre achievements, was unable to enable empowered women to ascend from the base to the top of the executive structure of the church. More to this is the fact that the empowerment of female Presbyterians through this programme was mostly beneficial to the elite class of women who quite often spoke and acted on behalf of the majority female folks in ways that amounted to marginalization.

Within the *Agenda 2000 and beyond Programme* and more specifically the 2003 gender policy, the PCC, among other things, had resolved to offer equal opportunities to men and women in employments and appointments. Surprisingly, the church had only three female principals and two vice principals in its secondary schools as well as three presbytery secretaries. Evidently, this administrative empowerment task did not reflect the commitment taken by the church to ensure gender equality in matters relating to employment and appointments. It is true that from 2003 to 2005, three female pastors were appointed to the position of presbytery secretary and one as presbytery treasurer. This was grossly insignificant given that the PCC had over 25 presbyteries at the time. Besides, the church had about 40 female pastors with the capacity to serve as secretaries and treasurers in the presbyteries. This is a pointer to the fact that there was persistent hesitation to place women in administrative positions. Female Presbyterians including pastors, teachers, nurses and those in other professions remained confined at the margins of the church's power structure. Positions such as Moderator, Synod Clerk, and the departments of the church such as communication, finance, presbook, medical, prescraft, education, scholarship, constitution, and theological seminary were consistently occupied by men. In the church's history, therefore, only the Women's Work Department has been successively headed by women, for obvious reasons. The Synod Office in Buea which hosts the central administration of the church is undeniably a male-dominated environment, with women serving as men's secretaries, liaison officers, cleaners and in other insignificant positions. Generally, the gender policy adopted in 2003 did not reform the marginalized status of women within the PCC administrative set up. Bettina describes the implementation of the gender policy as "still very timid", adding that "the church leadership is still widely male dominated."[159] Clearly, women's discrimination in employment and appointments in the church remains visible. The lack of sustained advocacy probably explains why the nearly all-male leadership of the church grossly violated its gender policy. Members of the CWF, female pastors and women who benefitted from the WEEP have tacitly accepted their exclusion from the church's executive structures.

It emerges from this chapter that despite the empowerment of women through the activities of CWF and programmes such as the Ecumenical Decade of Churches in Solidarity with Women and the Women's Education and Empowerment Programme, the PCC has not been able to rid itself of patriarchal ideology and its attendant practices of discrimination, domination, and disempowerment of women. Its power structure is still dominated by male Christians, with women consistently underrepresented in top decision-making organs. As a matter of fact, there is continuing subordination of women in the power structure of the PCC because the empowerment policies that have been implemented since 1957 have not been able to knock down the traditional barriers to female leadership and their holding of official authority in the church's organizational structures. The Christian Women Fellowship has not been able to empower women's capacity to confront patriarchy in the PCC. A female university lecturer who had been a member of the CWF doubted its potential to empower women for leadership in the church. She observed that "the mission of the fellowship and the nature of its work do not permit it to uproot the entrenched patriarchal culture in the church."[160] By focusing its activities on spiritual growth, sewing, and social work, the CWF lacked innovative initiatives capable of ending women's marginalization in the leadership of the church. The most visible contribution of the CWF to women's empowerment for leadership is the existence of

---

[159] Bettina, "Gender Justice," p. 198.
[160] Interview with Prof. Josepha Ngum Bih, Yaounde, 14 May 2019.

the Women's Work Department and its local organs within the organizational structure of the church. This has produced opportunities for leadership to women as bosses of the WWD, Church centres in Kumba and Bamenda and as leaders of CWF groups at congregational, zonal, and presbyterial levels. These are structures purposefully created for women. Sadly, as noted earlier, the structures have failed to promote women's equality with men in the leadership structures of the Presbyterian Church in Cameroon.

In recent years, some women who were encouraged to build on their self-confidence and self-esteem are challenging men in elective positions in the lower power structures of the church in congregations and presbyteries. This is evidence that increased empowerment has heightened the desire of women to play a greater role in the church. Many women have become conscious of how they were rendered subservient by the nearly all-male hierarchy. In many congregations, women leaders were able to exercise considerable authority over both their male and female congregants. There are many examples of female laity who have prospered in congregational and presbyterial leadership. A recent example is Elder Frida Ambanasom who was elected to the position of Chairperson in the Tubah-Boyo Presbytery. The manner in which she rose to this position was highlighted by a male elder in the CCAST Complex Congregation in Bambili, who implied that Elder Frida built on her empowerment in the church to challenge patriarchy in the presbytery.

It appears, then, that recourse to innovative gender reforms since the 1970s was intended to encourage the emergence of influential female leaders only at the base of the organizational structure of the church. It was not a gender ideology meant to prepare the vast female laity of the church for active participation in the top decision-making structures of the church. Little wonder women are still highly underrepresented in the Synod, considered as the highest decision-making organ of the church. Comparatively, the Presbyterian Church in South Africa (PCSA) has witnessed more progress in female leadership. In 2000, Rev. Diane Vorster was elected as the pioneer female Moderator of the General

Assembly of the PCSA.[161] Seemingly, there is a veiled agenda not to allow women to occupy top positions in the central administrative structures of the church like education, health, and communication as well as positions such as Moderator and Synod Clerk. Since the emergence of the PCC, the top-most elective positions of Moderator and Synod Clerk have never been occupied by a woman. It is even more disturbing that no woman has ever dared to vie for any of these positions. Surprisingly, the patriarchization of both positions is yet to amount to any organized dissent in the church. In fact, female pastors, whose numbers have increased in recent years, seem to have tacitly endorsed their marginalization in the power structure of the church. The next chapter provides more insight into the plight of female pastors in the PCC in an effort to appreciate why women's access to the ordained ministry has not come with more female leadership opportunities. It will argue that the presence of female pastors does not represent visible and sustainable female power in the PCC.

---

[161] Graham A. Duncan, "South African Presbyterian Women in Leadership in Ministry (1973-2018), *HTS Teologiese Studies/Theological Studies*, Vol. 75, No. 1, 2019, p. 7.

Chapter 6

Women in PCC's Ordained Ministry Leadership

In the 1971, the Synod of the Presbyterian Church in Cameroon recognized the biblical truth that women are called of God to roles of leadership in ministry. This formal acknowledgement that women have the same spiritual authority as men by the highest governing body of the church represented a significant shift in the status of women in the PCC. The Synod resolution came on the heels of two decades of biases against women in the ordained ministry. In 1957 when the PCC gained autonomy from the Basel Mission, the law barring women from the ordained ministry was upheld and strictly implemented. The church's theological college at Nyasoso (which was later relocated to Kumba) received only male candidates who studied for the pastoral ministry. This denial to train, ordain and engage women as pastors yielded a total male ministry leadership. While an all-male leadership was becoming the norm in the PCC, growing Christian feminism resulted in internal resistance to the powerlessness of women. This caused the PCC to be caught in a sustained struggle to open the ordained ministry to women and to allow them assume administrative pastoral roles in the church hierarchy from the congregations all through to the Synod Office. Trapped in these controversies over women's right to ministry leadership, the PCC authorities were obliged to take concrete measures aimed at eliminating decades of arbitrary rules against women in the ordained ministry. This led to the adoption of a policy of gender justice in the early 1970s which opened the ordained ministry to women.

The training and ordination of women as pastors from the 1980s were slow, with female pastors finding it difficult to rise to the top of clerical leadership. Hierarchical mobility within the power structure of the PCC was shaped by gender politics and patriarchy. This explains why ordained women hardly got access to hierarchical positions like Presbytery Secretary, Synod Clerk, and Moderator.

Decision making bodies like Synod, Synod Committees, and various departments: education, health services, Development, Communication, Youth, Women and Men's Work departments are headed by Executive Secretaries who have always been men with the exception of Women's Work Department. The management of the church's four business enterprises: Presbyterian Handicraft Centre (Prescraft), Presbyterian Printing Press (Presprint), Presbyterian Book Depot (Presbook), and Presbyterian Woodwork (Preswood) has consistently been male-dominated. Building on the foregoing scenario, this chapter critically explores the bases and changing trends of women's participation in the ordained ministry of the PCC in view of appreciating the extent to which it has enhanced the empowerment of female pastors for full participation in the leadership of the church. It pays particular attention to the extent to which elective and appointive leadership positions were accessed by female pastors.

Context of Women's Ordination in the PCC

The knocking down of sex-based restrictions to ordination in the PCC was not an isolated gender episode. It was inbuilt in global and local phenomena that served as provocation for raising the question of the ordination of women. Evidently, the opening of the ordained ministry to women in the PCC was a product of multiple forces that acted in combination, though at different times. The movement towards the ordination of women had a Biblical basis. Christian feminists who battled to open ordination to the ministry to women leaned on Biblical verses to make their case. They believed that the Bible is authoritative and that, if rightly understood, it supports the ordination of women. They described the mission of the church as grounded in God's mission in which all Christians irrespective of their sex must fully participate. The barring of women from the pulpit, they argued, prevented women from fulfilling their identity as being created in God's image as expressed in Gen 1:26. Building on this Biblical language, advocates of women's ordination noted that participation in God's mission to the world equally involves the fight for gender justice. As the latter gained acceptance in churches, controversies over women's right to ordination roiled probably every religious body. In the Western churches that opened theological education to women, a favourite text for sermons preached at ordination services of women candidates for the ministry was Galatians 3:28: "There is neither Jew nor Greek, there is neither slave nor free, there is neither male nor female; for you are all one in Christ Jesus." It is important to highlight that these doctrinal arguments were dragged into the debate on women's ordination in the PCC by Rev. Dr. Ruth Epting (ordained in 1947 in Basel) in her capacity as pioneer female lecturer at the Theological College of the PCC in Nyasosso where pastors were trained. Her role in ending PCC's custom excluding women from the priesthood will be discussed later in this section.

The ordination of women debate was equally dragged into the PCC, like in other churches, by the Christian feminist movement which was inbuilt in the successive waves of the feminism. Christian feminists such as Mary Daly, Rosemary Radford and Elisabeth Schussler Fiorenza aspired for women equality in the church especially at the pulpit.[162] These women voiced their frustration with the church's refusal to open the ordained ministry to women. Fiorenza particularly proposed a reconstructionist approach to recover women's Christian history and heritage that will serve as a live model of inclusive contemporary Christianity. Christian feminists stressed that male academics deliberately concealed women's history in scripture in view of perpetuating patriarchy. This was the context in which feminists brought to light the achievements, sufferings and struggles of women throughout the history of Christianity. The interesting tales of women saints contained in such literature made female Presbyterians to understand that there had always been a procession of radical women who loved God and were prepared to fight those men in ecclesiastical authority for the fulfilment of God's mission.[163] Female members of the PCC, especially the educated ones, perhaps found the stories of the women saints a real practical encouragement. As their feminism deepened and touched more and

---

[162] Wood, "Patriarchy, Feminism and Mary Daly", p. 85.
[163] Johnstone, *Religion in Society*, p. 207.

more areas of their life, they were challenged to examine things they would have preferred to have left unquestioned, and then goading them to act. One of such things was the custom barring women from ordination. The approval of the ordination of women by many Western churches in the early second half of the twentieth century (considered as an achievement of Christian feminism) was an added motivation for the PCC to consider the ordination of women. Thus, feminism caused controversies over women's right to ordination to roil the PCC.

The gender justice policy of the World Council of Churches (WCC) also had a bearing on the prehistory of the ordination of women in the PCC. Following its creation in 1948, the WCC started militating in favour of women's participation in the ordained ministry of the church. Indeed, the Council was conscious of the damage its member churches had done to women in the theologies. This made the fight for women's ordination rights its central drama. This struggle was heightened when the WCC called for an international forum on "The Life and Work of Women in the Church."[164] In 1961 when the PCC became a full member of the WCC, it had to join the struggle for inclusion of women in the ordained ministry. As Atem observes, the PCC signed on to the gender policy of the WCC as a member church.[165] This placed the PCC on the path to knocking down sex-based restrictions to the priesthood as it became unacceptable to have only men as pastors.

The birth and operation of the Women's Work Department (WWD) in 1961 was another contributory factor to the elimination of rules barring women from theological education and ordination in the PCC. With its activities carried out largely through the Christian Women Fellowship (CWF), the functioning of the WWD was an unintended step towards women's ordination in the ministry. Indeed, a logical consequence of the women's empowerment activities of this department was eventual consideration of women's participation in the ministry. It contributed in bringing the women's ordination debate to the

---

[164] Bendroth, "Gender and Twentieth-Century Christianity", p. 318.
[165] Atem, "Women's Empowerment", p. 25.

limelight of the church. As the women's empowerment efforts of the CWF gained momentum alongside the debate that had been initiated, the door to ordination and religious leadership remained close to women. In spite of this, the movement remained consistent as an ecclesial instrument through which women shaped their policies and channelled their ministry and mission visions and recommendations through the Synod of the PCC.[166] Expectedly, it challenged sex-based restrictions to ordination and recommended theological education for women. This triggered debate on the issue given that the synod was the highest organ of the PCC where debates and decisions regarding the wellbeing of the church were made. Generally, these debates ended with a critique of the Basel Mission gender legacy as it was argued by some women that the founding mission handed down to the PCC a tradition of women's inferior role.

As the PCC was beginning to discuss the women's ordination issue, more influence came from nuns at the Emmanuel Sisterhood in Bafut, the lone convent operated by the church. The articulate leader of the convent, Madeleine-Marie Handy, struggled to speak both to and for the many other women regarding empowerment in general and ordination specifically. It is important to mention that the practical autonomy with which these nuns acted was a contributory factor to the fading of established laws excluding women from ordination. There was a clear difference between the practical autonomy of the nuns and the constrained and dependent nature of the lives of the many other women in the PCC. The female Presbyterians who established links with the nuns became conscious of the need to challenge the patriarchy that underpinned the priesthood. Through the nuns, women internalized role models of how to have access to the pulpit.

On the overall, gender justice supportive Biblical texts, recovering of women's Christian history, the Christian feminist movement, the pursuance of a gender policy by the WCC, the women's empowerment activities of the WWD and CWF, and the opening of a convent in Bafut contributed in their own separate

---

[166] Ibid., p. 21.

ways to the rising of the women's ordination conundrum in the PCC. By 1969 when Rt. Rev. J. C. Kangsen became Moderator of the church, women simply were not a minority in the PCC. This was an added booster to the "feminization" of the pulpit. As this exclusion of women from priesthood maintained its status as a puzzling gender issue, foreign feminine clerical voices came in to peddle the debate. I am referring particularly to Rev. Dr. Ruth Epting, who was ordained in 1947 by one of the member churches of the Basel Mission (now Mission 21) and was sent to Cameroon to teach at the Presbyterian Theological College Nyasoso as an ecumenical co-worker.[167] Rev. Epting questioned why she was training only male pastors for the PCC. When interviewed on the issue in 2008 by Martina Heinriche, Epting noted that the male dominated leadership of the PCC even questioned why the Basel Mission had to send a woman as an ecumenical co-worker (teacher) at the theological college.[168] This was how this feminist got involved in the struggle to eliminate laws barring women from ordination in the PCC. Atem notes that Rev. Epting's presence and brilliant performance as a female lecturer at the theological college eventually amazed her male colleagues, students and the authorities of the institution.[169]

Born in 1919 in Basel, Switzerland, Rev. Epting completed primary school and then studied minor theology in Berlin where she was brought under the influence of women pastors, especially Anna Paulsen.[170] The outbreak of World War Two caused Rev. Epting to relocate to Basel where she pursued theological studies. She was ordained in 1947 and evolved to become President of the Young Women Christian Association (YWCA) in Switzerland. Ruth questioned why the Swiss Reformed Church upheld the discrimination of women in its leadership structures. She later joined the Basel Mission and served as Secretary for Women's

---

[167] Ibid., p. 28.
[168] Rev. Dr. Ruth Epting, Retired Theologian, Interviewed by Martina Heinriche at Chisinau-Moldova, March 2008.
[169] Ibid.
[170] Anna Paulsen was among the pioneer woman theologians in Germany. She challenged the women's restriction from the ordained ministry and inspired Ruth Epting to take interest in theological education.

Work in Asia, Latin America and Africa. This was the context in which she worked briefly in Cameroon as lecturer in PCC's Theological College 1971-72.[171] Her advocacy urged the officials of the PCC to initiate brainstorming on women's ordination.

Rev. Epting's presence in the PCC theological education system alongside Madeleine-Marie Handy who usually attended synod sessions as representative of Emmanuel Sisterhood dragged the debate on women's ordination into the Synod. Expectedly there were voices for and against women's ordination. In fact, the demand for women's ordination attracted a lot of criticism within and outside the church. But the advocates remained steadfast in battling this Basel Mission-inherited practice excluding women from the Eucharistic ministry. In further response, critiques maintained that ordination of women had no justification in either church tradition or its understanding of scripture; because Christ called only men to the apostolic succession. Advocates for the inclusion of women in the ordained ministry built on doctrinal texts such as Galatians 2:28 and Acts 2:17 to support the elimination of laws barring women from theological education. This made it clear that the PCC was already trapped in an irreversible course toward the ordination of women as bona fide pastors irrespective of the both male and female voices that continued in opposition.

The decades of arbitrary rules against women on the pulpit slowly began to erode when the Synod of the church yielded to the pressure in 1971 by lengthily discussing the issue. The Synod session welcomed the ordination of women and at the same time initiated the development of guidelines on how to practically open the priesthood to women. What generally emerged from the Synod was the unprecedented decision that the PCC opened its ordained ministry to women in pursuance of its policy of gender justice in theological education. The Synod argued that the ordination of women was a step towards the participation of women in the leadership of the church as parish pastors, presbyterial secretaries, synod clerk, moderator and other positions that were the preserve

---

[171] Roswitha Golder, "Farewell to Ruth Epting", *Women's Letter*, No. 53, October 2016. Women's Letter is written by women in Africa, Asia, Europe, and Latin America under the sponsorship of Mission 21.

of the ordained. Almost at the same time, the Presbyterian Church of Ghana also uplifted its ban on women's participation in the ordained ministry. This came after years of female advocacy and debates on the ordination of women.[172] This knocking down of the law excluding women from theological education and ordination represented a success of Christian feminism. It was an expression of the Christian feminist doctrine of the level playing field for men and women in the priesthood advocated by egalitarian theorists. From this moment measures were slowly and timidly taken to implement the synod decision.

Changing Trends of Women's Ordination: A Critique

The ordination of women had to be preceded by their training at the Presbyterian Theological College in Nyasoso. But it took seventeen years for the church to start admitting women into the theological college. This was, perhaps, because the decision to knock down laws barring women from ordination was reached at a time when the PCC was grappling with an unprecedented financial crisis. This was the outcome of a new labour code instituted by the Cameroon Government. The code obliged the PCC to place its workers on the same pay roll like government employees. The code stipulated that nobody shall be employed with a salary of below CFA 4800 francs.[173] Faced with this situation, the PCC opted for a retrenchment scheme as a remedy. It was not therefore logical for the church to start training female pastors in such times of crisis. Besides, the intake of male candidates in the theological college dropped drastically during this period. But this financial crisis is not tenable enough to justify the illegal refusal to enrol women in the theological college from 1971 to 1987. This is because the intake of male candidates continued throughout this period.

As a matter of fact, opposition to the ordination of women for religious leadership persisted after 1971. According to Atem, the door to enrolment in the theological college remained closed to

---

[172] Grace Sintim Adasi *et al.*, "Gender Politics and Social Change: The Status of Women Leaders in the Presbyterian Church of Ghana", *Canadian Social Science*, Vol. 9, No. 6, 2013, p. 105.
[173] Dah, "The Vision and Challenges", p. 63.

women because of entrenched cultural construction of women's roles and embedded church teaching that linked theological education with ordination and employment of men.[174] Simply put, it was men's desire to protect and sustain their domination of leadership that stalled the intake of female candidates into the theological college. Interestingly, this impediment did not silence pro-women's ordination voices, especially those of Rev. Epting and Handy. When the former returned to Switzerland, Handy continued with the struggle. Later in 1978, she was ordained as the pioneer female pastor of the PCC given that she had received theological education in Paris before founding the Emmanuel Sisterhood. By this, the PCC had practically accepted the ordination of women. But the battle for the latter's practical enrolment in the theological college was not yet won.

In 1985 when the long-serving Rt. Rev. Kangsen retired, Rt. Rev. Henry Awasom became the new Moderator. This forward-looking moderator enhanced the entry of women into the ordained ministry of the PCC by ordering the enrolment of women into the theological college in 1987 in spite continuing opposition. From this moment, women were given the opportunity for a career path into ministry, from seminary and ordination through parish placement. The brilliant performance of pioneer female pastors in congregations and other leadership positions, as will be argued later, represented an empirical rejection of the complementarianism theory postulation that the inclusion of women in the ordained ministry will result in dire consequences. Indeed, PCC's admission of women into the priesthood was supportive, and not disruptive, to the church. Of the thirteen candidates that were admitted into the theological college in 1987, two were women. The numbers grew slowly with three women against seven men in 1988.[175] This push came from the launching of the Ecumenical Decade of Churches in Solidarity with Women (1988-1998) by the WCC. As a member church, the PCC signed on to this programme. The offering of more opportunities to women for theological training

---

[174] Atem, "Women's Empowerment", p. 28.
[175] Atem, "Women's Empowerment", p. 28.

was one of the ways in which the PCC implemented the WCC programme. In 1998 when the programme ended, eighteen women had received training in the seminary.[176] These gains were also shaped by the Circle of Concerned African Women Theologians which was founded in 1989.[177] The Circle among other things aimed at contributing to research that leads to policies promoting the participation of women in religion. In collaboration with the All African Conference of Churches (AACC), the Circle argued that there is a contradiction in the way that the church in Africa has preached about the equality of all humanity in Jesus Christ while in practice excluding women from the Eucharistic ministry.[178] This was additional pressure on the PCC since it was a member of the AACC.

From 1998 onwards, progress in the ordination of women was underpinned by PCC's strategic planning for its ministry. In 1999 the church developed a strategic plan for its ministry and mission beyond the year 2000 in which the gender question was embedded.[179] These activities gained propensity in 2003 when the PCC fashioned a gender policy in the hope of further providing equal opportunities for male and female Presbyterians.[180] These reforms resulted in slight gains in the number of women in clergy positions. On the overall, 66 women were admitted into the PCC seminary as compared to 306 men from 1987 through 2014 (see table). The interesting reality is that almost all the women that enrolled in the seminary decided to pursue vocations in ministry and completed the curricular required as preparation for ordination. This was how the PCC had its female pastors participating in the ministry of the church despite persistent patriarchy.

---

[176] Ibid., p. 25.
[177] Mercy Amba Oduyoye, "African Women Theologians", in *A People's History of Christianity, Vol. 7, Twentieth-Century Global Christianity*, edited by Mary Farrell Bednarowski, Minneapolis, Fortress Press, 2008, pp. 88-91.
[178] Ibid., pp. 86-88.
[179] Atem, "Women's Empowerment", p. 2.
[180] Bettina, "Gender Justice", p. 197.

Table 1: Male and Female Enrolment in the PCC Seminary, 1987-2014

Year	Intake	Male	Female
1987	13	11	02
1988	10	7	03
1989	19	16	03
1990	13	13	-
1991	-	-	-
1992	14	12	02
1993	13	12	01
1994	18	18	-
1995	13	11	02
1996	15	14	01
1997	16	14	02
1998	15	12	03
1999	15	12	03
2000	17	13	04
2001	15	10	5
2002	20	17	03
2003	22	16	06
2004	12	10	02
2005	15	09	03
2006	20	13	02
2007	21	17	04
2008	22	17	05
2009	20	15	05
2010	22	16	06
2011	15	08	07
2012	20	16	04
2013	22	16	06
2014	22	11	11
Total	459	372	87

Source: Adapted from Michael Kpughe Lang, "The Long Trip to the Front Alter: Women in the Ordained Ministry of the Presbyterian Church in Cameroon, 1957-2010", *Ibadan Journal of Gender Studies*, Vol. 2, 2015, p. 154.

It is relevant to analyse the interesting trends that are evident in Table 1. The figures show that the long-term trend has been one of slight increases in women enrolment in the seminary. In spite of this growth, the table exposes that the number of women as a percentage of the total enrolment in the seminary is still strikingly small, when compared with that of male intake. The number of female enrolments dropped in the mid-nineties because no woman was admitted into the seminary in 1994. All the 18 candidates for that year were men. Evidently, the ordained ministry of the PCC is still male dominated. This relatively low proportion of clergywomen is accounted for by the persistence of opposition to the ordination of women. Indeed, many of the members of the PCC and even the Cameroonian society looked upon the women who pursued theological education to be not normal unlike the men. This explains why the first female pastors that were posted to parishes faced a lot of opposition, particularly from men.[181] In fact, the slow progress of women's ordination in the PCC is a signal that old-gendered division of labour, with men in leadership and women in silent service, is still very much in operation. Irrespective of this disturbing composite picture, PCC's knocking down of laws barring women from pursuing theological education made women to be able to respond to a sense of calling into the ministry by pressing for ordination. The latter, as argued in the next section, did not immediately translate into changes in the traditional attitudes about gender roles since ordained women became trapped in a plethora of dilemmas.

Post-Ordination Dilemmas and Response

The shift that permitted women to pursue theological education in the PCC produced female pastors who were exposed to an aura of dilemmas in the clergy profession. As already pointed out, almost all the women that enrolled in the seminary decided to pursue vocations in ministry and completed the curricular required as preparation for ordination. Upon their ordination, most of them were quite often deployed to parishes as bona fide clergywomen by the Staffing Committee of the church. Disturbingly, there was little or no guarantee that these female pastors will be accepted into the profession by laity in the congregations. There is evidence attesting that some women pastors faced professional marginality when they were deployed. Rev. Dr. Margaret Azange, who graduated from the

---

[181] Interview with Rev. Dr. Azange Margaret, *Presbyterian Messenger*, Interviewed by Achowah Umenei, December 2007.

seminary in 1993 and was successively posted to Likoko Membea, Buea, and Bonamoussadi (Douala) as parish pastor, argues that opposition to female pastors depended on the parish in question. She however agrees that some women pastors were fiercely opposed in their parishes. But she accuses the church for accepting women to be pastors without educating its Christians.[182] This is true because the church was supposed to have produced a document, educating the Christians on the bases for the ordination of women. The opposition sprang up because of this lack of sensitization. Indeed, there were evidences of ignorance in the rejection of some female pastors by Christians. Interestingly enough, most of the female pastors performed well in their parishes.

Another area of marginalization was the discrimination in the posting of female pastors whose husbands are pastors. The context of this practice was the pairing of female pastors and male pastors in marriage due to emotional ties probably traceable to the seminary where they were trained. As cases of pastor marrying pastor multiplied, it became the source of discrimination for such women pastors since they had to be posted to the parishes placed under their husbands.[183] In some cases, two very competent pastors had to be deployed to one place to the detriment of other places. Expectedly, women pastors were not happy with the law obliging them to work in the same places with their husbands.

The ordination of women was expected to surmount patriarchal leadership in the PCC since most key positions were/are the preserve of the clergy. The church custom which excluded women from ordination made positions such as Presbyterial Secretary, Synod Clerk and Moderator to be the preserve of men. The emergence of female pastors opened a range of parish leadership positions to women. On the overall, a majority of ordained women were deployed as parish pastors. Just like their male counterparts, the few female pastors serving as hospital or school chaplains and in ecumenical bodies to which the PCC belong have in most cases been parish priests at one time. So, most of the female pastors

---

[182] Idem.
[183] Idem.

started out in the pastoral ministry in theological leadership positions as heads of parishes. This represented a significant leadership shift given that the role of the parish minister had been the province of men before the approval and implementation of women's theological training and ordination.

In the face of the foregoing dilemmas, the clergywomen understood the need to emphasize their unique experiences and to develop their own agendas towards liberation from persistent marginalization. This was the context in which they created the Conference of PCC Female Pastors and Students in 1997. In the latter's annual meetings, women pastors perceived themselves as targets of discrimination in a church that was preaching gender justice, but marginalizing women. More emphasis was placed on female pastors' access to leadership and the difficulties they faced in the parishes and other places of work. It is therefore a forum where these pulpit women dialogue, exchange ideas and the problems they face back in their parishes in view of finding solutions. Amazingly, the church was/is slow in yielding to the demands of these ordained ministers in spite the fact that some have furthered their education. In 2007, for instance, Rev. Margaret Azange became the first female pastor of the PCC to obtain a PhD in theology.[184] Is it possible for male pastors and male laity who dominate the Synod to one day elect such a female pastor as Synod Clerk or Moderator? The contrary is very obvious if one should consider the manner in which these ordained women have been treated since 1978 when Rev. Handy became the pioneer clergywoman of the PCC.

Women Pastors in Elective Leadership Positions

The inclusion of women in the ordained ministry of the Presbyterian Church in Cameroon came with opportunities for them to occupy elective leadership positions in the power structure of the church. Although the existing elective power structures within the church are patriarchal, ordained women are permitted to contest for elective positions like Moderator and Synod Clerk.

---

[184] Interview with Rev. Dr. Azange Margaret, *Presbyterian Messenger*, Interviewed by Achowah Umenei, December 2007.

These two positions, according to the constitution of the church, can only be accessed by ordained ministers, be them male or female. In this section, an effort is made to analyse why the PCC has never had a female Moderator and Synod Clerk since the ordination of the first women pastors in 1991. Top elective positions in the PCC have remained the preserve of men because hierarchical mobility is shaped by gender politics and patriarchy.

Laid down procedures for holding the position of moderator did not exclude female pastors. The post of moderator was reserved for ordained ministers through an election which was done after every five years. The moderator's term of office was five years renewable once. According to Article 113 of the Constitution of the PCC, a candidate for the post of Moderator or Synod Clerk should be at least 40 years old and at most 55 years old. The first phase of the election was done at the presbyteries, after which the first three candidates in the elections moved to the next final phase in an Elective Synod Meeting. The moderator is the spiritual and executive head of the PCC.[185]

In 2014 when Rt. Rev. Festus Asana's tenure as Moderator came to an end, elections were organized from April to November that year. During the first phase of the election, all the candidates for the post of Moderator were ordained male pastors, with no woman featuring on the list. The three candidates who progressed to the second phase of the election were Rev. Johnson Tabe Besong, Rev. William Membong Abwenzo, and Rev. Samuel Forba Fonki. During the second phase, the Synod Executive Committee dropped Rev. Johnson Tabe Besong from the race in accordance with the Constitutional provision that one of the candidates is dropped after a thorough examination of their letters of faith. The remaining two candidates proceeded to the final phase of the election which took place during the Elective Synod Meeting held in Bamenda on 25 November 2014. At the end of the process, Rev. Fonki Samuel was elected as Moderator.

---

[185] Evangeline Ngwa Fomukong, "Stylistic Appraisal of 'Change' as an Ideology in the Presbyterian Church Day Speeches of Reverend Doctor Festus Ambe Asana, Moderator of the Presbyterian Church in Cameroon", *Journal of Applied Linguistics and Language Research*, Vol. 3, No. 7, 2016, pp. 132-150.

Ordained women did not also contest for the post of Moderator and Synod Clerk during the 2019 election. For the post of Moderator, the three candidates who moved to the second phase were Rev. Samuel Fonki, Rev. Jones Ayuk Ebot, and Rev. Christian Nganji. Rev. Miki Hans Abia, Rev. Hosea Ngwa, and Rev. Mokoko Mbue Thomas were the top finalists for the post of Synod Clerk. During the final phase of the election, the Elective Synod Meeting which held in Buea on 27 November 2019 re-elected Rev. Samuel Fonki to the post of Moderator. Rev. Hans Miki Abia was elected as the new Synod Clerk. Male domination of these top leadership positions is not the outcome of women's exclusion, but the absence of female candidates. The constitution permits women pastors to contest for these positions, but none has ever made the commitment to rise to the position of moderator or synod clerk. It appears female pastors have accepted their subordination to male pastors in the power structure of the church. A good number of these women like Rev. Dr. Perpetua Fonki, Rev. Dr. Florence Tache, Rev. Gladys Atem, Azange Margaret, Rev. and Yenchi Nukuna had the required qualification to occupy these top leadership positions. The absence of female candidates for these positions was probably because female pastors were conscious of the continuing patriarchy in the church and fear being beaten at the polls. They did not believe that their candidacies could sail through the male-dominated structures such as the Synod and Synod Executive Committee. Rev. Margaret says that female pastors were not treated justly as far as leadership was concerned, stressing that "the leadership of the church was/is probably not convinced about female pastors' skills."[186] Notwithstanding their motivation not to contest for these positions, the painful reality is that top elective leadership posts remained in the hands of male pastors since the opening of the ordained ministry to women. And these male leaders also ensured that female pastors were not appointed into key leadership roles.

---

[186] Interview with Rev. Margaret Azange, 3 February 2020.

Women Pastors in Appointive Leadership Positions

The ordained ministry was opened to women with the expectation that female pastors would be appointed to various administrative positions in the power structure of the church. It was hoped that ordained women had the capacity to play outstanding roles in the spheres of chaplaincy, administration of congregations, parishes, presbyteries, businesses and numerous departments operated by the church. This section examines the extent to which ordained women were associated with appointive leadership positions. It posits that while many women pastors played outstanding roles in low-ranking positions, juicy positions which came by appointment like Presbytery Secretary, Presbytery Treasurer, Church Treasurer, Education Secretary, Secretary for Health Services, Communication Secretary, and Financial Secretary were largely dominated by men since the beginning of women's ordination as pastors.

Historically, ordained women were conspicuous in low leadership places. They were most often engaged as chaplains and congregational and parish pastors. The first batches of ordained women ministers were appointed by the Staffing Committee of the church to function as chaplains in hospitals and schools. The church's chaplaincy ministry from the 1990s was almost the preserve of female pastors, appearing as if a decision had been taken to appoint ordained women only to chaplaincy positions. Seemingly, continuing opposition to the full inclusion of women in the ordained ministry was responsible for the church's reluctance to quickly accept them in congregational and parish leadership positions. The truism is that external pressure from the WCC through its Ecumenical Decade in Solidarity with Women (1988-1998) had forced the PCC to train and ordain female pastors. Little or nothing had been done to roll away the patriarchal beliefs which were responsible for the initial barring of women from the ordained ministry. Hence, the church ordained its pioneer female pastors in 1991 without being ready to accept their full participation in ministry leadership. No wonder Joseph Cheghe Nang describes the ordination of women as cosmetic, stressing that it was simply intended to satisfy the WCC which was disbursing some funds to the PCC for activities related to the ecumenical decade.[187]

As chaplains, female pastors served as a bridge between the schools and health facilities and the PCC. They were fully committed to work for the spread of the gospel and probably performed better than the few male pastors who served as chaplains at that time. Some female pastors spent many years serving as chaplains in various educational and health facilities. They proclaimed the Gospel through preaching and other tasks like organizing the liturgy for the schools as well as other daily activities deemed necessary for the proper upbringing of students. In PCC's health facilities, female chaplains cared for the sick and dying as a manifestation of Jesus Christ's good news. As noted by Rev. Ngwa Agnes, female pastors provided pastoral care to patients, supported their families through prayer and counselling. They worked in health facilities like Presbyterian General Hospital Acha-Tugi, Presbyterian Medical Institutions Manyemen, Presbyterian Hospital Nyasoso, and in various health centres. For example, Rev. Techa Florence who worked as a chaplain in the Presbyterian General Hospital Acha-Tugi provided pastoral care and biblical counselling to the sick, the terminally ill and their families. Female pastors also served as chaplains in prisons like the example of Rev. Mary Wose who played this role in the Buea Central Prison.[188] Rev. Cynthia Asenek worked as a chaplain in non-denominational secondary schools in Tiko, Limbe and Batibo from 2003 to 2008.[189] In Tiko, she taught moral education in the Government Bilingual High School and Government Technical College. Her chaplaincy work in Limbe consisted of teaching religious studies in Presbyterian Girls' Secondary School. Rev. Asenek also performed chaplaincy work at Presbyterian High School Batibo as a religious studies teacher in an effort to instil PCC's doctrines and disciplines in the students.

Female pastors were appointed to leadership positions such as Congregational and Parish Pastors. It was from the late 1990s that women were given charge of congregations and parishes in

---

[187] Interview with Joseph Cheghe Nang, Weh, 23 March 2018.
[188] Read Eden Newspaper, 25 August 2017.
[189] Interview with Rev. Asenek Cynthia Itih, Bamenda, 7 February 2020.

different parts of the country. They performed a plethora of functions such as proclaiming the gospel through preaching, worship, healing, evangelization, and counselling, and ensured that parishes placed under their headship were properly governed. There was indeed a high probability of having female pastors as parish leaders. For instance, Rev. Asenek Cynthia who was ordained in 2004 after graduating from the Presbyterian Theological Seminary Kumba in 2002, served as parish pastor of Diche I in Batibo Presbytery from 2002 to 2003. In this rural parish, Rev. Asenek controlled six congregations with the furthest located some seven kilometres away from the parish headquarters. She occupied similar functions in the Mbem, Ndzah, and Abangoh parishes. Rev. Asenek views the parish pastor position as an opportunity for female pastors to participate in the power structure of the PCC. "As parish pastor", notes Rev. Asenek, "I decided on the programs to carryout and the projects."[190] The position of parish leader has been occupied by many other female pastors like Reverends Theresia Uso, Perpetua Fonki, Immaculate Neba, Stephanie Ngang, Loveline Ndeleyen, Yenchi Nukuna, Priscilla Epiteme, Margaret Azanga, Grace Dashako, Comfort Nana, Elisabeth Ngu, Florence Ebango Sobe, Stella Teboh, among many others. This is evidence that the odds of female pastors leading parishes are giving way.

However, there are still visible signs of discrimination against female pastors regarding appointments to the parish leader position. In most cases, female pastors were placed at the helm of rural parishes, given that most parishes in urban locations were headed by male pastors. In fact, the likelihood of a female pastor being appointed to lead urban parishes like Azire and Ntamulung in Bamenda; Bastos, Nsimeyong, and Etug-Ebe in Yaounde; Bonamousadi in Douala, and the urban parishes in Kumba, Buea, and Limbe is very low. These big urban parishes, whose size is measured by the number of Christians and finances, have been consistently led by male pastors. For example, the Azire Congregation, considered as one of the largest in the PCC in terms of membership, has never been led by a female pastor. Recourse to

---

[190] Interview with Rev. Asenek Cynthia.

the policy of appointing associate pastors to assist parish pastors in large congregations further reveals discrimination against female pastors in congregational leadership. The position of associate pastor in large congregations was mostly occupied by female ministers, who were bossed by male pastors.

Ordained women were/are appointed to congregations and parishes as Associate Pastors under the total control of male pastors. The story of Rev. Cynthia Asenek and Rev. Theresia Uso offer an example of associate pastors who served under male pastors. Rev. Asenek was Associate Pastor of Ntaghem Congregation from 2015 to 2019. She was recently appointed to the position of second associate pastor in the Azire Congregation. Rev. Uso served as associate pastor in two urban congregations: Ntamulung in Bamenda and Nsimeyong in Yaounde.[191] This patriarchal practice was also common in congregations where there was a male and female pastor. Rev. Ngwa Agnes notes that in such congregations and parishes, the female pastor is automatically the associate pastor, while the male colleague is the parish pastor, and thus the boss. What made this practice even more disturbing to female pastors was the fact that senior female pastors were bossed by junior male pastors in congregations and parishes. The truism is that the inferior position of associate pastor in congregations and parishes having a male and female pastor has been consistently occupied by women ministers. Little wonder Barrister Nicholas Halle, President of the Christian Men Fellowship (CMF), criticized the low status given to women in the power structure of the PCC. In his presentation at the 2010 Annual Conference of PCC Female Pastors under the theme "The Ministry of Female Pastors within the Changing Times of the PCC", Barrister Halle challenged the female pastors to strive to assert themselves by making their impact felt in the church. He told the female pastors that "Even if you were to be 1000 female pastors in the PCC today, and you do not strive to assert yourselves, your impact will still not be felt."[192]

---

[191] Interview with Rev. Uso Theresia, Yaounde, 13 February 2020.
[192] The Post Newspaper, 22 March 2010.

Since the ordination of pioneer female pastors in 1991, appointive positions in the presbyteries like Presbytery Secretary and Presbytery Treasurer have largely remained in the hands of male pastors, with very few women having the privilege to be appointed. It is a known fact that not more than three of PCC's thirty presbyteries have been headed by women as presbytery secretaries at any given moment. Apart from serving as parish ministers and in ecumenical bureaucratic structures, ordination placed only a few women pastors in positions of authority and power. It was ordination that made it possible for Rev. Martha A. Essem to be appointed as the pioneer female Presbyterial Secretary in the Santa Presbytery. Later in 2004 the PCC got its second female Presbyterial Secretary, when Rev. Angela Ngwateche became the Secretary for the Ndop Presbytery in the Ngoketunje Division of the North West Region. In this Presbytery Rev. Ngwateche had fifty-five congregations under her control along with the over sixteen pastors she had to manage.[193] Good enough she was up to the task, due to the experience she had received as parish pastor in the Manyemen, Nguti and Tiko parishes.

It was in 2009 that the PCC got its third female Presbyterial Secretary in the person of Rev. Mary Ekinde Salle. The latter was appointed to the Meme North Presbytery, where she had to manage thirty-seven congregations and eight pastors.[194] After serving there for about four years, she went back to school to further her theological education which enabled her to earn a Masters in Theology. After leaving school she was reappointed by the Staffing Committee as the Presbyterial Secretary of the Fako South Presbytery in 2014. This time around she had the task of managing forty-five congregations and over nineteen pastors. Three recent appointments to the post of presbytery secretary include Rev. Mary N. Wose in Meme South Presbytery, Rev. Techa Florence in Tubah-Boyo Presbytery, and Rev. Rahel Nukuna Yenchi in Ndop Presbytery. This means that after ordaining women for 29 years, the PCC has made six out of over 80 female pastors presbytery

---

[193] Read *Presbyterian Messenger*, No. 5, July 2004, p. 8.
[194] See 2009 Diary of the PCC.

secretaries. This is clear evidence that the church is still feet-dragging regarding the holding of leadership positions by female pastors. In 2014, one out of the twenty-nine Presbyteries was headed by a woman. This means that they were twenty-eight male presbyterial secretaries and one female presbyterial secretary.[195] This is a disturbing statistic given that the PCC had over 80 female pastors, some of whom had worked with the church for a long time and had a wealth of experience. In this position, clergywomen were able to exercise administrative and spiritual authority over male pastors and the laity. Presently, the PCC has a total of thirty presbyteries with twenty-seven headed by male pastors. This accords credibility to Atem's observation that leadership positions in the PCC which are reserved for the clergy are dominated by male pastors. In an interview with Rev. Rachael Yenchi, Theologian Atem found that female pastors were not really represented in the high offices of the church.[196] This is further evidence that the church practiced bias, prejudice and discrimination in its gender approach which ensured that female pastors were not given the opportunity to be appointed to strategic leadership positions in presbyteries. No wonder top positions such as Presbytery Secretary and Presbytery Treasurer remained a preserve of male pastors since the institutionalization of women's ordination three decades ago. This discrimination against women regarding appointments to these positions evidenced the entrenched nature of gender insensitivity in the PCC.

---

[195] See 2014 Diary of the PCC.
[196] Atem, "Women's Empowerment", p. 41.

Photo 7: Rev. Grace Dashako and Church Elders at her Induction as Presbytery Treasurer, 2018. Source: Rev. Grace Dashalo's Album

Similarly, male pastors were favoured in appointments to prestigious departments in the central administration of the church. The post of Education Secretary is a good example of a high office role never occupied by a woman since the birth of the PCC in 1957. All previous Education Secretaries had been male in a church claiming to pursue a gender policy intended to promote complementarity between its male and female members. The current Secretary of the Education Department is Mola Kale Njie who was appointed in 2012 in replacement of Joseph Che Baboni who held the position from 1998 to 2012. Before Baboni and Kale Njie, the Education Secretary position was previously held by three male Christians like Eugene A. Ekiti (1968-1986), Abel N. Sumbele (1986-1994), and Chrispus Tunyi (1994-1997). It was a prestigious post of responsibility given that the Education Secretary coordinated all primary and secondary schools managed by the PCC. The Education Secretary was also in charge of transfers and recruitment of staff among other functions. This consistent appointment of only men to the post of Education Secretary resulted in the male domination of administrative positions in PCC secondary schools, especially the post of principal. In 2006 during the tenure of Baboni, there were fifteen secondary schools with only two led by female principals: Che Christina of PSS Nkwen and Kimah Constantine of PCHS Kumbo. In June 2012 when Kale Njie appointed new principals at the helm of secondary schools, only two of the nineteen secondary schools were headed by female principals, namely Lydia Penre of PCHS Azire and Kimah Constantine of PSS Mankon. Of the five Managers of schools that were appointed, there were two women, namely Nku Queen Rose and Ndip Martha.[197]

The post of National Secretary for Communication was consistently occupied by men like Rev. Nyansako-ni-Nku, Rev. Achowah Umenei, Rev. Edward Lekunze, Ikome Samuel Mbela, and the current Secretary, Rev. Mokoko Mbue Thomas. Never was a woman pastor appointed to this prestigious position in the central administration of the church. However, a few women were appointed to low office positions in the Communication Department. In 2017 for instance, Rev. Geraldine Fobang was appointed as the pioneer female Station Manager of the Christian Broadcasting Service (CBS) Radio Buea. Born in 1974, Rev. Geraldine Fobang graduated from the Presbyterian Theological Seminary (PTS) in Kumba in 2006. Ordained in 2008, she served in various congregations and parishes after which she was appointed Chief of Programmes at the Christian Broadcasting Service Radio Buea. The latter position together with her Bachelor of Technology in Journalism and Mass Communication obviously prepared her for appointment as Station Manager in 2017. Earlier, Rev. Perpetua Fonki had served as Communication Officer for the North West Region.

Similarly, the administration of the Health Department largely remained an all-male affair. Among other things, the Health Department strove to provide healthcare services wherever and whenever possible, and under appropriate conditions in a supplementary and complementary rather than competitive manner, and in compliance with all statutes governing healthcare delivery in

---

[197]Chronicle Newspaper, July 3, 2012.

Cameroon. While the proper administration of the department required the complementary engagement of competent male and female members of the church, top administrative positions in this department were consistently occupied by male Christians. In fact, women in leadership are in the minority in the entire power structure of the Health Department. From the inception of the department, only men successively occupied the position of Health Service Secretary: Nellis van der Stoep, Walter Zumbrennen, Jeremiah Ayangwe Ozimba, Ako-Egbe James Takor, and Nubed Godlove Tanyi.

Overall, it is obvious that ordained women in the PCC often found it difficult to be appointed to leadership positions. While a majority of them served as chaplains and parish pastors, very few were appointed to head larger congregations (Bastos, Nsimeyong, Bonamoussadi, Ntamulung, Azire, among others) and influential parishes and presbyteries. This is evidence of entrenched conservatism and a prevailing unwillingness, especially among male pastors, to allow female pastors to access leadership positions in the church. The male-dominated Staffing Committee charged with appointments in the church was, no doubt, comprised of powerful conservatives who endorsed the marginalization of female pastors. Evidence suggests that opposition to the leadership of ordained women was high among members of the Staffing Committee, which was chaired by the Moderator. But it would be erroneous to think that opposition to the appointment of female pastors to leadership positions came solely from the Staffing Committee. The successive moderators and synod clerks of the church since 1991 when the first female pastors were ordained did not take any bold step to appoint ordained women to important leadership positions. The Moderator plays an important role when it comes to appointments in the PCC. Moderators such as Henry Awasum, Nyansako-ni-Nku, Festus Asana, and Samuel Fonki had in separate ways encouraged the marginalization of female pastors. It is difficult to understand why in 2019 Rt. Rev. Samuel Fonki was heading a church with only three of its thirty presbyteries having female presbytery secretaries. The complicity of the moderators in the marginalization of female pastors is no longer to be doubted. This yields the thinking that the PCC opened its ordained ministry to women but put restrictions on their access to leadership positions. This discrimination was also an open violation of the 2003 gender policy which called for recourse to a non-discriminatory practice of employment and appointments to leadership positions of the church.[198]

Reactions to Female Pastors' Leadership Marginalization

Female pastors were not indifferent to their marginalization in the power structure of the PCC. In March 2010, during the Annual Conference of Female Pastors of the PCC, Rev. Ngwa Agnes, President of the Conference, lamented the marginalization of women pastors in the leadership structures of the church. Acknowledging the desire by female pastors to play a greater role in the church, she emphasized that women pastors wanted to see a change with their situation. "The Female Pastors' Conference", declared Rev. Ngwa Agnes, "wants to see that female pastors are no longer left behind. Our male counterparts are the ones who are projected as pastors of the PCC. They are many of them and they are everywhere. We are not only few, but are being pushed behind."[199]

---

[198] For details, read Presbyterian Church in Cameroon Gender Policy, 2003.
[199] Read The Post Newspaper, 22 March 2010.

Photo 8: Rev. Agnes Ngwa, Pioneer President of PCC Female Pastors' Conference. Source: Rev. Agnes Ngwa's Album

Later in October 2016 during the occasion of the 25th Anniversary of Women in the Ministry of Word and Sacrament in Kumba, the President of the PCC Female Pastors' Conference, Rev. Ngwa Agnes, openly urged the Moderator, Rt. Rev. Samuel Fonki, to appoint women pastors to key offices in the church like the National Sunday School Office, National Youth Office, Dean of the Seminary, Principals of colleges, managers of hospitals and businesses operated by the church. In reaction to this request, the Moderator stressed the commitment of the PCC to allow women to make their unique contributions to the betterment of society. He further observed that "female pastors have a key role to play; not as antagonists or competitors with men but as co-workers with men in God's vineyard."[200] Sadly, the side-lining of women in top appointive positions raised by the spokesperson of female pastors was not addressed by the Moderator. This probably explains why

---

[200] Read The SUN Newspaper, 17 October 2016.

the marginalization of female pastors in appointments to key positions has persisted under Rt. Rev. Samuel Fonki's tenure as Moderator. Obviously, Rt. Rev. Fonki inherited this culture of marginalizing clergywomen in executive structures from previous moderators: Henry Awasom, Nyansako-Ni-Nku, and Festus Asana. Rev. Awasum ordained pioneer female pastors in the early 1990s and decided to place them at the margins of power.[201] Throughout his tenure which spanned from 1985 to 1999, all executive structures of the PCC remained the preserve of men. Female pastors served either as chaplains or parish pastors mostly in rural areas. This overt discrimination against clergywomen was continued by Rt. Rev. Nku from 1999 to 2009. He violated the church's gender policy by ensuring that only a few female pastors were appointed to positions of responsibility.

The female pastors we interviewed expressed their desire to see more ordained women as Presbytery Secretaries, Presbytery Treasurers, executive heads of the church's departments, managers of the church's businesses, heads of educational and health institutions and as members of synod committees for the sake of the PCC becoming one whole church where ordained women are given the freedom to fulfil their pastoral and leadership gifts.[202] Some went as far as stressing that hard-line conservatives, most of whom are male pastors, need to abandon patriarchal beliefs and consider scriptural basis of God's call and approval of women as leaders in the church. Rev. Agnes Ngwa consistently used her position as President of PCC Female Pastors Conference to openly advocate for a gender sensitive leadership in the PCC. She questioned the assumption that women cannot be proportionately involved in decision-making structures of the church, and emphasizes that practical measures have to be taken to address

---

[201] Born on 6 October 1938 in Mankon, Rev. Awasom obtained the First School Leaving Certificate in 1956 from the Basel Mission School Mbengwi. He worked as a Catechist before obtaining admission into the Presbyterian Theological College Nyasoso in 1963. He graduated in 1963 and held various pastoral and administrative functions before his election as Moderator in 1985.

[202] Interview with Rev. Asenek Cynthia, Rev. Uso Theresia, and Rev. Ndiforngu Onorine.

gender imbalances within the church's governance structures.[203] Another critique of biases against female pastors in PCC's governance structures is Rev. Azange Margaret. She considers gender inequality, which is a defining feature of PCC's power structure, as detrimental to the growth of the church. She advocates recourse, through gender policy reforms, to a culture of complementary roles of male and female pastors.[204]

Photo 9: Female Pastors pose with Moderator, Synod Clerk and Secretary of PCC, 2016. Source: PCC Central Archive and Library, Buea, Cameroon

It emerges from the views of the above critiques that female pastors suffered marginalization and veiled oppression from men in congregations, parishes, presbyteries, and within the central governance structures of the church. The majority of female pastors remained relegated to inferior leadership positions as they were obstructed from holding high offices in the church. Sadly, the existence of the Female Pastors' Conference and ongoing opposing voices to biases against ordained women were futile efforts that were unable to cause the nearly all-male leadership of the PCC to fully involve women in the power structure of the church. The 2003

---

[203] Interview with Rev. Ngwa Aganes.
[204] Interview with Rev. Azange Margaret.

gender policy which required the leaders of the church to ensure that appointments to leadership positions where gender-sensitive was grossly contravened. Obviously, the church is not yet ready to abolish gender hierarchies and discrimination which have kept female pastors at the margins of its power structure. Yet, the PCC participated in the WCC's Ecumenical Decade in Solidarity with Women, 1988-1998 and continuously sent delegates to women's empowerment workshops organized by Mission 21 (former Basel Mission). As demonstrated already, the ecumenical decade and workshops were not able to address female pastors' lack of power in the PCC. In June 2019, participants at the Women's Pre-Synod of Mission 21 found that entrenched structural barriers were still limiting women's access to decision-making in Mission 21's partner churches. The statement released by the Pre-Synod emphasized the dilemmas of female pastors: "In some contexts, access to the ordained ministry is denied to women and even in churches where this possibility exists, women struggle to be treated in a fair way and remain subordinated to men's leadership."[205] The PCC fits squarely into this description. Its female pastors' lack of leadership is yet to be addressed by the church's male-dominated leadership. Female elders were also subjected to similar subordination, and their sad story is told in the next chapter.

---

[205] Read Message from the Women's Pre-Synod of Mission 21, Basel, 26 June 2029, In *Women's Letter*, No. 56, 2019/2020.

Chapter 7

Female Eldership in the PCC

Eldership is one of the rare spheres in which women are prominent in the power structure of the Presbyterian Church in Cameroon. Although the Presbyterian Church in Cameroon originated as a patriarchal institution with limited opportunities for female leadership, its recourse to an inclusive policy has placed many women in eldership roles in the church's congregations. Female elders, just like their male counterparts, had a certain amount of power and influence in each PCC congregation. The PCC inherited eldership as a non-ordained ministry role from the Basel Mission. Even though there was entrenched patriarchy and women's marginalization in the Basel Mission era, eldership was gender sensitive as it was opened to men and women[206] whose responsibilities ranged from preparing couples for Christian marriage, moral guidance, counselling of backsliders, collection of alms, to spiritual care. Elders worked collaboratively with ordained indigenous pastors and evangelists in congregations. According to Guy Alexander Thomas, elders were informal leaders in several Basel Mission congregations, stressing that qualification for eldership required weeks of preparation in training camps and retreats. He notes that "elders were, jointly with the teacher-catechists-in-charge, responsible for shaping the moral economy of the congregations. And this moral economy constituted the foundation for the transformation of converts into recognized adherents of the church."[207]

The PCC inherited a generous attitude towards women's eldership roles from the Basel Mission. Female eldership was further entrenched in the PCC thanks to its gender equality policy

---

[206] Basel Mission's admission of women into eldership was probably anchored on the fact that the concession was considered non-threatening to the male leadership. This explains why arguments against women pastors persisted given that this could upset the all-male leadership policy of the Basel Mission.

[207] Thomas, 2001, p. 231.

which came on the heels of increased requests for women's participation in the life of the church. It was clearly established that the participation of women in eldership roles is biblically legitimized as it does not conflict with scriptural interpretation. Women were seen by the Synod of the church as being able to fulfil the requirements for the eldership listed in 1 Timothy verse 3. Phrased differently, the office of elder is not gender specific and qualified women were encouraged to contest for elections to become elders. However, it is important to stress that there is no universal acceptance of women's participation in eldership roles. Some churches have placed a ban on female elders on grounds that the Bible does not recognize the existence of women as elders.[208] They seemingly ignore the biblical antecedent for women as apostles, deacons, and prophets in the early church.

Church eldership is presented in this chapter as one of the rare spheres in which women were prominent in the power structure of the PCC. It is argued in this chapter that although patriarchy remained entrenched in the PCC system, women's participation in the eldership revealed the remarkable gifts and skills they possessed. This is a clear case of how male-female complementarity can be beneficial to church governance and growth. To better articulate this argument, the chapter opens with a discussion on the requirements for the eldership. It further examines the responsibilities of female elders and their participation in decision-making structures of the church. A final section analyses the limitations of eldership as a tool for women's association with the church's power structure.

The Process of Choosing Elders

The PCC was generous towards women's participation in eldership roles. The process of choosing elders was gender sensitive, with equal opportunities offered to male and female Christians. In the PCC, it was the congregation that determined the

---

[208] For a full discussion on the scriptural debate on the validity of female elders, see Jamin Andrew Hubner, "A New Case for Female Elders: An Analytical Reformed-Evangelical Approach", PhD Thesis in Theology, University of South Africa, 2013.

number of elders it needed, depending on its size. Elders were chosen through elections for a renewable five-year term of office. The constitution of the PCC provided that, after every five years, there was reorganization within the church and the mandate of elders ended for new ones to be elected. Some were usually re-elected since there was no limit to the number of terms an elder stood for election. As a matter of fact, male and female Christians could serve as elders as long as they worked well, and the people desired them enough to be re-elected. The Constitution emphasized in its Article 47 that "An elder may be male or female, married or unmarried, spiritually mature, and of reasonable age, and who has been a member in good standing in the congregation for not less than three years."[209] Thus, women were given the opportunity to be elected as elders on condition that they fulfilled the qualifications laid down in the Constitution. This section seeks to demonstrate how this gender sensitive procedure made it possible for many women to become elders in all PCC congregations.

Elders were therefore elected from suitable members of the congregation through an open election conducted after every five years. The election was conducted by a Selection Committee set up by the Congregational Meeting. The Constitution of the PCC required that Christians be allowed to nominate persons they deemed fit for the eldership. All nominations were published by the Selection Committee in preparation for the election proper. Mbamoh Simon, an elder in the CCAST Complex Congregation in Bambili, stressed that the selection procedure was gender sensitive as no restrictions were placed on the nomination of women.[210] The key qualifications to be fulfilled for nomination included God's call and gifts of the Holy Spirit. It was also a requirement for candidates to be able to teach, be above reproach, sensible, dignified, hospitable, and gentle. Simply put, potential elders were expected to possess moral integrity, knowledge of the Bible, managerial skills, and a sincere pastoral concern. Article 46 of the 1998 Constitution summarized these qualifications as follows: "To be eligible for

---

[209] For details on the conditions governing the election of elders, see Constitution of the Presbyterian Church in Cameroon, 1998, pp. 20-28.
[210] Interview with Elder Mbamoh Simon, Bambili, 7 February 2020.

election as an Elder, a member of a congregation shall be a full and participating communicant whose life and character are estimated to be exemplary in keeping with the Holy Scriptures as recorded in 1 Timothy 3:1; Titus 1:5-9."[211] The Selection Committee advised Christians to nominate only those who possessed these qualifications. These qualifications, it should be stressed, were possessed by both men and women. Little wonder many women were usually nominated for election as elders. Women were recognized as having been called by the Holy Spirit to serve as elders. Nominations for the office of elder were gender friendly, as women were always shortlisted for election. There was scarcely an all-male list of nominees published by the Selection Committee in any congregation.

Nominations were followed by elections in the Congregational Meeting. The latter was comprised of all members of a given congregation who were empowered to elect members to serve as elders. The election was preceded by the publication of the list of nominated candidates by the Selection Committee. Those who were elected could serve as elders for longer than five years on re-election. The congregation then pledged to respect elected elders who were charged with a plethora of responsibilities. Since the birth of the PCC in 1957, many women have been elected and dedicated into the eldership.

In 2019 for instance, more women than men were elected as elders in most PCC congregations. In the Barakwe Congregation in the Meta Presbytery, three of the five elected elders were women. Reacting to the election in the Meta Presbytery, Elder Frida Mbong noted that "in all the congregations, women have been leading. Most of the elders are women."[212] However, the success of women in eldership election was at times associated with the high rate of bribery and vote buying which have gained prominence in the PCC. According to Isidore Abah, eldership elections were plagued by vices like bribery and buying of the electorate. He further reports how a member of the PCC Action Transparency observed on

---

[211] Constitution of the Presbyterian Church in Cameroon, 1998.
[212] Interview with Frida Mbong, Bamenda, 20 December 2019.

condition of anonymity that election malpractices stained the selection of elders, stressing that "It is very common in our congregations today to see people fighting, raining abuses on each other, some even go as far as blackmailing, witch-hunting and sometimes refusing to talk to their fellow brethren in the same congregations because of the quest for eldership in the church."[213] These problems notwithstanding, the stark reality is that the election and dedication of women as elders came with opportunities for them to participate in the leadership structures of the church.

Responsibilities of Elders

Women, just like their male counterparts, legitimately served as church elders. Their chief responsibility was to assist the pastor in the management of the congregation. They were empowered to perform an aura of functions like serving within pews during worship services, supervising the activities of Christian groups, teaching of catechumens and Sunday School, preserving communion vessels, and assisting in administering Holy Communion. It was also the responsibility of elders to settle misunderstandings and quarrels between Christians and to resolve matrimonial disputes. The winning of non-Christians for Christ also featured among the duties of elders as they were called upon to proclaim the Gospel to non-Christians. The Constitution stresses that "The task of elders is to be, in their whole behaviour, a good example to both Christians and non-Christians. It shall be their zeal to attend Divine Services, congregational meetings and other gatherings in the Church, hallow the Lord's Day, sacrifice and pray for the advancement of the gospel, and be God's witnesses before other members of the congregation."[214] The most important duty of the elder was to follow the will of Christ for the Church.

It emerges from the foregoing responsibilities that elders where called by God to a special vocation and office within the church. They worked collegially with the ordained pastors to watch over the flock placed under their charge. In short, they ensured that God's

---

[213] Isidore Abah, "Bribery, Vote Buying Infiltrate the PCC, *The Post Newspaper*, 21 May 2014.
[214] Constitution of the Presbyterian Church in Cameroon, 1998.

word was purely preached, the sacraments rightly ministered, and the discipline within the congregation maintained. This emphasis on the administration of discipline, word, and sacrament in the congregation offered female elders an opportunity to participate in the governance of the church. Elder Lilian Njalla Quan explains that eldership is an indispensable office in PCC congregations given the key roles assigned to those who are elected. She notes that elders' role in the administration of discipline, word, and sacrament positioned them at the centre of power in congregational leadership.[215] "The role of elders in the Presbyterian Church in Cameroon is crucial," says Joseph Ndong who fellowships in the Azire Congregation in Bamenda.[216] Certainly, eldership was a major office in the Presbyterian Church in Cameroon, and women took advantage of its responsibilities to gain access into decision-making structures of the church from the Session of the congregation all through to the General Synod. The remaining sections of this chapter will reveal how women's admission to eldership enabled female elders to express their gifts of leadership within the church.

Female Elders in Decision-Making

The gender-sensitive nature of eldership permitted women to access decision-making structures of the Presbyterian Church in Cameroon from the congregation all through to the Synod. At the congregational level, eldership made it possible for women to be prominent in the Session which was the executive organ of the congregational meeting. The latter was comprised of all members of the congregation, and it was responsible for overseeing the entire life and mission of the congregation. The functions of the governing organs of the congregation were enshrined in Article 61 of the Constitution. The Session was the executive organ of the congregational meeting, with a membership that consisted of the pastor in charge, elected elders, and other elected officials of the congregational meeting. The organ was responsible for the spiritual oversight of the congregation, the maintenance of order and

---

[215] Interview with Elder Simon Mbamoh.
[216] Interview with Joseph Ndong, Bamenda, 8 February 2020.

discipline, the administration of congregational property and finances among other duties. Officers of the Session were elected by the congregational meeting and were comprised of the pastor in charge as ex-officio, the Chairperson, the Vice Chairperson, the Secretary, the Treasurer and the Finance Secretary. While the Chairperson and Vice-Chairperson were elected from among the elders, the Secretary, Treasurer, and Finance Secretary could be elected from either elders or from suitable members of the congregation. The existence of these congregational leadership positions in the Session and the congregation at large facilitated the involvement of female elders in the administration of the church.

In many congregations of the PCC, female elders served in the Session as Congregational Chairpersons, Vice-Chairpersons, Secretaries, Treasurers, and Finance Secretaries. As elders, women stepped into new leadership roles in congregations were they formally sat in the pews to be led by male pastors and elders. They attended and chaired Session meetings and took decisions that affected the entire congregation. This is evidence that the entrenched pattern of a nearly all-male congregational leadership in the PCC was giving way to a more inclusive and gender sensitive leadership. This shift at the lowest level of the church's power structure, though intended, was fed by the desire of local Christian women to exercise roles previously occupied by men. Besides occupying key positions in the Session, female elders played other roles in the congregation by assisting Christians in their reception of the word. They were involved in teaching and sowing the seed of the word, ensuring that special attention was given to members who had gone astray. They also proclaimed the Gospel to non-Christians and cared for Christian children whose parents failed to live up to the vows they made when their children were baptized as infants. Clearly, the period when women cleaned and cooked in the church and merely sat in pews during worship services was brought to an end by their inclusion in the eldership.

From the 1980s when the WCC's Ecumenical Decade in Solidarity with Women was launched, there was hardly a PCC congregation without female elders. These congregations depended on the labours of male and female elders who provided the services that were required for the proper functioning of the church. "The commitment of female elders to the administration of the sacraments and pastoral care," notes Emilia Tamungang, former elder in the Mulang Congregation, "kept congregations alive."[217] Elder Emilia Tamungang adds that "women were endowed with leadership skills which enabled them to be elevated to eldership roles in their congregations." The stark reality is that inclusion of women in eldership increased the percentage of women on congregations' governing boards, with a resultant efficacy in congregational governance and output. In fact, the PCC was using the gifts of men and women to better manage its congregations and to preach the Word. To put it another way, the church affirmed through its gender-friendly eldership that both men and women were indispensable for the health and ministry of the church. Female elders found appropriate places to use their leadership gifts within the congregation.

There are hundreds of examples of female elders who participated in the leadership of congregations in exceptional ways. It is necessary to make an excursion into the practical connection between eldership and women's participation in the power structure of the church as narrated by female elders. Such life histories, I believe, can accord credibility to the contention that the election and dedication of women as elders exposed them to leadership roles in the church. Matina Tangie insists that her membership in the Session of the Mambu Congregation and other leadership positions were the direct result of being elected as an elder by the Congregational Meeting. She served as an elder in the Mambu Congregation for ten years, from 2009 to 2019. This female elder was successfully re-elected in 2014 because she performed her roles effectively in ways that maintained the congregation on a growth path. She participated in pastoral care, proclaimed the Gospel of Christ, served in the pews during service, shared communion, supervised activities of church groups, and attended Session meetings.

---

[217] Interview with Emilia Tamungang, Bamenda, 20 June 2019.

Gladys Shang Viban has served as Elder in the Presbyterian Church, Bastos Congregation since 2004. Serving as Elder in the Bastos Congregation exposed Gladys Viban to leadership roles in the congregation. She was involved in varied areas of Kingdom service: Music Ministry (with the then Junior Choir – Now the Transformational Youth Choir), Youth Elder, church programs and events coordinator, sanctuary decorations and decorum, and Secretary of the congregation for 10 years; just to mention these. Her successful participation in congregational leadership anchored on the wide and varied experiences she had gained as Elder. These experiences spanned from spiritual growth and maturity to personal development, leadership skills and the purpose of service in God's vineyard.[218] "I have learned the value of compassionate service, servant leadership, listening skills, and above all that availability is the key to ALL service," said Elder Gladys Viban. She inherited a love for the eldership and the church as a whole from her mother, Elder Olive Shang and from Elder Lydia Belle Effimba. Elder Gladys notes how her mother inspired her to take interest in church leadership, emphasizing that "as a mother and an elder of PCC Bastos, and President of the CWF Bastos; as producer of one of the longest running radio programs of the CRTV (Calling the Women) she has left and is still leaving a mark on my trajectory in the church and has shaped the lives of many women nationwide."

Gladys Viban, in other words, absorbed the dedication of her mother and Elder Lydia Effimba's mentorship to take interest in church leadership. She then worked hard as Elder, doing what many women have done in the church, using eldership to access a congregational power structure which had been dominated by men. Little wonder her re-election into eldership in 2009, 2014 and 2019 was mostly non-incidental, from the nomination process or pre-selection process to the actual elections. "I cannot say with exact figures and numbers, but I always featured among the top five during the pre-selection and after the elections," Gladys Viban remembers, "except for the most recent elections which were

---

[218] Gladys Shang Viban, Reply to Questionnaire "Female Eldership in the PCC", Yaounde, 4 March 2020.

checkered by a lot of misinformation, malice and misgivings, as was witnessed even at the national level of the PCC Synod elections." By exercising her eldership and ensuing congregational leadership functions with devotion and commitment, Elder Gladys Viban was overwhelmingly elected as Chairperson of East Mungo North Presbytery in 2014. In her capacity as Chairperson, Elder Gladys Viban ensured that the over 52 congregations of the presbytery were properly managed. Working closely with the Presbyterial Secretary and other officials of the Presbytery Committee, Elder Gladys recorded some commendable contributions to the growth of the Presbytery and the church at large. "When we took office in 2014 our mission was couched in the vision of the Moderator of the PCC- The Rt. Rev. Fonki Samuel Forba - to be: Transformed Transformers," Gladys said. "In this direction, we used transformation as a cross-cutting dynamic for church growth and church health in our Presbytery. Our vision focused on Purposeful Transformation to stimulate impact through spiritual empowerment, church planting, financial stewardship and capacity building for Pastors and congregational leadership - to engender this as a shared vision and to motivate the Christians of the East Mungo North Presbytery to embrace that vision."[219]

Elder Gladys and her team sought to reshape the narrative and thinking of the East Mungo North Presbytery across the board. The Pastors had workshops to hone and harness their spiritual awareness, pastoral comportment, collegiality, team spirit and professionalism. This in turn trickled down to congregational leadership and then to the Christians. Accruing from this governance approach were achievements in the spheres of membership, infrastructure, land acquisition, and financial stewardship. From 2014-2018, membership growth rose from 25,000 to about 30.000, with an accompanying growth of congregations from 34 to 52. In the Yaounde area alone, Elder Gladys Viban led a team that succeeded in planting congregations/Prayer cells in Emana, Odja, Akok Ndoe, Nyom, Mbankolo, Nkoabang, and Mfou. Sunday School/Young

---

[219] Ibid.

Presbyterians also witnessed an increase in enrolment from 2674 to 5130. Regarding infrastructural development in the East Mungo North Presbytery, a mission secondary school went operational in Mfou while an ultra-modern health facility was opened at Nsimeyong in Yaounde. In 2018, the East Mungo North Presbytery contributed an extra 20 million FCFA to the central church.

These unprecedented achievements recorded by the East Mungo North Presbytery in the areas of spiritual, infrastructural and financial growth were products of a female leadership. Before her election as Presbytery Chairperson, Elder Gladys Shang had garnered broad expertise and knowledge, established vital networks and contact base which she used to improve on the management of the presbytery. She is described by HOFNA, an NGO charged with the empowerment of women, girls and their communities, as someone with "solid experience in supervisory roles in areas of project conception, management, execution and monitoring, and rigorous work ethics that will help any institution and organization meet their objective in an efficient and timely fashion." It is obvious that the PCC was able to tap from Elder Gladys' experience to attain growth in many spheres. After obtaining a Bachelor of Arts and a Master of Arts in Foreign Languages and Literatures from the Washington State University, Pullman (Washington) in 1979 and 1982 respectively, Gladys Viban proceeded to the University of Montreal in Canada where she obtained a Master of Arts in Translation in 1987. In addition to these academic strides, Gladys received training in Project and Proposal Writing in 1990. She also obtained a diploma in Public Administration and Management from the Higher Institute of Public Management, Yaounde in 1998.[220]

---

[220] For more information on the biography of Gladys Shang Viban, read Vanessa Munge Mbong, "Yaah Gladys Shang Viban: Promoting Gender Equity in Cameroon", *Success Story*, No. 007, March 2008, p. 14.

Photo 10: Elder Gladys Shang Viban, Chairperson, East Mungo North Presbytery. Source: Gladys Shang's Online Album

Gladys Viban's contribution to the growth of the East Mungo North Presbytery is evidence that she put her expertise at the service of the PCC. Beyond the presbytery level, Gladys Viban was/is a member of Synod which is the supreme governing body of the PCC. Besides, she currently seats in the Synod Executive Committee which implements important resolutions taken by the Synod. Clearly, Gladys Viban's involvement in the eldership of the Church contributed in enabling her to access the supreme power organ of the PCC. Thanks to the eldership, Gladys, like other women, has been able to serve the PCC from the congregational level right up to the most supreme organ of the church. The Synod, it should be stressed, is charged with addressing issues affecting the entire church. The Synod elected the moderator and synod clerk and addressed theological issues, appointments, healthcare, education, church businesses, ecumenical partnerships, infrastructural development, and many other things relating to church governance. Considering that Gladys Viban served in both the Synod and Synod Executive Committee, she, no doubt, played a frontline role in decision-making and execution in the church.

A similar example is that of Elder Lilian Njalla Quan whose eldership came with opportunities for participation in the power structure of the church. Being an elder moulded and empowered Lilian Njalla Quan with some leadership qualities. She first became an elder in the PCC Beach Congregation in Limbe in 2004. Lilian Njalla Quan stressed that being elected as an elder came with leadership opportunities in the church, especially at the congregational level. "As an elder and member of Beach Congregation Session", says Elder Lilian, "my work consisted of cleaning and preparing the church premises for Sunday and special services, helping the pastor(s) in serving communion and performing other church duties like marking communion cards, teaching catechumen classes to prepare candidates for baptism and confirmation. I also organized meetings with Christians in my neighbourhood every three months. During this time, we did some Bible study and I explained what was not understood in church at a particular time."[221]

It was this commitment to eldership that enabled Elder Lilian to serve as Congregational Chairperson in Beach Limbe Congregation for two terms of five years each. In this position, Elder Lilian chaired Session meetings, and she ensured that the congregation was maintained in the path of spiritual, financial and infrastructural advancement. During her first term as Congregational Chairperson, Elder Lilian introduced the culture of uniform outfit for elders, which was won under the robes. Other congregations in the Fako South Presbytery copied this example by also introducing uniforms for their elders. To this should be added the fact that Lilian encouraged other female elders to have a voice in decision-making in the congregation. The exercise of power in the Beach Limbe

---

[221] Lilian Njalla Quan, Reply to Questionnaire "Female Eldership in the PCC", Yaounde, 20 February 2020.

Congregation thus ceased to be male-dominated. There were more women in the Session than men, and decision-making was consensual. Under Elder Lilian's leadership, women's voices were heard in all local church matters, including finances and infrastructure development. To put it another way, Beach Limbe became an inclusive congregation, where men and women worked collegially for the growth of the church.

By expressing her leadership gifts in ways that were beneficial to the Beach Limbe Congregation, Elder Lilian was elected as pioneer female Presbytery Chairperson of Fako South Presbytery in 2014. The election to this higher office came with more leadership opportunities as she had to manage a presbytery of 50 congregations. Lilian's first five-year term was incredible, owing to the achievements which accrued from her leadership at the helm of the Fako South Presbytery. Little wonder Christians are so generous in their evaluation of the work carried out by the Presbytery governing staff under the headship of Elder Lilian Njalla Quan. George Etuge, a former member of Beach Limbe Congregation, described Elder Lilian as "a female Christian leader who leads with integrity, inclusivity and accountability."[222] Among other things, Elder Lilian initiated a Congregational Chairpersons meeting which brought together chairpersons from the 50 congregations of the Fako South Presbytery. It was at such meetings that problems facing various congregations were discussed and solutions sought from pastors and other persons who could be of help. "Such meetings", says Elder Lilian, "served as forums for harmonization of programs and proper management of the presbytery."[223] She achieved good outcomes in her role as Presbytery Chairperson and was re-elected for a second term in 2019 on grounds of these contributions to the growth of the Fako South Presbytery.

As Presbytery Chairperson, Elder Lilian was/is member of the supreme governing organ of the church, the Synod. Delegates represent their presbyteries at the synod, which operates on the basis of collegiality. Each presbytery is represented in synod by

---

[222] Interview with George Etuge, Bamenda, 10 March 2020.
[223] Lilian Njalla Quan, Reply to Questionnaire "Female Eldership in the PCC", Yaounde, 20 February 2020.

three delegates (presbytery chairperson, presbytery secretary and the synod representative). This collegiality permits the voices of female delegates to be heard during deliberative sessions of the synod. Elder Lilian attended synod meetings as one of the delegates from the Fako South Presbytery and made valuable contributions during deliberations on matters relating to various departments of the church: education, health, evangelism, etc. It is interesting to stress that Elder Lilian's participation in church decision-making institutions from the Session of the congregation all through to the Synod positioned her as a role model for many Christian women. This probably urged her to seek to achieve above expectations in any role. Her impact in the PCC, as evaluated by one female Christian who begged to remain anonymous, "is one of significance and excellence." Elder Lilian notes that her achievements as Congregational Chairperson, Presbytery Chairperson and as Synod member were products of the motivation and guidance she received from mentors, especially Elder Ida Mallett. "I admire and see Mrs Ida Mallett", says Elder Lilian, "a very dedicated elder, activist, and a great voice for women's empowerment in the PCC, as a role model."[224]

How Elder Ida Mallett became a role model for many women in the PCC is traced to her contributions to the empowerment of women in the church. Ida Mallett studied in Basel Mission schools at Nyasoso and Kumba in the late 1930s and early 40s before passing through Edgerley Memorial School in Calabar. She was later trained as a teacher at the Teacher Training College Shagamu, Nigeria.[225] In addition to her teaching career, Mallett played a frontline role in the organization of women's work in the Basel Mission, which at that time was unfortunately limited to domestic science. When the Basel Mission Church in Cameroon gained independence as the PCC in 1957, Ida Mallett became a promoter of women's empowerment for leadership in the church. She advocated powerfully for the inclusion of women in the ordained ministry of the church. As member of the Committee of the

---

[224] Ibid.
[225] Thomas, 2001, p. 213.

Ministry, she consistently lobbied for the admission of women into the Presbyterian Theological Seminary in Kumba. Her pressure yielded in 1988 when the pioneer female candidates were admitted into the seminary to be trained and ordained as pastors. Elder Lilian Njalla Quan notes that "Ida Mallett helped with her foreign friends and partners to build the very first girls' hostel in the PCC in Limbe. It was used as the first hostel for Presbyterian Girls' Secondary School Limbe, and presently it is being used by our medical department as a hospital."[226] These contributions to the growth of the PCC earned Mallett the Certificate of Meritorious Service at the Silver Jubilee of the church in 1982. She was also recognized with a Certificate for Outstanding Contributions towards the growth of the PCC on the occasion of the Basel Mission's Centenary in 1986.[227]

Elder Justine Abeng is another woman who used her eldership to access institutional power in the PCC. She held numerous positions of great leadership in the church. Elder Justine served the church at the frontline for more than 25 years. Born into a Christian family and baptized into the Basel Mission Church in a tender age, Justine Abeng rose from an ordinary Christian to become an elder in the Bonamoussadi Congregation in the East Mungo South Presbytery. The loyalty and commitment she manifested as an elder propelled her to occupy leading positions at various levels of the church's power structure: congregation, presbytery, and synod. She was a committed member of the Bonamoussadi Congregation, whose roots are traced to 1969 when it started as a prayer cell. In 1970, the prayer cell gained the status of a congregation under the cover of *Eglise Evangélique du Cameroun* (EEC), PCC's ecumenical partner. Later in 1989, the Bonamoussadi Congregation came under the direct administration of the PCC under the newly created East Mungo Presbytery.[228] The foundation stone of the church was laid in 1990 by the Moderator of the PCC, Very Rev. Henry A.

---

[226] Lilian Njalla Quan, Reply to Questionnaire "Female Eldership in the PCC", Yaounde, 20 February 2020.
[227] Thomas, 2001, p. 214.
[228] This was PCC's pioneer presbytery in the French-speaking zone of Cameroon, and it covered the eight administrative provinces in this part of the country.

Awasom.[229] This was the congregation which Justine Abeng joined in 1990 and worked hard for it to grow numerically and spiritually. Working closely with other women, particularly Elizabeth Samkoh, she constituted the CWF group in the congregation and was eventually elected as its president.

In 1996 when the Bonamoussadi Congregation became the seat of the newly created East Mungo South Presbytery which was carved out from the East Mungo Presbytery, Elder Justine Abeng worked committedly with other elders towards the growth of the young presbytery. This commitment helped Justine to serve two terms as Vice Chairperson of the presbytery from 2004 to 2014. Elder Justine served in this administrative position in collaboration with pastors and elders such as Rev. Samuel Fonki, Rev. Ignatius Jum, Rev. Daniel Mokake Kulu, and Elder Abiyah Moise. This enabled the number of congregations and Christians in the presbytery to increase in an unprecedented manner. These achievements did not go unnoticed by the central administration of the church. Little wonder Elder Justine became a member of the Synod Executive Committee, where she served for ten years before retiring from active service in 2015. As member of the prestigious Synod Executive Committee, Elder Justine brought a rare female voice into decision-making and implementation in the church, given that her opinion on issues such as the creation of new congregations and presbyteries and the management of church schools and health facilities was sought. She participated in the making of policies that helped in shaping the church in many spheres. The Synod Executive Committee, it should be stressed, oversees the implementation of church policies defined by the Synod. This fascinating institution serves the church in many ways. It plays an important role in the election of moderators and synod clerks and executes decisions on important issues in the spheres of health, education, businesses, ecumenism, and communication.

At the international level, Elder Justine served in the World Council of Churches (WCC) as a Commissioner of Churches in the

---

[229] Samuel Fonki, "Facts about East Mungo South Presbytery 29th September 1996 till 2006", in Jonas N. Dah, ed., *Presbyterian Church in Cameroon: 50 Years of Selfhood 1957-2007*, Limbe, Presprint, 2007, p. 93.

International Affairs Committee, during which she visited many countries including Brazil, Norway, China and Switzerland. Her membership in the International Affairs Committee was made possible by her commitment in the PCC. Elder Justine's services to the church at the congregational, presbytery, and synod levels caused the leadership of the PCC to recommend her to the WCC. During a special church service at the Bonamoussadi Congregation of the PCC to celebrate Elder Justine's life of service to the Lord and the PCC for over 25 years, Rt. Rev. Festus Asana, PCC's former moderator, said he was so impressed by Justine's character, when they worked together for many years in the church, including trips they made abroad in the service of the PCC. Rt. Rev. Asana stressed that "We took note of her honest attitude and frank talk. She would present the truth firmly, but calmly, no matter the situation. She faced some very tough challenges in life, but maintained her faith and calm."[230] On his part, the Chairperson of the Bonamoussadi Congregation, Thaddeus Fon, said "the Christians were finding it difficult to see the congregation without Justine at the frontline." Without doubt, Elder Justine stands tall as a healthy role model for younger women in the PCC. Her contribution to the growth of the PCC cannot be gainsaid and stands as evidence that the absence of restrictions against women in eldership increased their presence in the power structures of the church.

Elder Elizabeth Mbiwan's leadership journey in the PCC is also fascinating and rich. Born in 1929 to Thomas Mbongo, a catechist and Sophie Namondo, Elizabeth was baptized in 1930 as an infant and was nurtured as a Christian in the Buea Congregation of the Basel Mission Church in Southern Cameroons. Elder Elizabeth attended Basel Mission Girls School in Victoria before proceeding to the Teachers Grade Three Training School in Oron, Nigeria. After completing her studies in this institution, she returned to Cameroon and taught in the Basel Mission Girls School Victoria for one year and enrolled in Umuahia Teachers Training College in

---

[230] For details on Rt. Rev. Festus Asana's remarks about Elder Justine, read *The Post Newspaper*, 9 February 2015.

Nigeria. Upon her graduation, she resumed teaching at the Basel Mission Girls School Victoria. She served the church as Sunday School teacher, choir mistress, elder, and CWF leader. As a Sunday School teacher, Ma Mbiwan, as she was widely known, offered Biblical knowledge and grounding in the faith to young Christians of the Presbyterian Church in Cameroon. Tall and slim, Ma Mbiwan, as described by Rt. Rev. Nyansako-ni-Nku, "was exquisite in beauty, refined in manners, diligent in her faith and elegant in her gait."[231] As an Elder, Elizabeth Mbiwan contributed to the growth of the church in Yaounde and Buea. Peter Mafany Musonge recalls her contribution to the church, stressing that "she was a strong, devoted and committed Christian of the Presbyterian Church in Cameroon; she led many to Christ including children and family members."[232]

---

[231] Nyansako-ni-Nku, Sermon Delivered at the Funeral of Elizabeth Mbiwan on 14 September 2012.
[232] Peter Mafany Musonge, Tribute to Elizabeth Mbiwan, September 2012.

Photo 11: Elder Elizabeth Mbiwan, Teacher at Basel Mission Girls' School, Victoria. Source: PCC Central Archive and Library, Buea, Cameroon

Besides these prominent female leaders, there are several lesser known others serving in congregations and presbyteries whose stories are worth telling. Christina Yah is well known in the Ntigi Congregation, Tubah-Boyo Presbytery. She served as an elder in the congregation for fifteen years since 2004. During this period, she was active in the executive structure of the congregation as member of Session, Vice Chairperson and Chairperson of the congregation. Eldership, says Christina Yah, "helped me to gain self-control, patience and tolerance. Without these qualities, an elder or anybody in a post of responsibility cannot succeed. I have always come up with a vision and stood firm on it and at a long run, the Christians worked together with me because I sacrificed a lot."[233] These qualities, vision and collaboration of the Christians enabled Christina Yah to contribute towards the growth of the Ntigi Congregation. During her tenure, work on the church building continued unperturbed. She worked closely with her executive and bought chairs, canopies, a band and piano for the church. Through her, the Session applied for a parish status which was granted by the central administration of the church. The successful transformation of the Akou Prayer Cell into a congregation was thanks to the efforts of Elder Christina and her collaborators. The spiritual and numerical growth of the Ntigi Congregation and the Tubah-Boyo Presbytery in general, notes Elder Christina, are products of shared leadership between men and women. She singles out male and female elders such as Victor Tuijah, Gideon Tantoh, Cecilia Mofor, and Frida Ambanasom as people who toiled for the progress of the PCC in this part of the country. The last two female elders have served successively as Presbytery Chairpersons and members of Synod. The current leadership of the Tubah-Boyo Presbytery is significantly dominated by women given that the Presbyterial Secretary and Presbytery Chairperson are women, namely Rev. Florence Tache and Elder Frida Ambanasom. Besides, the number of women in eldership in this presbytery outweighs men. In fact, ten of the fifteen congregations in the presbytery are headed by female chairpersons.

There is a similar trend in the Mezam and Meta Presbyteries. Mezam Presbytery which is home to the largest congregations in the PCC has a female Chairperson and many female congregational chairpersons. The Meta Presbytery has had Elder Catherine Njweng Tamanji as Presbytery Chairperson since 2014. This female mathematics teacher doubles as Chairperson in the Mbengwi Station Congregation. "These positions", says Elder Catherine, "have given me room to contribute to the growth of the congregation, presbytery and the church as a whole. Attending Synod meetings chaired by the Moderator enhanced my growth and

---

[233] Interview with Elder Christina Yah, Bambili, 8 February 2020.

improved my leadership."[234] In Elder Catherine's assessment, "the PCC has empowered women for leadership in all areas that you can think of. If women do not sit up, they have themselves to blame." Little wonder she thanks the PCC for giving women the opportunity to work as elders, emphasizing that "Women are allowed to express their views and contribute to the growth of the church."

It emerges from the foregoing life histories of female elders that eldership is one of the rare sectors with equal gender relations. This has brought many women into various roles of leadership in the power structure of the church. This female agency in the governance of the PCC would not have existed if not for the gender sensitive eldership system, which permitted women to become elders. The significant growth the PCC has recorded in the last four decades as evidenced by the number of Christians, congregations, presbyteries, schools, healthcare facilities, businesses and especially its expansion to Europe and North America is partly due to the presence of female elders in its executive structures. Slowly, the church is abandoning the false belief that a woman's place is in the home. "Should female elders suddenly vanish from the scene", notes Elder Bertha Sume Mukwele, Kumba Presbytery Chairperson, "the church will probably cease to grow."[235] The evidence this chapter has uncovered on women's involvement in the power structures of the church accords credence to Elder Bertha's claim. Clearly, eldership has brought women to the frontline of leadership, but not without shortcomings.

Limitations of Eldership as a Tool for Women's Empowerment for Leadership

Although the PCC has used eldership to enable women express their leadership abilities in the church, women are not uniformly represented in the hierarchical power structures. While the involvement of female elders in congregational leadership is robust, their participation in higher executive structures of the church is insignificant when compared with roles played by their male

---

[234] Interview with Elder Catherine Njweng Tamanji, Mbengwi, 10 February 2020.
[235] Interview with Mukwele Bertha Sume, Kumba, 23 February 2020.

counterparts. According to Elder Gladys Viban, the huge presence and achievements of women in church leadership has sadly not been reflected above congregational level. "There has been some improvement at the congregational level, actually I can say much improvement," says Elder Gladys, who however goes on to observe that "if we were to go by numerical strength, output and dedication, we should have at least a 50/50 breakdown at all levels." Simply put, Elder Gladys is putting forth the argument that the numerical strength, output and commitment of female elders and women as a whole ought to have yielded a gender balance in the executive structures of the PCC. Female elders enjoy a comfortable majority and have carried out their duties with a lot of devotion and commitment. Unfortunately, this gender balance is yet to progress beyond the congregational level, which is the lowest power structure in the church. These elders in congregational leadership, most of whom are women, do not receive any salary or allowance from the Church (with the exception of the congregational pastors) and therefore usually shoulder their expenses like telephone calls, transportation, and other needs related to their functions in the congregation.

Elder Christina Yah is therefore right when she says that the Synod which is the supreme power structure in the PCC is dominated by men. All presbytery chairpersons are members of Synod and only about 25% are women. Statistically therefore, there are seven female presbytery chairpersons and 23 males in synod. Women's marginalization in synod is aggravated by the fact that all thirty presbyterial secretaries, only three of whom are women, are members of this supreme executive structure. Another source of marginalization of women at synod level is the fact that most of the synod representatives drawn from the presbyteries are male. Clearly, the domination of leadership at the presbytery level by men amounts to a prominent male voice in synod. This underutilization of female elders' potentials represents an impediment to the growth of the church. No wonder Elder Gladys Viban believes that "the health and growth of the PCC will be determined by the degree of involvement of women in the church at all levels."[236] It is therefore necessary for the church to encourage women to take interest in leadership. They should use their numerical strength in the pews to place more elders at the helm of congregations and presbyteries. This is the easiest means through which the percentage of women in synod can be increased. Other higher echelons of the church's hierarchy such as Synod Executive and heads of various departments can be accessed by female elders if they make it their priority. Regrettably, leadership of the various departments such as health, education, presprint, prescraft, presbook as well as some central administrative positions like financial secretary and development secretary are accessed only through appointments made by the Moderator. For the church to benefit more from female elders' leadership gifts, the Moderator should place them in positions of responsibility. The church needs to commit itself to the policy of gender balance in its executive structures for this to happen. Also, troubling is the fact that elders are restricted from vying for the positions of moderator and synod clerk which are the preserve of ordained ministers. Even female pastors, as discussed already, have not been able to access these positions despite their eligibility. The Emmanuel Sisters, whose presence in the church is traced to 1971 when its lone nunnery or convent was established in Bafut, are also discriminated in the power structure of the PCC. This is the subject of the next chapter.

---

[236] Gladys Shang Viban, Reply to Questionnaire "Female Eldership in the PCC", Yaounde, 4 March 2020.

Chapter 8

Called to Serve: Nuns in the Presbyterian Church in Cameroon

Since 1975, female members of the Presbyterian Church in Cameroon have had the option of becoming nuns following the opening of the Emmanuel Sisterhood. Founded by Sister Madeleine-Marie Handy and operated by the Presbyterian Church in Cameroon, the convent offered female Presbyterians an opportunity for training as sisters and to contribute to the growth of the church and the society as a whole. It has ever since admitted and trained women as nuns who were expected to play influential roles in the life of the church and society at large. The establishment of the convent came on the heels of debates on women's role in the power structures of the church. This pioneering initiative in Protestant monasticism in Africa was preceded by the knocking down of laws barring women from the ordained ministry of the PCC. Both reforms eventually brought into existence two categories of women in the church, namely, the female pastors and nuns. The latter, it was hoped by feminists in the church, would play an active role in the life of the PCC. Many Christians saw the presence of nuns as a rare opportunity for women to share with men in the decision-making in the church as well as in other spheres of ministry like education and health. The main goal of this chapter is to examine the extent to which the existence of the Emmanuel Sisterhood has enabled nuns to play active roles in the PCC. I argue in the chapter that although nuns of the Emmanuel Sisterhood responded to the human and societal needs of Presbyterians and non-Presbyterians, they were consistently placed at the margins of church leadership. The vowed sisters were not assigned to positions of responsibility and their leadership roles were mostly limited to the administration of the convent. Just like the female pastors, Emmanuel Sisters did not question the institutional structures that perpetuated their marginalization in the church. Simply put, the nuns were meek servants who consistently displayed submission to the church patriarchy.

Genesis of the Emmanuel Sisterhood in Bafut

The Emmanuel Sisterhood in Bafut originated from diverse sources. The determination of Madeleine-Marie Handy to become a nun alongside PCC's commitment to embrace monasticism was one of the contributing factors to the creation of the convent. Handy originated from Makak in the Centre Region of Cameroon and was born in 1932[237]. After completing her secondary education, the French colonial government granted her a scholarship to study nursing in France in 1951. While in France, she developed interest in theology with the hope of becoming a nun. Consequently, Handy was admitted into the Deaconesses Sisterhood in Paris, France where she studied nursing and theology. In November 1952, a spiritual retreat involving deaconesses from across France was held in the sisterhood under the theme "Our consecration is a total consecration". The insistence of the officiating clergy, Pastor Bourque, that all sisters must belong entirely to God motivated the young Handy to develop more interest in becoming a nun[238]. This was when she informed her family back in Cameroon about her decision to train as a sister. Although her family frowned at the decision, Handy pursued her training. When she visited Cameroon in 1958 for holidays, she successfully persuaded her family, and obtained her father's permission to continue with the training. Handy's father declared that "Let us dedicate our daughter to God. We merely wanted to see her commitment. She is not seized from our hands, we voluntarily give her away.[239]" Two years afterwards, Handy completed her training and was consecrated as a sister on 6 November 1960. From this moment, she took the decision to

---

[237] Jonas N. Dah, *Christianity and Tradition in Bafut-Tubah 1911-2011* (Bamenda: Presbyterian Church in Cameroon Department for Men's Work, 2011), p. 93.

[238] A. P. Ashu, "Celibacy and Religious Order of the Presbyterian Church in Cameroon", Bachelor Diss., Presbyterian Theological Seminary Kumba, 2002, p. 29.

[239] Emmanuel Sisterhood Archives Bafut (ESAB), Monastic Life in the Presbyterian Church in Cameroon, p. 2.

return to Cameroon with the hope of eventually opening a community.

When she returned to Cameroon in 1967, the *Eglise Presbytérienne du Cameroun (EPC)* employed her in the Department of Christian Education. Later in 1971, Sister Handy's family offered her a piece of land in Makak on which she began a community with some sisters dispatched by the Deaconesses Sisterhood. This pioneer Protestant religious community in Cameroon was given the name Bethany Sisters[240]. But the authorities of EPC did not welcome the community in their church. They argued that it was abnormal for a Protestant church to operate a community. Besides, the Makak people, especially Presbyterians did everything to keep their female children away from the community. It was therefore difficult for the Bethany Sisters to pursue their activities in Makak under the EPC[241]. It was against this backdrop that Sister Handy started exploring how the community could be placed under a different Protestant church.

In 1973, Sister Handy submitted an application to the authorities of the PCC in which she requested for permission for her community to operate under their church. After receiving the appeal, the Moderator of the PCC, Rt. Rev. J.C. Kangsen and Rev. Aaron Su visited the Bethany Sisters in Makak. Confronted with the problems of the sisters, the Moderator resolved that the issue be discussed in the Synod Meeting of March 1974. So, the General Secretary of EPC, Rev. Jonas Bokagne and Sister Handy were invited to the Synod Meeting in an effort to find a lasting solution to the problems plaguing the young community. During this Synod Meeting which held in Bamenda from 28 to 30 March 1974, the application and problems between the EPC and Bethany Sisters were examined. The Synod then resolved to create a committee comprising Rev. Gerhard Vohringer, Rev. Gerhard Rhim, L. Miesch and Rt. Rev. Kangsen to insightfully study Sister Handy's

---

[240] Ashu, "Celibacy", pp. 30-31.
[241] Judith Nyemb and Nche Henuck, "Emmanuel Sisterhood Bafut," in *The Centenary of the Gospel in Bafut-Tubah Presbytery 1911-2011*, ed. Joseph Mfonyam, Bamenda, Unique Printers, 2011, p. 179.

appeal[242]. The committee visited the Bethany Sisters in Makak and advised that the PCC should consider Sister Handy's application. This urged the Synod Committee to resolve in its meeting of April 1974 that Sister Handy and her community be transferred to the PCC. In addition, the General Secretary of the EPC, Rev. Bokagne, welcomed the decision of the Synod Committee by officially approving that the community should be affiliated to the PCC[243].

The decision by the PCC to operate a monastery was not surprising given that the church had developed interest in monastic life a few years after gaining independence from the Basel Mission. It should be stressed that Rt. Rev. Kangsen visited a Roman Catholic seminary in Germany in 1971 and admired the lifestyle of the seminarians. Besides, Rev. Gerhard Rhim, a missionary of Lutheran background who worked with the PCC from 1962 to 1982 as an ecumenical co-worker sent by the Basel Mission was a celibate. His presence in the PCC especially during the Synod meeting of March 1974 might have influenced the authorities of the church to embrace monasticism. Rev. Rhim even acknowledged that he was once dispatched to Europe alongside Moderator Kangsen to visit some religious communities and to explore ways of inviting them to establish a monastery in Cameroon to be operated by the PCC[244]. During their stay in Europe, they visited Protestant monasteries like the Evangelical Sisterhood of Mary, Christ Brotherhood, Community of Jesuhausen, and Christ Bearers. But, as reported by Rev. Kangsen and Rev. Rhim after returning to Cameroon, the communities they visited were not willing to open branches in Cameroon. So, Sister Handy's application came at a time when the PCC was eager to open a monastery.

After accepting to operate the community, the authorities of the PCC began looking for a comfortable site for the Bethany Sisters. The Director of the Presbyterian Church Centre, Mankon-Bamenda, Rev. Su, was commissioned to negotiate land from the

---

[242] Presbyterian Church in Cameroon Central Archive Buea (PCCCAB), File No 2772, Minutes of Synod Meeting held in Kumba, 28-30 March 1974.
[243] PCCCAB, File No 2772, Minutes of Synod Committee Meeting held in Buea in April 1974.
[244] Interview with Rev. Gerhard Rhim, Limbe, 2011.

traditional authorities of the Bafut Fondom. After Rev. Su's discussion with Fon Abumbi II of Bafut in late 1974, the latter offered a vast parcel of land at Agyati-Bafut to host the community. It was within this context that four sisters (Judith Nyemb, Anne Etienne, Heidi Rubli and Madeleine- Marie Handy) left Makak and arrived in Bafut on 18 February 1975[245]. They were later joined by sisters Martha, Paul, and Rachael. The sisters were provided temporal accommodation by Rev. Su. It was only in 1976 that they relocated to the permanent site following the construction of two thatch houses. These nuns, considering the suitability of the site, accepted to perform service to God there. On 19 December 1976, the Moderator of the PCC, Rev. Kangsen, inaugurated the nunnery under a new name, Emmanuel Sisterhood[246].

Emmanuel Sisterhood was a community of Presbyterian women religious who expressed their mission of being freed and assisting others to enjoy freedom in service to God's people. Originally, the mission of the Emmanuel Sisterhood was directed towards perpetual training in view of helping those who feel called to dedicate their lives to Christ. Its key goal was to assist its members and candidates willing to embrace monastic life to be more attached to God by removing all obstacles to loving Christ. So, the major aim of the monastery was prayer, preaching and teaching with the hope of overcoming greed and leading souls to God. No wonder all members of the convent were required to take the vow of renunciation so as to remain committed to God[247]. Besides, the community was to undertake measures aimed at aiding the missionary works of the PCC. According to the founder of the community, Sister Handy, the base of a monastery is its evangelistic life which leads people to renounce life. As time went on and the Emmanuel Sisterhood became firmly established, it extended its aims to include the general welfare of its members and the society as a whole. Thus, it was also to be at the service of mankind

---

[245] Nyemb and Nche, "Emmanuel Sisterhood Bafut", p. 179; Dah, *Christianity and Tradition*, p. 93.

[246] Ibid.

[247] Samuel Kilo, "Emmanuel Sisterhood Bafut: The only Convent in the Presbyterian Church in Cameroon", *Presbyterian Messenger*, No. 2, 2002, p. 13.

through involvement in varied socio-economic activities. Finally, it was to ensure its existence through improved standards following the extension of its activities[248]. The aims of the community were therefore a dynamic process with inbuilt regenerative mechanisms. Overall, the nuns' roles included teaching, ministering to the helpless and nursing. Their core values were deep-seated in the word of God, the operational rules of the convent, and the PCC. This mission and values influenced the community's organization and sources of finances as they responded to dire human situations.

Administrative Structures and Sources of Finances

The administrative structures of Emmanuel Sisterhood evolved with time and circumstances. The community was headed by a Prioress who, in consultation with the other sisters and senior officials of the PCC, ensured the smooth functioning of the institution[249]. The Prioress was empowered to take decisions affecting the community and to represent the institution during Synod Meetings. She was also charged with the duty of convening meetings, negotiating and communicating with partners and reporting all affairs connected with the institution to the Synod Office of the PCC. Sister Madeleine-Marie Handy served as the Prioress of Emmanuel Sisterhood from 1975 to 1999 when she passed away. She was replaced by Sister Judith Nyemb, the current Prioress of the convent[250]. The involvement of the sisterhood in diverse socio-economic activities at the turn of the seventies necessitated the establishment of specialized departments since it obliged the sisters to distribute functions amongst themselves. As a result, a finance department was established and headed by an Account Mistress who managed all the finances of the community. Sister Heidi Rubli held the position of Account Mistress for so many years[251]. There also existed other departments like the post card, sewing, cattle rearing, bakery, and marketing departments. Each department was headed by a manager who ensured its day-to-

---

[248] Ibid.; Interview with Sister Judith Nyemb, Bafut, 2012.
[249] ESAB, Monastic Life in the Presbyterian Church in Cameroon, p. 2.
[250] Interview with Sister Judith Nyemb, Bafut, 2012.
[251] Interview with Sister Angel Sohlee Sighan, Bafut, 2012.

day functioning and reported to the Prioress during meetings. For instance, the Manager of the Guest House Department took care of all guests and acted as the link between the convent and the public. The pioneer Manager of the Guest House Department was Sister Anne Etienne.

The finances required for the day-to-day running of the convent came from varied sources. Originally, all the finances came from the various departments run by the institution. In fact, profit from its commercial activities was an important source of its finances. For example, it earned some money from the sales of cattle and its by-products, postcards, bread, and liturgical material used by some Protestant churches in Cameroon. The community also received special financial donations from well-to-do Presbyterian Christians in and around Bafut. To add, the PCC allocated specific budgets for the convent as circumstances arose[252]. The convent equally obtained funds from friends and ecumenical partners like the Circle of Friends of Emmanuel in Switzerland and the *Communauté des Diaconesses de Reuilly* in France. It was with these finances that the authorities of the monastery strove to attain the spiritual and socio-economic aims of the institution through diverse projects.

Religious Activities of the Monastery

The Emmanuel Sisterhood, as already noted, was aimed at helping its members, candidates and public to be more attached to God by removing all obstacles to loving Christ. So, the main base of the community was commitment to religious issues. Spiritual life in the convent was comprised of prayers, public divine services and retreat related activities. When the convent was moved to Bafut in 1975, it had only six sisters who committed themselves to God's work and took vows like chastity (celibacy), poverty and obedience. The chastity vow required the sisters to offer their hearts to the Lord in an exclusive manner. The vow of poverty required of them to live a life of poverty. Thus, they never had personal property and spent much of their time in the convent. With regard to the vow of obedience, the sisters obeyed Biblical principles alongside rules and

---

[252] Idem; Nyemb and Nche, "Emmanuel Sisterhood Bafut", p. 182.

regulations governing the community. These vows were referred to as Evangelical Counsels[253].

Training of candidates as nuns was an important religious activity in the Emmanuel Sisterhood. The training comprised an intensive study of monastic life and the history of the PCC. Generally, the training had four successive stages. After receiving God's call to become a nun, the person got in contact with the authorities of the institution. The candidate was then invited to spend one year in the community as an aspirant. The next stage, Noviciate, lasted for two years and ended with the taking of a simple vow by the candidate. In the third stage, Temporary Professed, the would-be sister studied for three years which permitted her to enter the final stage. It was at this final stage (fourth) that the student monastic took the last vow and was given a cross to wear. A ring was put on her married finger and she given a white veil indicative of her marriage to Christ. From the second to the fourth stages of the training, candidates wore blue, green, and white gowns respectively. After completing the training, the candidates were consecrated as sisters in a ceremony presided by authorities of the PCC[254]. Since its birth, many women have been consecrated as sisters and the monastery has grown. For example, the first batch of sisters was consecrated on 24 November 1985 by Moderator Henry Awasom. They included Sisters Judith Ngo Nyemb, Joy F. Joy, Jane Manka'a, Ann Emmanuel, Martha Ngo Nge and Regina Shu[255]. Also, Moderator Nyansako-ni-Nku consecrated three sisters on 21 January 2005 in a ceremony that was attended by hundreds of people[256]. The most recent consecration into the convent was in 2015 in a great ceremony overseen by Rt. Rev. Samuel Fonki.

---

[253] Ibid., p. 180.
[254] ESAB, The Community of Emmanuel Sisterhood Silver Jubilee in 1997, p. 4. In 1978, Sister Handy was trained and ordained as the pioneer female pastor of the PCC partly in an effort to boost the religious vocation of the monastery.
[255] Nyemb and Nche, "Emmanuel Sisterhood Bafut", p. 183.
[256] Sigfred Sinior, "Three Presbyterian Sisters make Final Profession", http://www.leffortcamerounais.com/2006/02/three-presbyter.html (Accessed May 10, 2012).

Prayer was also an important religious activity in the convent. Like in other monasteries, prayer was done seven times a day in the Emmanuel Sisterhood. The sisters got up for prayers as early as 4:30 am and went to bed at 8 pm after the evening prayer (compline), and ensured that the convent's daily prayer program was strictly followed. According to the program, the sisters followed seven different types of prayers everyday (Vigils at 4:30 am, Laud at 5:30 am, Terce at 7:20 am, Sext at 12 noon, None at 2:15 pm, Vespers at 5:00 pm, and Compline at 8:00 pm)[257]. During prayers, the nuns took different postures like kneeling, bowing, standing and raising hands up. In addition to this, they meditated, chanted and recited Psalms. People visited the monastery with prayer requests for their loved ones, businesses, examinations, illnesses among others. The nuns addressed such external prayer requests during the 5:30 am and 5:00 pm prayer sessions. Besides, they prayed for the PCC every day during the 7:20 am prayer. Thus, the sisters spent a greater portion of their time raising their arms in prayer, conscious that in this prayerful attitude one obtains victory. These incessant prayers enabled them to spiritually impact the lives of many. Through these prayers, therefore, Presbyterian Christians felt the presence of these monastics wherever their spiritual contribution was needed.

Apart from prayers, the sisters organized divine church services which were opened to the public. The chaplain which was constructed by the sisters was managed by a pastor stationed by the PCC. During such services, the public was not allowed to mingle with the nuns except after the service. It is important to point out that the liturgy used in the Emmanuel Sisterhood during Sunday services slightly differed with that used in the other congregations of the PCC. According to Sister Ruth Laka, the monastery employs the original liturgy of the PCC while the rest of the congregations use a modified liturgy that suits the activities of their services.[258] From 1980 to 2010, nine pastors served in the convent's chaplain. They include Revs. Gerhard Rhim, Dr. David S. Gana, Joe Set Aji-

---

[257] Interview with Sister Ruth Laka (2012), Bafut.
[258] Interview with Sister Ruth Laka.

Mvo, Lucas Asamba, Henry Fomuso, Samuel Kilo, Godlove Nsai, David Mebeng, and Henuck Nche[259]. It is relevant to point out that, prior to PCC's stationing of chaplains in the community, chaplaincy work in the monastery was done by Rev. Sister Handy after her ordination in 1978.

Finally, the Emmanuel Sisterhood set up a Guess House in 1978 with the aim of hosting guests who visited the convent for retreat purposes. The Guest House which was well equipped was opened to the public at all times. The sister charged with the running of the Guest House received guests and provided them all necessary assistance. As recounted by Sister Ruth Laka, the Guest House served a good purpose as it met the spiritual needs of guests through retreat, counselling and reconciliation. Thus, most visitors went to the convent mostly for religious considerations as revealed by the visitors' book of the convent. In January 1999, for example, some six student pastors from the Presbyterian Theological Seminary in Kumba visited the convent for a spiritual ordination retreat. Also, the Mezam Presbytery executive board of the Christian Women Fellowship visited the Emmanuel Sisterhood on 13 February 1999 for a spiritual retreat[260]. At the end of the retreat, the sisters prayed with the women. So, the Guest House received people of diverse backgrounds who sought spiritual solutions to various categories of problems.

Socio-Economic Activities

In monasteries, as earlier noted, religious activities are matched with labour. The nuns in the Emmanuel Sisterhood were massively involved in external labours of the most varied character, not only to sustain the monastery, but also to be able to raise resources with which to assist the poor. But this productive work, argues Nyemb and Nche, was extrinsic to the real essence of the monastery[261]. Since its establishment, the convent has been involved in multiple social and economic works. It operated production units like tailoring workshop, cattle ranch, postcard production, bakery, wafer

---

[259] Interview with Moncha Abongta.
[260] ESAB, Visitors' Book of Emmanuel Sisterhood Bafut.
[261] Nyemb and Nche, "Emmanuel Sisterhood Bafut", pp. 181-182.

department, provision store, farms, and an orphanage. By engaging in socio-economic works, the Emmanuel Sisterhood hoped to improve its lot and the general welfare of its nuns and of the society as a whole.

As concerns cattle rearing, it was introduced in the convent in 1977 by Sister Handy in an effort to check some of the economic problems of the sisters. The sisters purchased a small herd which enabled them to set up a cattle ranch in the monastery. The ranch, which was expected to serve as a source of raw material for the manufacturing of varied products, was managed by Sister Rachael. Apart from serving as a permanent source of meat, the cows in the ranch produced milk from which the sisters manufactured cheese, butter and yogurt. These goods were not only consumed in the monastery, but also sold in markets in and around Bafut. Thus, the cattle ranch was one of the monastery's sources of income. In order to further improve on their quality of life, the sisters kept domestic animals like fowls and pigs. The modern piggery, as noted by Sister Nyemb, is a secured source of protein intake[262].

Apart from cattle rearing, the Emmanuel Sisterhood operated a farm were the sisters cultivated various crops. The farm originated from the necessity to find a solution to the problem of lack of food in the early years of the monastery. Prior to the establishment of the farm, the sisters largely depended on well-wishers for food. Farming effectively started in the community in 1975. In the course of time, following the consecration of many other sisters, the size and productivity of the farm tremendously increased. The sisters cultivated crops such as plantains, sugar cane, pineapple, maize, coco yams, and vegetables. The farm produce was used not only for the sisters' daily food, but also as raw materials for the production of goods like jam, fruits juice, postcards and greeting cards. The pioneer manager of the farm, Sister Anne, collaborated with the authorities of the Presbyterian Rural Training Centre, Mfonta-Bafut to educate the sisters on appropriate agricultural practices.[263]

---

[262] Interview with Sister Judith Nyemb, Bafut, 2012.
[263] Established in 1968 by the PCC, the mission of the Presbyterian Rural Training Centre, Mfonta, was to promote sustainable agriculture in the North West Region of Cameroon through a combined training and extension

Further, the determination of the sisters to render the monastery self-supporting and self-reliant motivated them to set up a tailoring workshop in 1979. This was preceded by the training of some sisters in the art of sewing and designing to enable them run the tailoring workshop. Sister Anne Etienne, who was charged with the management of the workshop, did everything to acquire sewing machines and other equipment needed in the workshop. The Emmanuel Sisterhood's ecumenical partners in Europe (the Circle of Friends of Emmanuel in Switzerland and the *Communauté des Diaconesses de Reuilly* in France) contributed financially and materially towards the construction and equipment of the workshop. This gave the workshop, just like other production units, the potential to enable the monastery gain a self-supporting status. In this workshop, the sisters produced cassocks for pastors and priests, lay preacher gowns, choir gowns, academic robes and liturgical vestments used for the decoration of churches. These goods were displayed in the workshop for pastors, priests, elders, teachers and students. According to Abongta Moncha, most of the cassocks, robes and liturgical vestments used in the PCC are supplied by the sisters in Bafut[264].

The bakery was another important production unit in the Emmanuel Sisterhood. It was opened in 2004 with funds allotted by the Circle of Friends of Emmanuel in Switzerland. In order to ensure its existence, the sisters recruited ten workers to operate the bakery and commercialised its products. The products from the bakery (bread and cakes of all sorts) were not only consumed in the monastery, but also sold in boarding schools and markets in and around Bafut. Apart from the bakery, the Emmanuel Sisterhood operated a wafer department that produced the bread or host used during Eucharist (Lords supper) in all PCC congregations. This sector was established in 1980 through the efforts of Rev. Gerhard Rhim. It was the latter who proposed to the PCC that the nuns in

---

approach for maintaining the yields of crops and livestock. For a history of the centre, see Noela Nwiselie Manka'a, "The Presbyterian Rural Training Centre, Mfonta 1968-2010: A Historical Appraisal", DIPES II Dissertation in History, The University of Bamenda, 2016.

[264] Interview with Moncha Abongta.

Bafut be permitted to produce communion bread for the church. With the consent of the Synod of the PCC, Rev. Rhim worked in collaboration with the sisters and set up the wafer department in 1980. The PCC then compelled all her congregations to purchase communion bread from the Emmanuel Sisterhood[265]. Recently, the Synod authorized the sisters to produce olive oil that is used in the PCC. It is worth pointing out that the sisters were not allowed to supply communion bread and olive oil to any other church.

Also, during the early years, the Emmanuel Sisterhood established a paper department that produced paper from local materials like sugar cane and elephant grass stalk. The sisters then used the sugar cane paper to manufacture greeting cards and postcards of all sorts. Besides, they produced handmade matted pictures printed on sugar cane paper and necklaces from glass beads. These goods were marketed locally and internationally. In an effort to better market all the goods from its production units, the sisters opened a provision store (Magda Shop) in Meta Quarters, Bamenda in 2005[266]. It is in this shop that goods like bread, cakes, cheese, yogurt, butter, milk, postcards, and greeting cards were marketed. The funds emanating from these production units and provision store did not only enable the community to gain a self-supporting status, but also provided it the potential to indulge in social and humanitarian services.

The Emmanuel Sisterhood did a lot to improve the general welfare of orphans and children with disabilities. It all started when an extremely impoverished widow visited the convent during its early years with children asking for assistance. The sisters, despite their financial constraints, did their best to extend financial and material assistance to this family. The children lived in the monastery from where they went to school under the sponsorship of the sisters. By living in the convent for many years, one of the children eventually trained as a sister and was consecrated. The other children are still receiving assistance from the sisters and are on the path to successful professional lives[267]. It was against this

---

[265] Interview with Rev. Gerhard Rhim, Limbe, 2011.
[266] Interview with Sister Ruth Laka, Bafut, 2012.
[267] Interview with Sister Marie-Joel Bongnavti, Bafut, 2012.

backdrop that the sisters envisaged the establishment of an orphanage for handicapped children. Created on 6 October 2009 at Akum, the orphanage trained girls with disabilities in different crafts in an effort to render them self-reliant. Generally, the centre was host to deaf and crippled parentless children. To add, the monastery has been providing health services to the Bafut people. As a matter of fact, Sister Samuella Mban, who trained as a nurse, sponsored works in the Presbyterian Health Centre at Nsem-Bafut.

Sisters' Leadership Role in the Church

The history of nuns assuming leading roles in the executive structures of the PCC is not impressive. Since their inception in the church in 1975, a policy of marginalizing and preventing them from assuming leadership positions has been pursued by the patriarchal hierarchy of the church. With their voices marginalized, sisters could not question their gross underrepresentation in the power structure of the church. The presence of the sisters in the church's power structure has not gone beyond their representation in the Synod. Initially, Emmanuel Sisterhood had one representative in Synod, who usually was the Prioress. Successively, therefore, sisters Madeleine-Marie Handy (1975-1999) and Judith Nyemb (2000-20014) attended Synod Meetings as delegates representing the convent. They usually drew the church's attention to the challenges of the nunnery and also made their voices heard on important issues that were discussed. Recently, especially from when Sister Shalom Kiven assumed the function of Prioress, the nunnery has been sending two delegates to the Synod Meetings. In November 2019 for example, the Prioress Sister Shalom and Sister Angele attended the Synod Meeting and participated in the re-election of Rt. Rev. Samuel Fonki as the Moderator of the church. They also participated in the election of Rev. Hans Miki as new Synod Clerk.[268]

---

[268] Sister Shalom Kiven, Annual Newsletter from the Community of Emmanuel Sisters Bafut for Year 2019.

Photo 12: Sisters at Emmanuel Sisterhood in Bafut
Source: PCC Central Archive and Library, Buea, Cameroon

Emmanuel sisters were also represented in the Presbytery Meeting of the Bafut Presbytery. Their delegates to the Presbytery Meeting usually present a report on the activities and challenges of the convent. They were also given an opportunity to actively participate in this decision-making body by contributing to discussions on matters of health, education, evangelism, among others. Generally, the nuns had a limited voice in the policies and formal administration of the PCC. However, they constituted a special category of people within the PCC and intervened in the spheres of education, health, evangelism and social work. The substantial increase in the membership of the church, which now stands at about 1.5 million, is partly thanks to the pastoral service of the nuns. Also, worth mentioning is the fact that the nuns pressurized the PCC to open its ordained ministry to women. The founder of the nunnery, Sister Handy, urged the PCC to reconsider its position on the ordination of female pastors. She was involved in the meaningful and intense discussions over the role of women with the church. Working closely with another woman, Rev. Ruth

Epting, Sister Handy dragged the debate on the admission of women into the theological college into the Synod. Following Synod's endorsement of women's ordination, Sister Handy was ordained in 1978 as PCC's pioneer female pastor. Today, the church has about 80 female pastors who are associated with its power structure, though mostly at the base.

Pressing Problems

The Emmanuel Sisterhood was affected by a multitude of problems. Most often, the authorities of the monastery took some measures to check these difficulties. The major problem faced by the community was the reluctance of female Presbyterian Christians to be trained as nuns. The sisters faced resistance from female Presbyterians in Bafut and the environs who wanted their female children to get married instead of becoming nuns. Thus, it was very difficult for the sisters to have candidates to train. Given that this problem risked the life of the young monastery, the sisters, with the total backing of the Synod of the PCC, decided to resolve the problem by publicizing the institution. Some sisters were occasionally dispatched to worship in some congregations on Sundays and special days. The Synod also resolved that some sisters be allowed to always accompany the Moderator during some of his tours[269].

The Emmanuel Sisterhood also suffered from the shortage of funds. Its finances were very limited and did not permit the community to meet up with some of its goals. To check this problem, the institution entered into ecumenical relations with the Circle of Friends of Emmanuel in Switzerland and the *Communauté des Diaconesses de Reuilly* in France from whom it occasionally obtained financial assistance. To add, the sisters initiated economic projects (cattle rearing, piggery, sewing, and bakery) with the hope of transforming them into permanent financial assets for the monastery. The foregoing measures alongside others enabled the

---

[269] Ibid.

monastery not only to roll back its financial difficulties, but also to become financially autonomous[270].

Another serious problem that was encountered by the monastery was the lack of potable water. This resulted from the non-extension of the Bafut community water to the monastery. So, the sisters trekked for long distances to fetch water from streams. The sisters solved the problem by constructing a borehole which permitted them to constantly have water. Besides, the land of the monastery was quite often encroached by some Bafut indigenes. This was a serious problem given that the sisters needed this land for economic activities like agriculture and cattle rearing. The sisters therefore identified the need to check such encroachments. They engaged in frank dialogue with such individuals in an effort to protect the monastery's land. In some cases, they contacted the Fon of Bafut and the Bafut Traditional Council. Finally, the Emmanuel Sisterhood suffered from numerous cases of theft from men of the underworld. This resulted to psychological pain in the minds of the sisters. For example, thieves visited the monastery in 2008 and made away with money, a laptop and five cell phones. To prevent further harassments from men of the underworld, the security in and around the monastery was stepped up with the recruitment of some credible security guards[271]

---

[270] Nyemb and Nche, "Emmanuel Sisterhood Bafut", 181-182.
[271] Interview with Sister Marie-Joel Bongnavti, Bafut, 2012.

Chapter 9

Conclusion: Women's Role Reconsidered

Towards the end of the nineteenth century, the Basel Mission commenced its mission work in Cameroon, which among other things focused on the transformation of local women. From 1957, this transformation of women's status was continued by the PCC which had emerged from Basel Mission's ecclesiastical mould. This book has argued that both the Basel Mission and PCC had entrenched patriarchal cultures which contributed in keeping women at the margins of their power structures despite the transformations they were subjected to. Under the weight of patriarchy, the Basel Mission enforced a controversial "Christian home ideal" in Cameroon, which was intended to propagate Western notions of domesticity. From 1886 to 1957, missionary wives and single female missionaries to Cameroon trained women in various fields: motherhood, domestic science, and marriage. Drawn from a female-hostile Western context, domesticity demoted women's status by yielding little or no occupational options and opportunities for local women to participate in the power structures of the Basel Mission. The home thus became the narrowed space for women who had once enjoyed a privileged status in indigenous religious structures. This complicity of the Basel Mission in the demotion of women's status and their subservience in its executive structures characterized the entire missionary era. Women who had played frontline leadership roles in African Traditional Religion became members of a mission church that perpetuated their marginalization and oppression.

In fact, women received a new status often defined in terms of dressing, cooking, and child-rearing; not full participation in church leadership. Plainly put, the diffusion of Western women's emancipation norms by European missionaries narrowed local women's sphere of activity to the home and family, which could be described as the "housewifisation of women." Domesticity skills like laundry, cookery, gardening, hygiene, and sanitation permitted female missionaries to fulfil their task of turning local Christian women into "good" wives and mothers. In missionary women's homes and girls' schools, local women received lessons on women's reproductive and nurturing skills, with emphasis on Christian marriage ideals, childrearing, husband care, and handicrafts. The Basel Mission thus limited women's space which contributed to their near absence in its leadership structures. Clearly, domesticity yielded a pattern of predominantly male leadership in the structures of the Basel Mission in Cameroon.

Little or no participation was available to women in the hierarchical structure of the mission church. From the congregational level all through to the central administration, men were preponderant in structures like Session of the Congregation, District Synod, District Synod Committee, and General Synod. This discrimination could also be explained by the barring of women from participating in the ordained ministry as they could not be trained and engaged as catechists, evangelists, and pastors. Denied power and responsibility, women were subordinated to structures that were in the hands of men who defined and implemented the policies of the church. As emphasized already, catechists, evangelists, and pastors were given leadership responsibilities in congregations, presbyteries, church districts, and central administration of the church. They had influence, responsibility, and hierarchical authority, given that they carried a clerical function in terms of representing people to God and God to people. Women also had limited space in education and healthcare leadership. However, there were isolated cases of local women who were placed in education leadership roles, mostly as teachers and school heads. These were Elizabeth Mbonifor, Ruth Ndando, Sophie Limunga Ndando, Ida Mallett, B. Forbang, and Catherine Musoko.

After close to seventy years of leadership masculinization, the Basel Mission ended its mission enterprise in Cameroon by granting independence to the indigenous church under the name Presbyterian Church in Cameroon. The transition, from which local Christian women were completely excluded, yielded an autonomous indigenous church led by men. It was an all-male General Synod that proclaimed the birth of the PCC on 13 September 1957. This was preceded by a slow transfer of executive responsibilities in Basel Mission's power structure, from the congregational meeting through to the central administration, to Cameroonian pastors, catechists and evangelists, all of whom were men. With such an all-male pioneer leadership, the PCC had therefore inherited an entrenched patriarchal culture from the Basel Mission. Male members of the young Church assumed the power bestowed on them by the founding mission agency, and sought to legitimize the exclusion of women from the Church's leadership.

The PCC continued the controversial empowerment of women along domesticity lines, while ensuring that the power structure was not at their reach. Domesticity skills like laundry, cookery, gardening, hygiene, homecare, Christian marriage ideals, childrearing, husband care, and handicrafts became the hallmark of the Christian Women Fellowship. By acquiring these skills, CWF empowered its members for more space within their homes and families, while unknowingly limiting their access to the church's leadership structure. Although the Basel Mission patriarchal legacy had been inherited and perpetuated by the PCC, growing Christian feminism occasioned internal opposition to women's lack of power. The barring of women from the ordained ministry and their near lack of power were brought under attack. This was a significant shift from the Basel Mission era given that its patriarchal practices coursed unopposed. Caught in this struggle of empowering women and placing them in leadership positions, the PCC opened it ordained ministry to women in 1971, though admission of female candidates into its theological college commenced only in the late 1980s.

This training and ordination of women as pastors was occasioned, no doubt, by the WCC's Ecumenical Decade in Solidarity with women, which spanned from 1988-98. Funds provided by this ecumenical body were injected into the activities of the Women's Work Department and the training of female pastors. Unfortunately, the church's two Women's Work Centres seated in Kumba and Bamenda did not deviate from the domesticity empowerment approach. Despite calls by the WCC and Mission 21 for women to be granted more access to leadership, the WWD and its affiliated structures such as women centres and CWF did not retailor their work towards women's empowerment for leadership. Later in 2003, pressure from ecumenical partners obliged the PCC to acknowledge that women were still at the margins of its leadership structures. This yielded the 2003 gender policy whose implementation was timid, partial, and unsuccessful, and was visible only through the Women's Education and Empowerment Programme (WEEP) launched in 2005. Female pastors, whose number remained inferior to that of male pastors, found it difficult to acquire power and responsibility. While they were/are preponderant in chaplaincy and parish leadership, power in the presbyteries, synod, and synod committee largely remained in the hands of male pastors. Appointments to key departments of the church quite often favoured male pastors. The PCC Female Pastors' Conference, which was created on the premise of checking such discrimination, lacked the capacity to place more women in leadership roles. Little wonder the church is yet to have its pioneer female moderator and synod clerk, while only three of its thirty presbyteries are headed by female presbytery secretaries.

Female elders, however, succeeded in accessing some positions of leadership in the church. Since the purpose of eldership was to involve the laity in church governance, the inclusion of women came with opportunities for them to step into elective positions of responsibility. It revealed the remarkable gifts and skills female elders possessed, which were harnessed for the growth of the church. In all PCC congregations, women became members of the governing body called Session. The latter, in most cases, was headed by women who were elected as Congregational Chairpersons. Some served in the Session as Vice-Chairpersons, Secretaries, Treasurers, and Finance Secretaries. Commitment to the eldership also permitted some women to be elected as Presbytery Chairpersons, which gave them rare access to the Synod, the supreme governing body of the church. These were Gladys Shang Viban, Lilian Njalla Quan, Frida Ambanasom, Esther Tegha, Justine Abeng, Catherine Njweng Tamanji, Bertha Sume Mukwele, among others. But while the involvement of female elders in congregational leadership was robust, their participation in higher executive structures of the church was insignificant when compared with roles played by their male counterparts.

The Emmanuel Sisters, whose presence in the church is traced to 1971 when the lone convent was established, were also discriminated in the power structure of the PCC. Although nuns responded to the human and societal needs of Presbyterians and non-Presbyterians, they were consistently placed at the margins of leadership in the church. Nuns' representation in the Synod made it the lone institutional connection between the PCC and Emmanuel Sisterhood. They were meek servants who consistently displayed submission to the church patriarchy.

Overall, women had limited opportunities to hold administrative positions in the power structures of the Basel Mission and PCC. As a highly patriarchal mission agency, the Basel Mission lacked the necessary structures within which local Christian women could acquire power and responsibility. Its domesticity empowerment approach produced Christian wives who were kept at the margins of the leadership structures. The PCC inherited and perpetuated this patriarchy, and resisted calls for women's inclusion in leadership by its ecumenical partners such as WCC and Mission 21. Thus, not many women were found in the hierarchy of the PCC owing to resistance from male authority. This deprived the church of women's contribution and may explain its long-dragging leadership crises and misuse of funds. In fact, women have not been permitted to put their remarkable gifts and skills at the service of the church. The architects of this exclusion failed to realize that the growth of the church was being stalled by the absence of women in most of its decision-making structures. Trained female pastors, elders, nuns, and CWF members were underrepresented in the church's executive structures. Their power and influence remained largely at the base, with the higher echelons of the church's hierarchy dominated by men.

Clearly, the PCC, just like many other traditional Protestant churches in Africa, failed to respond adequately to the dearth of women in positions of leadership. This is evidence of continuing opposition to the full participation of women in the church, peddled probably by those we may describe as complementarians, who feel that power should not be equitably shared between male and female members of the church. Simply put, complementarians believe that the differentiation of leadership roles should favour men, since women cannot live up to certain tasks of church leadership. Unfortunately, egalitarians who believe that both men and women are suitable for church leadership have always been in the minority. Their advocacy for equal distribution of power has not achieved much as women's underrepresentation in leadership remains the norm.

It is necessary to reconsider the place of women in the PCC in view of bringing them into the mainstream of leadership. Though the PCC has not pursued an exclusive male leadership agenda, its Women have been repressed through discrimination and underrepresentation in leadership structures. The advocacy for the full association of women in PCC's power structure, so far expressed only through timid action by PCC Female Pastors' Conference, is yet to end the consistent overlooking of the 2003 gender policy. For the immediate future, the lack of overt advocacy in the work of the Female Pastors' Conference renders a committed implementation of the 2003 gender policy improbable. At the same time, no female pastor is willing to challenge patriarchy outside the purview of the Conference. Most are still hopeful that the Female Pastors' Conference would one day free them from subordination to the longstanding male leadership. No wonder some think that there are feminist voices in the Conference capable of rolling away biases against female pastors. But a few have lost hope in the capacity of the Conference to end their exclusion from leadership, preferring to objectively describe the institution as "a toothless bulldog." Given this inability to live up to the premise on which it was created, the Female Pastors' Conference needs to rethink its approach and adapt to the hesitation of the current male-dominated structures to place more female pastors in positions of responsibility. In the years ahead, women's representation in the power structure might further shrink, should the Female Pastors' Conference continue with its docility, without rising up against this patriarchal culture.

Female elders, nuns, and the thousands of CWF members also need to end their docile attitude and advocate for the involvement of more women in the leadership of the PCC. Unless nuns and female elders learn to speak up in Synod against restrictions against women, the current male authority would persist for a long time. The few female members of the Synod and Synod Committee, including some who have gained reputation as advocates of women's empowerment, have scarcely challenged the masculinization of these structures. This culture of silence, which has dragged on for decades, has to be broken. Constant declarations by the male authority, especially the Moderator, that the church has placed many women in positions of responsibility, have to be questioned and labelled as baseless. PCC's male leaders are conscious of the international movement to bring more women into church administration, but are exploiting the silence of its female members to hang on. It is time for the PCC to aim at ending gender hierarchies and discrimination. It has to initiate something new capable of rolling away the patriarchal order.

But the current absence of institutions and people with a commitment to eliminate women's lack of power makes the years ahead more challenging for women in the PCC. The most visible failure of the post-ecumenical decade generation of PCC moderators (Henry Awasom, Nyansako-Ni-Nku, Festus Asana, and Samuel Fonki) was their inability to recognize that, unless the gifts and skills of women were fully exploited, the church would not be able to achieve substantial growth. Without the full participation of women, the PCC could run into managerial dilemmas greater than what it currently faces. The poor governance which the current male leadership is accused of, especially the improper use of funds[272] could be addressed through collegial leadership involving men and women. At a time when the PCC is part of a strong international ecumenical network, which is encouraging advocacy for gender mainstreaming, it must prove its willingness to end the

---

[272] For details, read Michael Kpughe Lang, "The Patterns of Corruption in Christian Churches of Cameroon: The Case of the Presbyterian Church in Cameroon", *Transformation: An International Journal of Holistic Mission Studies*, Vol. 31, No. 2, 2014, pp. 132-144.

preponderance of men in leadership. The fact that women dominate the pews, which has been so since the Basel Mission era, is enough reason for their dearth in the power structure to be addressed. According to Suzan Mark, "Women's empowerment is very important in this time of building a better church and a better society."[273] She recommends that churches in Africa should reap women's talents and gifts by placing them in positions of leadership. "Jesus", says Suzan Mark, "respected women and gave them power and strength, just as he did with men."[274] Christians ought to follow this example set by Jesus Christ. The PCC should come to the realization that women can serve in all positions of leadership. All its members, both male and female, should be supported to live out their calling. In fact, placement in positions of church leadership should no longer be determined by gender identities. The time has come for members of the Presbyterian Church in Cameroon to stop believing in a male headship in the church. As Gretchen Ziegenhals puts it, "No role or position in the church is limited to just one gender."[275]

Sadly, many people in PCC's Synod Office[276], including the current Moderator, Rt. Rev. Samuel Fonki, believe that the church has already placed many women in positions of leadership. Responding to a rare request for more female pastors to be placed in top positions by the President of the Female Pastors' Conference, Moderator Samuel Fonki observed, with no backing, that gender identities have never been a hallmark of PCC's power structure. Other Synod Office officials also believe that the church's empowerment of women for leadership is going in the right direction, toward a more gender inclusive church. They do not

---

[273] Suzan Mark, "Empowering Women for a Better Africa/World", *Women's Letter*, No. 55, 2018/2019, 9.
[274] Ibid.
[275] Gretchen Ziegenhals, "Women in Ministry: Beyond the Impasse", In *Women and the Church*, Edited by Robert B. Kruschwitz, *The Centre for Christian Ethics at Baylor University*, 2009, p. 77.
[276] The Synod Office is an institution with a complex bureaucracy, housing central administrative structures of the church such as the Office of the Moderator, the Office of the Synod Clerk and a plethora of departments (Communication, Health, Education, Development, Finance, and Archive).

accept that the church has faltered in the implementation of its women's empowerment policies, insisting rather that power has this far been distributed to both men and women. This flawed assessment, intended or not, places women's future on a bad course. The years ahead may see the limiting of more female pastors, elders, nuns, and CWF members from filling top leadership roles in the church. But a quick shift from docile to radical advocacy, as already pointed out, may push the male authority to take actions capable of ending the underrepresentation of women.

A radical advocacy might come with opportunities for female members of the PCC to demand a fifty-fifty sharing of power. Such a request, if expressed with force and anger, might motivate some male pastors to question the church's position on female leadership. In making such a case, these advocates could build upon women leadership examples in the Bible. "The Bible", as Linder Belleville explains, "does not limit women from filling certain leadership roles." If this is emphasized by Christian feminists, more women will gain consciousness of how they have been kept subservient to male authority. Presently, Synod Office officials are not taking feminism seriously, but this will change as a nearly all-male leadership will not continue to please women. More recently, the church has witnessed a decline in the number of women willing to train as nuns and pastors, probably because of the alienation of these categories of female Presbyterians. Reversing this trend through inclusive leadership is imperative, given its predicted adverse bearing on the church's social and evangelism programmes.

Many churches, including the Roman Catholic Church, have grappled with the issue of women's underrepresentation in positions of leadership. In most of these churches, feminism has brought women into leadership roles as pastors, theologians, elders, and administrators of educational, medical, and humanitarian programmes. International ecumenical bodies in the example of the WCC have pressed for a reconsideration of scriptural justifications for inclusive leadership in Christian organizations. While some churches heeded to feminists' demand for women to be given more leadership opportunities, others have fit-dragged, choosing to act slowly, while still keeping more decision-making positions in male hands. But this struggle, as church history teaches us, will not end any time soon. Women will forever remain a force to reckon with within Christianity, and the future of the church must be shaped taking this reality into consideration. Women, no doubt, will continue to dominate the pews in Christian churches around the globe, and the resistance against their participation in leadership cannot survive in a Third Millennium characterized by radical feminist advocacy. The Presbyterian Church in Cameroon cannot thrive in this millennium without women in the higher echelons of its power structure. Women's consistent underrepresentation in positions of leadership is a trend that needs to be reversed through increased commitment to gender inclusiveness. There is need for its current leadership to believe in the equal worth of its female and male members.

Bibliography

Primary Sources

Archival Materials
a) Presbyterian Church in Cameroon Central Archive and Library, Buea

File No. 22, Grassfield Synod Meetings, 1948-1958.
File No. 723, Minutes of the General Synod, 1948-1957.
File No. 596, Minutes of General Synod Meeting at Buea, April 1954.
File No. 1613, Minutes of the Manyemen Hospital Staff Meeting, 7 February 1958.
File No. 1616, Minutes of Medical Board meeting at Bamenda, 18 September 1968.
File No. 1616, Minutes of Medical Board meeting at Buea on June 1969
File No 2772, Minutes of Synod Meeting held in Kumba, 28-30 March 1974.
File No 2772, Minutes of Synod Committee Meeting held in Buea in April 1974.
Annual Report of the Community of Emmanuel Sisters Bafut, 2019.
Constitution of the Presbyterian Church in Cameroon, 1998.
Constitution of the PCC, 1957.

b) Emmanuel Sisterhood Archives, Bafut

ESAB, Visitors' Book of Emmanuel Sisterhood Bafut.
ESAB, The Community of Emmanuel Sisterhood Silver Jubilee in 1997
ESAB, Monastic Life in the Presbyterian Church in Cameroon

Newspapers
Cameroon-Info-Net, 3 April 2019.
Presbyterian Messenger, No. 5, July 2004.
Eden Newspaper, 25 August 2017.

The Post Newspaper, 22 March 2010.
Read *Presbyterian Messenger*, No. 5, July 2004.
See 2009 Diary of the PCC.
Chronicle Newspaper, July 3, 2012.
The SUN Newspaper, 17 October 2016.

Informants

Akwo Taiheart, Member of Ndau-tse, Interview, Weh, 27 April 2013.

Akwa Miselele, Weh Notable, Interview, Weh, 27 April 2013.

Mbamoh Simon, Elder, P.C.CCAST Complex Bambili, Interview, Bambili, 28 December 2019.

Kum Moses Mughe, Chief Priest of purification rituals in Weh, Interview, Weh, 25 April 2013.

Nnam Christiana, Notable in Weh Chiefdom, Interview, Weh, 22 March 2013.

Big Ejuh, Weh Notable, Interview, Weh, 27 April 2013.

Nkoh Joseph, Finge Notable and Practitioner of Traditional Religion, 86 Years, Interview, Finge, 20 August 2017.

Toh Linus, Teacher and Catholic Christian, 47 Years, Interview, Finge, 20 August 2017.

Beryl Esino, aged 43, Project Coordinator, Interview, Buea, 25 February 2017 (by Ngam Valery Etanefilla).

Wose Mary, WEEP Coordinator, Interview, Buea, 20 February 2019 (by Ngam Valery Etanefilla).

Agbor Gladys, Councillor, Interview, Limbe, 20 February 2017 (by Ngam Valery Etanefilla).

Ndifor Patiance, aged 49 years, SIRDEP Coordinator, Interview, Buea, 22 February 2017 (by Ngam Valery Etanefilla).

Ikome Vivian, aged 48 years, WEEP Board Member, Interview, Buea, 20 February 2017 (by Ngam Valery Etanefilla).

Rev. Dr. Azange Margaret, Female Pastor, Interview, Buea, 23 December 2007 (by Achowah Umenei).

Joseph Cheghe Nang, Christian of the PCC, Interview, Weh, 23 March 2018.

Asenek Cynthia Itih, Rev. Pastor of the PCC, Interview, Bamenda, 7 February 2020.

Uso Theresia, Rev. Pastor of the PCC, Reply to Questionnaire, 13 February 2020.

Ndiforngu Onorine, Rev. Pastor of the PCC, Reply to Questionnaire, 13 February 2020.

Frida Mbong, Christian of the PCC, Interview, Bamenda, 20 December 2019.

Joseph Ndong, Christian of the PCC, Interview, Bamenda, 8 February 2020.

Emilia Tamungang, Christian of the PCC, Interview, Bamenda, 20 June 2019.

Shang Gladys Viban, Chairperson, East Mungo North Presbytery, Reply to Questionnaire "Female Eldership in the PCC", 4 March 2020.

Njalla Quan Lilian, Chairperson, Fako South Presbytery of the PCC, Reply to Questionnaire "Female Eldership in the PCC", 20 February 2020.

Etuge George, Christian of the PCC, Interview, Bamenda, 10 March 2020.

Christina Yah, Former Chairperson, Ntigi Congregation, Reply to Questionnaire, 8 February 2020.

Tamanji Catherine Njweng, Female Elder and Chairperson of Meta Presbytery, Reply to Questionnaire, 10 February 2020.

Mukwele Bertha Sume, Elder and Chairperson, Kumba Presbytery, Reply to Questionnaire, 23 February 2020.

Gerhard Rhim, Rev. Pastor and Former Ecumenical Co-worker to Cameroon, Interview, Limbe, 2011 (by Same Elvis Nkumbe).

Judith Nyemb, Nun at Emmanuel Sisterhood, Interview, Bafut, 14 June 2012 (by Same Elvis Nkumbe).

Angel Sohlee Sighan, Nun at Emmanuel Sisterhood, Interview, Bafut, 14 June 2012 (by Same Elvis Nkumbe).

Sister Ruth Laka, Nun at Emmanuel Sisterhood, Interview, Bafut, 14 June 2012 (by Same Elvis Nkumbe).

Sister Marie-Joel Bongnavti, Nun at Emmanuel Sisterhood, Interview, Bafut, 14 June 2012 (by Same Elvis Nkumbe).

Ruth Epting, Former Lecturer at the Theological Seminary in Kumba, Interview, Chisinau-Moldova, March 2008 (by Martina Heinriche).

Secondary Sources

a. Books

Amadiume, Ifi, *Male Daughters, Female Husbands: Gender and Sex in an African Society*, London, Zed Press, 1987.

Amadiume, Ifi, *Re-Inventing Africa: Matriarchy, Religion, and Culture*, London, Zed Press, 1997.

Anderson, Gerald H., (ed.), *Biographical Dictionary of Christian Missions*, Cambridge, William B. Eerdmans Publishing Company, 1999.

Chilver, E. M. and Kaberry, P. M., *Traditional Bamenda: The Precolonial History and Ethnography of the Bamenda Grassfields*, London, 1967.

Dah, Jonas N., *Christianity and Tradition in Bafut-Tubah 1911-2011*, Bamenda, Presbyterian Church in Cameroon Department for Men's Work, 2011.

Falvey, J. Lindsay, *Religion and Agriculture: Sustainability in Christianity and Buddhism*, Adelaide, The Institute for International Development, 2005, Online: http://www.iid.org, Accessed on 8 May 2014.

Fanso, V. G., *Cameroon History for Secondary Schools and Colleges, Vol. 1, From Prehistoric Times to the Nineteenth Century*, London: Macmillan, 1989.

Finch III, Charles S., *Echoes of the Old Darkland: Themes from the African Eden*, Decatur, GA, Khenti, Incorporated, 1991.

Goldberg, Stevens, *The Inevitability of Patriarchy*, New York, William Morrow & Company, 1973.

Grudem, Wayne, *Evangelical Feminism and Biblical Truth*, Multnomah, Inter Varsity Press, 2004.

Guthrie, Stan, *Missions in the Third Millennium: 21 Key Trends for the 21st Century*, Cumbria, Paternoster Publishing, 2000.

Gwanfogbe, Mathew Basung, *Basel Mission Education in Cameroon, 1886-1968*, Bamenda, Quality Printers, 2018.

Hallden, E., *The Culture Policy of the Basel Mission in the Cameroons 1886-1905*, Lund, Berlingska Boktryckeriet, 1968.

Hunter, Jane, *The Gospel of Gentility: American Women Missionaries in Turn-of-the-Century China*, New Haven and London, Yale University Press, 1984.

Johnstone, Ronald L., *Religion in Society: A Sociology of Religion*, Fourth Edition, New Jersey, Prentice Hall, 1992.

Japinga, L., *Feminism and Christianity: An Essential Guide"*, Nashville, Abingdon Press, 1999.

Kaberry, Phyllis M., *Women of the Grassfields: A Study of the Economic Position of Women in Bamenda, British Cameroons*, New Edition, London, Routledge, 2004.

Kah, Henry Kam, *The Sacred Forest: Gender and Matriliny in the Laimbwe History (Cameroon), C. 1750-2001*, Munster, LIT Verlag, 2015.

Lehman, Edward, *Women's Path into Ministry: Six Major Studies*, Pulpit and Pew Research Reports, No. 1, Fall 2012, www.pulpitandpew.duke.edu, Accessed on 16 August 2014.

Mbuy, Tatah, *The Faith of Our Ancestors: New Perspectives in the Study and Understanding of African Traditional Religion*, Bamenda, Archdiocesan Print Media, 2012.

Mbaku, John Mukum, *Culture and Customs of Cameroon*, London, Greenwood Press, 2005.

Mbiti, John S., *Introduction to African Religions*, London, Heinemann, 1975.

Mougoue, Jacqueline-Bethel, *Gender, Separatist Politics, and Embodied Nationalism in Cameroon*, Michigan, University of Michigan Press, 2019.

Ndi, Anthony, *Mill Hill Missionaries in Southern West Cameroon*, Nairobi, Paulines Publications Africa, 2005.

Nelson, Steven, *From Cameroon to Paris: Mousgoum Architecture In and Out of Africa*, Chicago, Chicago University Press, 2007.

Nkwi, Paul Nchoji, *The German Presence in the Western Grassfields 1891-1913: A German Colonial Account*, Leiden, African Studies Centre, 1989.

Nkwi, Paul Nchoji and Warnier, Jean-Pierre, *Elements for a History of the Western Grassfields*, Yaounde, SOPECAM, 1982.

Nson, Joseph, *The Modern Kom Society: Culture, Customs and Traditions*, Yaounde, Nyaa Publishers, 2015.

Nyansako – Ni – Nku (ed.), *Journey in Faith: The Story of the Presbyterian in Cameroon*, Yaounde, Buma Kor, 1982.

Oakley, Ann, *Sex, Gender and Society* (Revised Edition), Farnham, Surrey, Ashgate, 2015.

Oduyoye, Mercy Amba, *Beads and Strands: Reflections of an African Woman on Christianity in Africa*, Yaounde, Editions Cle, 2002.

Okkenhaug, Inger Marie, ed., *Gender, Race and Religion: Nordic Mission, 1860-1940*, Studia Uppsala, Missionalia Svecana XCI, 2003.

Omgba, B., *Histoire de l'Eglise Catholique au Cameroun*, Yaoundé, SOPECAM, 1985.

Peach, Lucinda Joy, *Women and World Religions*, Paris, Pearson, 2001.

Pourchez, Laurence, *Women's Knowledge: Traditional Medicine and Nature - Mauritius, Reunion and Rodrigues*, Paris, UNESCO, 2017.

Sackey, Brigid, *New Directions in Gender and Religion: The Changing Status of Women in African Independent Churches*, Lanham, MD, Rowan and Littlefield, 2006.

Sill, Ulrike, *Encounters in Quest of Christian Womanhood: The Basel Mission in Pre-and Early Colonial Ghana*, London, Brill, 2010.

Asante, Molefi Kete and Mazama, Ama, eds., *Encyclopedia of African Religion*, London, SAGE Publications Ltd., 2009.

Vubo, Emmanuel Yenshu, ed., *Gender Relations in Cameroon: Multidisciplinary Perspectives*, Bamenda, Langaa RPCIG, 2012.

Werner, Keller, *The History of the Presbyterian Church in Cameroon*, Victoria, Presbook, 1969.

b. Articles and Theses

Abah, Isidore, "Bribery, Vote Buying Infiltrate the PCC", *The Post Newspaper*, 21 May 2014.

Abdekhodaie, Zohreh, "Letty M. Russell: Insights and Challenges of Christian Feminism", Master of Theology Studies Thesis, Waterloo, Ontario, Canada, 2008.

Adams, Melinda, "Colonial Policies and Women's Participation in Public Life: The Case of British Southern Cameroons," *African Studies Quarterly*, Vol. 8, No. 2, 2006.

Adasi, Grace Sintim *et al.*, "Gender Politics and Social Change: The Status of Women Leaders in the Presbyterian Church of Ghana", *Canadian Social Science*, Vol. 9, No. 6, 2013, pp. 105-110.

Adeney, Miriam, "Do Missions Raise or Lower the Status of Women? Conflicting Reports from Africa," In Dana Robert, (ed.), *Gospel Bearers, Gender Barriers: Missionary Women in the Twentieth Century*, Maryknoll NY, Orbis Books, 2002.

Anti, Kenneth Kojo, "Women in African Traditional Religions", Presentation Prepared for the Women's Centre, Eastern Washington University, http://www.mamiwata.com/women.html, Accessed in May 2013.

Arrey, J. A., "Missionary Activities in the Upper Cross River Region: The Basel Mission in the Banyangland 1912-1957", Maitrise Dissertation in History, University of Yaounde, 1991.

Asare-Danso, Seth, "Historical Study of Girl Child Education in Ghana (1828-2014): A Review of Basel Mission Educational Policy," *International Journal of Scientific Research and Management*, Vol. 5, No. 4, 2017, pp. 7437-7448.

Ashu, A. P., "Celibacy and Religious Order of the Presbyterian Church in Cameroon", Bachelor Dissertation in Theology, Presbyterian Theological Seminary Kumba, 2002.

Asongwe, Christian, "Healthcare Delivery in British Southern Cameroons, 1922-1961: A Historical Investigation", PhD Thesis in History, The University of Yaounde I, 2018.

Atem, Gladys Ekone, "Women's Empowerment for Leadership Position Within the Presbyterian Church in Cameroon: A Missiological Exploration", MA Dissertation in Theology, School of Religion and Theology, University of Kwazulu-Natal, 2011.

Baber, H. E., "Feminism and Christian Ethics", Paper Presented at the April 1993 Meeting of SEAD at Virginia Theological Seminary.

Babila, George Fochang, "An Exploration of the Conception of God among the Bali Nyonga and its Impact upon Their Contemporary Christian Practice with Particular Reference to Hymnody and Prayer," Masters Dissertation in Theology, University of KwaZulu Natal, 2004.

Banadzem, Joseph Lukong, Catholicism and Nso' Traditional Beliefs", In Fowla, Ian and Zeitlyn, David, (eds.), *African Crossroads: Intersections between History and Anthropology in Cameroon*, Oxford, Berghahn Books, 1996, pp. 125-140.

Bankole, Katherine Olukemi, "Goddesses" in Asante, Molefi Kete and Mazama, Ama, (eds.), *Encyclopedia of African Religion*, London, SAGE Publications Ltd., 2009, pp. 293-295.

Becker, Sascha and Ludger Woessmann, "Luther and the Girls: Religious Denomination and the Female Education Gap in 19th Century Prussia", *Scandinavian Journal of Economics*, Vol. 110, 2008, pp. 777-805.

Bendroth, Margaret, "Gender and Twentieth-Century Christianity", in Mary Farrell Bednarowski, (ed.), *A People's History of Christianity, Vol. 7, Twentieth-Century Global Christianity*, Minneapolis, Fortress Press, 2008, pp. 307-326.

Betoto, Joseph Ebune, "Missionary Activity in Bakunduland, Cameroon, 1873-1960: An Historical Appraisal," *Global Advanced Research Journal of History, Political Science and International Relations*, Vol. 1, No. 2, 2012, pp. 048-055.

Bettina Beer, "Gender Justice-An Issue of Mission", in Jonas N. Dah, (ed.), *Mission in a Post Missionary Era*, Limbe, Presprint Plc, 2008.

Blackstone, Amy, "Gender Roles and Society", In *Human Ecology: An Encyclopedia of Children, Families, Communities, and Environments*, Edited by Julia R. Miller, Richard M. Lerner, and Lawrence B. Schiamberg, Santa Barbara, CA, ABC-CLIO, 2003, pp. 335-338.

Bowie, Fiona, "Reclaiming Women's Presence", In Fiona Bowie, Deborah Kirkwood and Shirley Ardener, (eds.), *Women and Missions: Past and Present: Anthropological and Historical Perceptions*, London, Bloomsbury Publishing, 1993, pp. 1-19.

Bowie, Fiona, "The Elusive Christian Family: Missionary Attempts to Define Women's Roles: Case Studies from Cameroon", In Fiona Bowie, Deborah Kirkwood and Shirley Ardener, (eds.), *Women and Missions: Past and Present: Anthropological and Historical Perceptions*, London, Bloomsbury Publishing, 1993, pp. 145-164.

Clark Elisabeth A., "Women, Gender, and the Study of Christian History", *Church History*, Vol. 70, No. 3, 2001, pp. 395-426.

Dah, J. N., "Missionary Motivations and Methods: A Critical Examination of the Basel Mission in Cameroon 1886-1914", PhD Thesis in Theology, University of Basel, 1983.

Dah, Jonas, "The Vision and Challenges of an Autonomous Church", In Jonas N. Dah (ed.), *Presbyterian Church in Cameroon: 50 Years of Selfhood*, Limbe, Presprint, 2007), pp. 15-55.

Duncan, Graham A., "South African Presbyterian Women in Leadership in Ministry (1973-2018), *HTS Teologiese Studies/Theological Studies*, Vol. 75, No. 1, 2019.

Eneme, Grace, "Women's Work Department", In Nyansako-Ni-Nku, (ed.), *Journey in Faith: The Story of the Presbyterian Church in Cameroon*, Yaounde, Buma Cor, 1982.

Felix, Paul W., "The Hermeneutics of Evangelical Feminism", *The Master's Seminary Journal*, Vol. 5, No. 2, 1994, pp. 159-184.

Fomukong, Evangeline Ngwa, "Stylistic Appraisal of 'Change' as an Ideology in the Presbyterian Church Day Speeches of Reverend Doctor Festus Ambe Asana, Moderator of the Presbyterian Church in Cameroon", *Journal of Applied Linguistics and Language Research*, Vol. 3, No. 7, 2016, pp. 132-150.

Fonchingong, Charles Che, "Religiosity and Existentialist Approach to Poverty in North-West Cameroon", *International Journal of Religion and Society*, Vol. 4, No. 3, 2013, pp. 165-179.

Fonki, Samuel, "Facts about East Mungo South Presbytery 29th September 1996 till 2006", In Jonas N. Dah, (ed.), *Presbyterian Church in Cameroon: 50 Years of Selfhood 1957-2007*, Limbe, Presprint, 2007.

Gana, E., "History of CWF as a Development Agent", In Gana E., ed., *Christian Women Move on in Hope and Hope in Christ*, Limbe, Presbook Print, pp. 69-69.

Geary, Christraud, "Traditional Societies and Associations in We (North West Province, Cameroon)", *Paideuma*, no 25, 1979, pp. 53-72.

Golder, Roswitha, "Farewell to Ruth Epting", *Women's Letter*, No. 53, October 2016.

Gordon, April A., "Women and Development", In April A. Gordon and Gordon, Donald L. (eds.), *Understanding*

Contemporary Africa, Second Edition, London, Lynne Rienner Publishers, 1996, pp. 249-272.

Haas, Waltraud, "The 19th Century Basel Mission and its Women Missionaries," *Mission History from the Woman's View*, No. 13, Basel, Basel Mission, 1989.

Halsall, Paul, "Early Western Civilization under the Sign of Gender: Europe and the Mediterranean", In Teresa A. Meade and Merry E. Wiesner-Hanks (eds.), *A Companion to Gender History*, Melbourne, Blackwell Publishing Ltd, 2005, pp. 285-304.

Hubner, Jamin Andrew, "A New Case for Female Elders: An Analytical Reformed-Evangelical Approach", PhD Thesis in Theology, University of South Africa, 2013.

Jenkins, Paul, "Everyday Life Encapsulated? Two Photographs Concerning Women and the Basel Mission in West Africa, c. 1900," *Journal of African Cultural Studies*, Vol. 15, No. 1, 2002, pp. 45-60.

Kasomo, Daniel, "The Role of Women in the Church in Africa," *International Journal of Sociology and Anthropology*, Vol. 2, No. 6, 2010, pp. 126-139.

Kilo, Samuel, "Emmanuel Sisterhood Bafut: The only Convent in the Presbyterian Church in Cameroon", *Presbyterian Messenger*, No. 2, 2002.

Kilson, Marion, "Women in African Traditional Religions," *Journal of Religion in Africa*, Vol. 8, No. 2, 1976, pp. 133-143.

Klingorova, Kamila and Havlicek, Tomas, "Religion and Gender Inequality: The Status of Women in the Societies of World Religions," *Moravian Geographical Reports*, Vol. 23, 2015, pp. 2-11.

Koloss, Hans-Joachim, "Kefuh Myin: A Therapeutic Medicine in Oku," *JASO*, Vol. 26, No. 1, 1995, pp. 69-79.

Lang, Michael Kpughe, "The Long Trip to the Front Alter: Women in the Ordained Ministry of the Presbyterian Church in Cameroon, 1957-2010", *Ibadan Journal of Gender Studies*, Vol. 2, 2015, pp. 147-172.

Lang, Michael Kpughe, "The Menchum-Boyo Presbytery-Goppingen Deanery Partnership 1968-2008: A Historical Investigation" Ph.D. Thesis in History, University of Yaounde 1, 2012.

Lang, Michael Kpughe, "The Plight of German Missions in Mandate Cameroon: An Historical Analysis," *Brazilian Journal of African Studies*, Vol. 2, No. 3, 2017, pp. 111-130.

Lang, Michael Kpughe, "Religious Diversity in Cameroon: A Historical Survey," *African Humanities Review*, Vol. 1, No. 1, 2015, pp. 55-71.

Lang, Michael Kpughe, "World War One in Africa: Implications on Christian Missions," *Contemporary Journal of African Studies*, Vol. 4, No. 2, 2017, pp. 37-65.

Lang, Michael Kpughe, "The First World War in Cameroon: An Historical Analysis of its Implications on the Territory's Christian Religious Landscape", In *Cameroon and the Great War (1914-1916)*, Proceedings of the 1st National Colloquium of Military History, Douala, 05-08/08/2014, Paris, L'Harmattan, 2017, pp. 241-258.

Lawyer, Linda Ankiambom "The Christian Women Fellowship of the Presbyterian Church in Cameroon and Women Empowerment in the Bamenda Grassfields, 1961-2001," *Pan-Tikar Journal of History*, Vol. 1, No. 2, 2013, pp. 24-41.

Lewis, Jane, "Women and Society: Continuity and Change since 1870," *Refresh* 1, 1985.

Mark, Suzan, "Empowering Women for a Better Africa/World", *Women's Letter*, No. 55, 2018/2019.

Mbiti, John, "The Role of Women in African Traditional Religion", *Cahiers des Religions Africaines*, No. 22, 1988, pp. 69-82.

Mbong Vanessa Munge, "Yaah Gladys Shang Viban: Promoting Gender Equity in Cameroon", *Success Story*, No. 007, March 2008.

Mellemsether, Hannah, "African Women in the Norwegian Mission in South Africa", in Inger Marie Okkenhaug, (ed.), *Gender, Race and Religion: Nordic Mission, 1860-1940*, Studia Uppsala, Missionalia Svecana XCI, 2003.

Miles, Carrie A., "The Church Versus the Spirit: The Impact of Christianity on the Treatment of Women in Africa," Paper presented at the SSSR/ASREC, 2007.

Moyo, Ambrose, "Religion in Africa," In April A. Gordon & Donald L. Gordon, (ed.), *Understanding Contemporary Africa*,

Second Edition, London, Lynne Rienner Publishers, 1996, pp. 273-301.

Ndenecho, Emmanuel Neba, "Traditional Health Care System and Challenges in Developing Ethnopharmacology in Africa: Example of Oku, Cameroon," *Ethno Med.*, Vol. 5, No. 2, 2011, pp. 133-139.

Neculaesei, Angelica-Nicoleta, "Culture and Gender Role Differences", *Cross-Cultural Management Journal*, Vol. 1, No. 7, 2015, pp. 31-35.

Ngwainmbi, Emmanuel Komben, "Bali", In Asante, Molefi Kete and Mazama, Ama, (eds.), *Encyclopedia of African Religion*, London, SAGE Publications Ltd., 2009, pp. 95-97.

Njoh, Ambe J. and Akiwumi, Fenda A, "The Impact of Religion on Women Empowerment as a Millennium Development Goal in Africa," *Soc Indic Res*, Vol. 107, 2012, pp. 1-18.

Njoku, Chukwudi A., "The Missionary Factor in African Christianity: 1884-1914," In Ogbu U. Kalu, (eds.), *African Christianity: An African Story*, Pretoria, University of Pretoria Press, 2005, pp. 218-255.

Nyemb, Judith and Nche Henuck, "Emmanuel Sisterhood Bafut," In Joseph Mfonyam, (ed.), *The Centenary of the Gospel in Bafut-Tubah Presbytery 1911-2011*, Bamenda, Unique Printers, 2011.

Oduyoye, Mercy Amba and Kanyoro, Musimbi R. A., (eds.), *The Will to Arise: Women, Tradition, and the Church in Africa*, Maryknoll, New York, Orbis Books, 1992.

Oduyoye, Mercy Amba, "African Women Theologians", In Mary Farrell (ed.), *A People's History of Christianity, Vol. 7, Twentieth-Century Global Christianity*, Bednarowski, Minneapolis, Fortress Press, 2008, pp. 83-106.

Ojong, H. O., "Missionary Activities in Kumba Division 1916-1961: A Study of their Presence", Maitrise Dissertation in History, University of Yaounde, 1987.

Pawlikova-Vilhanova, Viera, "Christian Missions in Africa and their Role in the Transformation of African Societies," *Asian and African Studies*, Vol. 16, No. 2, 2007, pp. 249-260.

Predelli, L. Nyhagen, "Contested Patriarchy and Missionary Feminism: The Norwegian Missionary Society in Nineteenth

Century Norway and Madagascar", Faculty of the Graduate School, University of Southern California, 1998.

Presbyterian Church in Cameroon (PCC), Women's Education and Empowerment Program (WEEP), Gender and Human Rights Manuel for Grassroots Population, First Edition, January 2017.

Razak, Arisika, "Sacred Women of Africa and the African Diaspora: A Womanist Vision of Black Women's Bodies and the African Sacred Feminine," *International Journal of Transpersonal Studies*, Vol. 35, No. 1, 2016, pp. 129-147.

Robert, Dana L., "The 'Christian Home' as a Cornerstone of Anglo-American Missionary Thought and Practice," In Dana L. Robert (ed.), *Converting Colonialism: Visions and Realities in Mission History, 1706-1914*, Grand Rapids, Michigan/Cambridge, UK, William B. Eerdmans Publishing Company, 2008.

Segueda, Wendpanga Eric, "Imported Religions, Colonialism and the Situation of Women in Africa," *Schriftenreihe Junges Afrikazentrum*, Vol. 3, 2015, pp. 1-21.

Shenk, Wilbert, "The Contribution of Henry Venn to Mission Thought", *Anvil*, Vol. 2, No. 1, 1985, pp. 25-42.

Slowinski, Amanda, "Christian Feminism: Women Pastors and Feminism", *MSU Journal of Undergraduate Research*, Spring 2007, pp. 1-18.

Spinks, Charlotte, "Panacea or Painkiller? The Impact of Pentecostal Christianity on Women in Africa", *Critical Half*, Vol. 1, No. 1, 2003, pp. 21-25 (Special Issue on *The Impact of Religion on Women in the Development Process*).

Stark, Rodney, "Reconstructing the Rise of Christianity: The Role of Women," *Sociology of Religion*, Vol. 56, No. 3, 1995, pp. 229-244.

Thomas, Guy Alexander, "Why do we Need the White Man's God? African Contributions and Responses to the Formation of a Christian Movement in Cameroon, 1914-1968," PhD Thesis in History, School of Oriental and African Studies, University of London, 2001.

Towns, Ann E., "The Status of Women as a Standard of 'Civilization'," *European Journal of International Relations*, Vol. 15, No. 4, 2009, pp. 681-706.

Vubo, Emmanuel Yenshu, "Matriliny and Patriliny Between Cohabitation: Equilibrium and Modernity in the Cameroon Grassfields," *African Study Monographs*, Vo. 26, No. 3, 2005, pp. 145-182.

Wetuh, V. Q., "From a Local Church Group to a Movement for Women's Empowerment and Societal Transformation; A Case Study of the CWF of the Presbyterian Church in Likomba-Tiko, Cameroon", Master's Thesis in Theology, MF Norwegian School of Theology, 2017

Wood, Johanna Martina, "Patriarchy, Feminism and Mary Daly: A Systematic-Theological Enquiry into Daly's Engagement with Gender Issues in Christian Theology", Doctor of Theology Thesis, University of South Africa.

Woodberry Robert and Timothy S. Shah, "The Pioneering Protestants", *Journal of Democracy*, Vol. 15, No. 2, 2004, pp. 47-61.

Xiang-yu, Cai, "Christianity and Gender in South-East China: the Chaozhou Missions (1849-1949)", PhD Thesis, Leiden University, 2012, http://hdl.handle.net/1887/18940, Accessed 23 December 2015.

Ziegenhals, Gretchen, "Women in Ministry: Beyond the Impasse", In Robert B. Kruschwitz, (ed.), *Women and the Church*, The Centre for Christian Ethics at Baylor University, 2009.

www.ingramcontent.com/pod-product-compliance
Lightning Source LLC
Chambersburg PA
CBHW050532300426
44113CB00012B/2060